Hollywood Speaks Out

To Mary Ellen for imbuing Mark and Mara, and Linda for imbuing Carl, with the understanding of and passion for protest;

to Mark, Mara, and Carl for opening their hearts and minds to the reasons for protest;

to Mara and Carl for implementing the meanings and purposes of protest and passing them on to the next generation through Marlowe;

to Zeke, as Shakespeare wrote, play on!

Robert L. Hilliard

Hollywood Speaks Out

Pictures that Dared to Protest Real World Issues

WILEY-BLACKWELL

A John Wiley & Sons, Ltd., Publication

This edition first published 2009
© 2009 Robert L. Hilliard

Blackwell Publishing was acquired by John Wiley & Sons in February 2007.
Blackwell's publishing program has been merged with Wiley's global Scientific,
Technical, and Medical business to form Wiley-Blackwell.

Registered Office
John Wiley & Sons Ltd, The Atrium, Southern Gate, Chichester, West Sussex,
PO19 8SQ, United Kingdom

Editorial Offices
350 Main Street, Malden, MA 02148-5020, USA
9600 Garsington Road, Oxford, OX4 2DQ, UK
The Atrium, Southern Gate, Chichester, West Sussex, PO19 8SQ, UK

For details of our global editorial offices, for customer services, and for information
about how to apply for permission to reuse the copyright material in this book please
see our website at www.wiley.com/wiley-blackwell.

The right of Robert L. Hilliard to be identified as the author of this work has been
asserted in accordance with the Copyright, Designs and Patents Act 1988.

Wiley also publishes its books in a variety of electronic formats. Some content that
appears in print may not be available in electronic books.

Designations used by companies to distinguish their products are often claimed as
trademarks. All brand names and product names used in this book are trade names,
service marks, trademarks or registered trademarks of their respective owners. The
publisher is not associated with any product or vendor mentioned in this book. This
publication is designed to provide accurate and authoritative information in regard
to the subject matter covered. It is sold on the understanding that the publisher is
not engaged in rendering professional services. If professional advice or other expert
assistance is required, the services of a competent professional should be sought.

Library of Congress Cataloging-in-Publication Data

Hilliard, Robert, 1925–
  Pictures of protest : Hollywood films that dared to deal with real world issues /
Robert Hilliard.
    p. cm.
  Includes bibliographical references and index.
  ISBN 978-1-4051-7899-0 (hardcover : alk. paper) — ISBN 978-1-4051-7898-3 (pbk. :
alk. paper)
  1. Social problems in motion pictures. I. Title.
PN1995.9.S62H55 2009
791.43′655—dc21

                                                                                2008041542

A catalogue record for this book is available from the British Library.

Set in 10/13pt Palatino by Graphicraft Limited, Hong Kong
Printed in Singapore

001   2009

"If all mankind minus one were of one opinion, and only one person were of the contrary opinion, mankind would be no more justified in silencing that one person than he, if he had the power, would be justified in silencing mankind."

John Stuart Mill (1806–73)

"Millions of tons of celluloid for millions of people to see and hear. But what do they see and hear? And does it make them and the world any better?"

From Robert Hilliard, *The 48th Parallel* (a play)

Contents

List of Figures

Foreword

In Hollywood, political films traditionally were often considered "box-office poison." Then along came Gillo Pontecorvo with *Battle of Algiers* (1965) and Costa-Gavras with *Z* (1968). Both – ironically, from across the Atlantic – were considered box-office successes internationally. *Battle of Algiers* was even shown in the White House in September of 2003 to "educate" the staff and others on aggressive tactics against guerrilla warfare which they could apply in Iraq. *Z* was awarded an Oscar for Best Foreign Language film in 1969 and was censored by the Greek junta until 1974. The floodgates were opened. Robert Hilliard's book documents the evolution of political film. Although political films emerged with D. W. Griffith's controversial Civil War classic *The Birth of a Nation* in 1915, as Robert Hilliard points out, they have covered many and diverse areas. A study of them can become a veritable labyrinth. Hilliard's approach is a thematic one, creating an umbrella for each category of political film . . . war, racism, sexism, homophobia, anti-Semitism, to name just a few of the dozen topics Hilliard confronts.

Robert Hilliard's knowledge of the films is very extensive. He has lived through most of the protests represented in the book from World War II (GI with a Purple Heart), through the Cold War, Vietnam, and currently the war in Iraq. Hence he comes to the book with rich personal experiences that amplify the narrative. The chapter on war, for example, is very enlightening, given Hilliard's World War II action in the Battle of the Bulge and his very well-articulated antiwar stance today. In another instance, in the chapter on anti-Semitism dealing with such films as *Gentleman's Agreement* or *Crossfire*, Hilliard has a keen historical approach with a current concern about more subtle prejudices against Jews, as well as other minorities throughout the text. The chapter on racism is a very good microcosm of the history of race as depicted generally in society, on television, and in today's controversial and complicated films by Spike Lee, *Do the Right Thing* and *Bamboozled*. Hilliard's lament is that Hollywood and society in general downplay racial issues in film, although as we have seen, it was a big issue in the Democratic nomination in 2008 – "playing the race card" – and the subsequent election of the first African-American as President of the United States.

With respect to the chapter on labor vs. management films (*Salt of the Earth* and *Norma Rae*), the book offers excellent examples of two films, two decades apart, which reflect a strong plea for unionizing against harsh labor conditions either in the mines or textile factories. (Hilliard has seen close-up the retaliation of institutions against union activity.) He makes the union concerns of *Salt of the Earth* very relevant by shedding light on the immigrant workers' situation in 2008.

As a Professor of Communications before his recent retirement, Hilliard has taught many of these movies, revealing the profound issues presented dramatically in the film and showing their relevance today. His course on "Pictures of Protest" brought to light for a younger generation many of the issues depicted in this book. Here Hilliard has grounded his observations in solid research. One needs only to look at all the resources he has at hand in the endnotes of each chapter, for example, film critics, film historians, and general newspaper articles from the respective time period. This will certainly help the reader pursue each of the issues touched upon in the text.

Throughout the text, Hilliard is realistic enough to see that Hollywood has on occasion invested in protest films, but for financial or other reasons, does not go far enough to have a strong "bite" to them and make an extensive impact upon the audience. His concern is voiced near the close of his text: "Where have all the protest films gone?", echoing the antiwar song of the Vietnam era. His conclusion is that Hollywood remains conservative and unwilling to go out on a limb to make a provocative and timely film that would generate true social action. We have miles to go before we sleep . . .

John J. Michalczyk (author of *French Literary Filmmakers*,
Costa-Gavras: The Political Fiction Film,
and *Italian Political Filmmakers*)

Introduction

One can't say enough bad things about Hollywood and one doesn't say enough good things about Hollywood. Hollywood has entertained and Hollywood has bored. Hollywood has educated and Hollywood has obfuscated. Hollywood has stimulated and Hollywood has fed us pap. Hollywood has produced films that have dealt with critical issues in society and Hollywood has deliberately avoided controversial subjects. Hollywood has dealt with reality and Hollywood has retreated into fantasy.

Hollywood has tried to be everything to everybody. And sometimes it has succeeded in being nothing to nobody. Before radio and then television challenged its influence, Hollywood's feature films were the most powerful factors for affecting people's minds and emotions – and even actions. Hollywood had – and still has – the power to cloud people's minds on one hand and to open and excite them on the other. With such power comes responsibility. Has Hollywood lived up to its responsibility?

Some will look at films such as "Gentleman's Agreement," which dealt with anti-Semitism at a time when such bigotry was openly rampant in America; "Do the Right Thing," made when institutional racism kept the urban streets of America on fire; "The Grapes of Wrath," made when America's great depression created millions of Joad families throughout the country struggling for survival; and "Fail-Safe," made when the Cold War prompted people all over the world to go to bed wondering whether a button pushed during the night would atomize them, their families, and most of civilization before the next morning. ("Dr. Strangelove: or, How I Learned to Love the Bomb" is usually thought of as the seminal protest film against nuclear war, yet it was not a Hollywood film, but a British production.) And there are dozens more.

Some critics believe that every movie advocates something. For example, Richard Corliss wrote:

> Every movie is propaganda. Every character is a walking placard – for capitalism or idealism or monogamy or the status quo. Every shot, by its placement and rhythm and duration, is one more Pavlovian command to the viewer. A narrative movie is usually successful to the extent that it obscures these facts, transforms the thesis into entertainment and the placards into persuasive semblances of human beings.[1]

But the other side of the picture shows thousands and thousands of feature films dealing with pure escapism or pretending to deal with reality by dealing with controversial subjects at a safe time and distance from when the issues or events had occurred. For example, no amount of rationale can absolve Hollywood from its failure to make a single picture about the World War II Nazi Holocaust – the deliberate and systematic murder of at least eleven million people – while the Holocaust was happening. Decades later Hollywood made numerous films about the Holocaust, too late to influence the world to try to stop that genocide. It has too often acted similarly in regard to other genocides. Entrepreneur Jeffrey Skoll, founder of Participant Productions, designed to develop socially pertinent films, discussed the scarcity of Hollywood movies with political messages: "The system's set up for safe bets: sequels, superheroes, romantic comedies . . . All the people I met [in Hollywood] had a particular interest in doing something more meaningful. I thought if I could start a company [Participant Productions] that takes risk out of doing these films, they'll get done."[2]

Similar to the two-faced symbol of thespis, comedy and tragedy, Hollywood has shown two faces in its productions, sometimes using its power to try to change society for the better, but most often abandoning its responsibility to society by deliberately avoiding content relating to the real world.

That is not to say that Hollywood should have spent all its time making feature films oriented to political or social or economic issues. Hollywood has offered much psychological surcease to its patrons with comedies and family drama unrelated to any of society's problems. It is to say that Hollywood has had incredible opportunity to influence the world we live in for the better, but has chosen to do so only sporadically and too rarely when an entertainment film on a given subject could have had an immediate positive impact on people's lives.

Why? The bottom line says it all. A common perception in show business, attributed to Sam Goldwyn, one of the great movie moguls, is, "Pictures are for entertainment. Messages should be delivered by Western Union." (For some of the younger people reading this, Western Union was once the premier agency through which one sent messages via telegraph.) That "message movies" don't make money is part of the general wisdom of Hollywood. More accurately, many message movies don't make money; some do. Conversely, movies made for the lowest common denominator – third- or fourth-grade intelligence – usually make a lot of money, so a lot more of them are made. If you have any doubts, just check out the biggest grossing releases of any given week.

There is a distinct difference, however, between documentary films and feature films. Many documentary films deal with real extant issues. Robert Flaherty is a seminal figure in the development of the documentary films. His "Nanook of the North," in 1922, established a pattern for the documentary that went beneath the exterior of life and carefully selected those elements that dramatized peoples' relationships to the outer and inner composition of their worlds. Flaherty eulogized the strength and nobility of his subjects struggling against a hostile or, at the least, difficult environment. Pare Lorentz, noted for his documentary productions of "The Plow That Broke the Plains" and "The River" under President Franklin D. Roosevelt's administrations in the 1930s, presented problems that affect numerous people and showed ways in which the problems can be solved. Lorenz's documentaries called for positive action by his viewers to remedy an unfortunate or critical situation. A third documentary type is exemplified by the work of John Grierson in England. In the film "Night Mail" he presented the details of ordinary, everyday existence – in this case the delivery of night mail in the UK – in a dramatic but non-sensational manner, showing us people and things as they really are without an obvious political or social message. In all such documentaries, however, the producer has a purpose, a point of view that he or she wishes to convey to the audience. There is an old saying that to make a good documentary, you need to have a "fire in your belly." Documentaries go beyond entertainment alone, and therefore can be and have been, in many cases, realistic pictures of protest.[3]

In this book, however, we are not dealing with documentaries, but with the Hollywood genres that have had the most influence, reaching the largest audiences – feature entertainment films. We are dealing with those feature entertainment films that represent the needs, struggles, failures, and achievements of individuals and groups who fought and continue to fight to overcome prejudice, discrimination, injustice, poverty, and physical and emotional violence by challenging America's status quo in regard to race, religion, lifestyle, and economic, social, and political beliefs and practices. As noted earlier, many Hollywood films have been about these controversial subjects at a "safe" time and distance. We will deal principally with films that protested conditions that existed at the time the films were made and released. In some cases the current issue is confronted through analogy to a comparable situation in the past – or in the future – presented in the given film.

This is a selective process. We cannot cover all the films in the "protest" category, so we will use examples from a number of genres and try to relate them to the genre as a whole. Some of the films we will deal with in detail, others we'll mention in passing. Hopefully, all the films we select will in some way represent some degree of protest within the particular genre and give a sense of the protest within the genre as a whole. We know that many readers will be concerned that their favorite films may not be included within a given genre. But, just as everyone's list of the greatest fifty or one hundred films ever made will always have some differences compared to anyone else's list, so too will the films chosen here have some differences from the films anyone else might have selected for inclusion.

Some of the categories this book will cover are war, anti-Semitism, the justice and prison system, labor vs. management, poverty, racism, politics, homophobia, technology, and sexism. Where appropriate, we will set a given film in the context of the times it was made, the status of the given issue, the critical judgment of and impact of the film, and the application of that film and issue to comparable films and issues today – that is, the first decade of the twenty-first century.

Why the emphasis on the historical context? History moves the media and the media move history. To study the media, one must understand the context and the issues of the times in which a given media event or production took place, whether a television series (e.g., "Roots" or "All In The Family"), a radio play (e.g., Norman Corwin's scripts for the CBS Radio Workshop), a TV news and public affairs special (such as any of many Edward R. Murrow's and Fred Friendly's "See It Now" programs), or the Hollywood films discussed in this book. (Can you think of any television programs you've seen in recent years that fall into these categories? "Boston Legal"? "Frontline"? "Now"? "Bill Moyers"?)

This book developed out of a course that I taught for some years at a college in Boston, "Pictures of Protest." In this course I emphasized the historical context. I have encountered too many college students who are abysmally ignorant of the world that existed before they became aware of the world in which they are living. Platitude or not, Santayana was right in saying that those who do not know history are doomed to repeat it. In another course I taught entitled "History of Broadcasting," when we chronologically reached the infamous blacklisting period of the 1950s, I would ask the students, "Who knows who Joe McCarthy was?" Rarely did anyone know. Sometimes an answer would be, "wasn't that the dummy with that ventriloquist?" (Charlie McCarthy and Edgar Bergen, if you're stumped.) Sometimes I'd get a correct answer, but the wrong person: "Joe McCarthy was the New York Yankees manager who won four straight World Series." Thus, the necessity of making students aware of the real world of the past that established the foundation for the world in which they are living and in which they will produce the new media content or, at the very least, will be affected by it.

In the course, therefore, the students' research, writing, and reports were a mixture – depending, as other professors know, upon the size of the class and the orientation and capabilities of individual students – of critical and historical analysis. The course organization included research into all legitimate sources and verification, when possible, of secondary sources used, shared in class through papers and reports; lectures primarily used to motivate class discussions; and viewing of at least one film illustrative of the genre being studied.

A filmography – that is, basic information about the key films in the various genres – is useful for students. Rather than try to include it in this book, it is strongly recommended that in a course using this book an additional reference be considered: one is *Leonard Maltin's Movie Guide*. The current, 2009 edition is published by Signet Books in New York. Its 1,664 pages include, for each film listed, the film's name, year produced, director, key cast, short description, awards, and Maltin's quality rating. Another is *VideoHound's Golden Movie Retriever*, edited by Jim Craddock and published by GaleCengage. Its 2009 edition is available in book and e-book versions.

I am grateful to the students who took my "Pictures of Protest" classes for the motivation, stimulation, ideas, and information through their discussions and research. I think it appropriate to acknowledge them by name, with apologies for any inadvertent omissions: Dylan Allen, Jefferson Allen, Ana Aragon-Tello, Odalix Bautista, Christopher Bazaz, Carol Brohm, Robert Buckley, Trevor Byrne-Smith, Kiri Clemence, Patrick Creedon, Andrew Curtis, Chris De La Torre, Joseph del Buono, Sarah Dewart, Lydia Fantozzi, Sam Fels, Scott Friedman, Cameron Gay, Marie Gillis, Evan Goldman, Keith Gormley, Joshua Grayson, Jonathan Hanka, Michelle Hanson, Rachel Hungerford, Christopher Irr, Gabriel Karter, Vanessa Knoll, Casey Krier, Jessica Lauer, Evan Levine, Dimitris Los, Timothy Luke, Jeffrey Maker, James Meegan, Chris Moscardi, Jana-Lynne Mroz, Aguren Nikolov, Andrea O'Meara, James Palmer, Christopher Peck, William Popadic, Jeremy Powers, Iso Rabins, Danielle Randall, Evan Roberts, Tom Rossini, Kristy Rowe, Tim Silfies, Kief Sloate-Dowden, Matthew Smith, Andrew Stefiuk, Spencer Strayer, Yetunde Thompson, Tanya Townes, Daniel Ucross, Mary Walsh, Edward Wendell, Timothy Whitney, and/Robert Wilson, Chad Yavarow. In a number of instances I have, with their permission and with attribution to the specific student source in the text or the notes, adapted a research finding or statement or the writer's observation for this book.

I am grateful to Carla Johnston for her editorial comments. I appreciate Mark Hilliard's research and suggestions concerning film genres and examples. I thank Christina Braidotti for her research recommendations and genre commentaries. I am also grateful to the editors at Wiley-Blackwell, not only for their expertise, but also for their personal courtesies, warmth, and consideration. My special thanks to Margot Morse, my principal editor, editor Jayne Fargnoli, and project manager Juanita Bullough. I am appreciative, as well, to Dr. John Michalczyk, film producer and professor at Boston College, for his critique of the manuscript.

One of the students in my "Pictures of Protest" course, Kief Sloate-Dowden, wrote in a class paper, "Many of the themes and issues can be applied to the state of the world today. By viewing these protest films and understanding the problems with society that they bring up, one can be influenced to take action to change the conditions that are presented in these 'pictures of protest.' " What more could a professor want from a student? Hopefully, this book will make some of its readers feel the same way!

Notes

1 Corliss, Richard, "Persuasive Pictures," *Time*, January 30, 2006, p. 11.
2 Hempel, Jessi, "Lights, Action, and Bleeding Hearts," *Business Week*, November 7, 2007, p. 102.
3 The material on documentaries is taken from Robert Hilliard, *Writing for Television, Radio, and New Media* (9th edn, Boston: Wadsworth/Thomson, 2007).

1

O*verview*

But who will come to see it?

Two quotes define the basis of this book. The first, from John Berger:

> Ever since the Greek tragedies, artists have, from time to time, asked themselves how they might influence ongoing political events. It's a tricky question because two very different types of power are involved. Many theories of aesthetics and ethics revolve around this question. For those living under political tyrannies, art has frequently been a form of hidden resistance, and tyrants habitually look for ways to control art.[1]

The second quote, from Ed Lasky, brings Berger's statement into the specific context of the proposition that although Hollywood very often can be very shallow in its messages that address our quality of life, "it wields a power which defines America abroad [and] influences our own self-image: a power that can create desires, influence opinions, distort history and create facts."[2]

We could go down a long list of films that deal with social, political, economic, and other critical issues in our society and out of them select a fair number that not only addressed crises that existed at the times the films were made, but also had greater or lesser impact on the public by drawing their attention to the given problem and/or having an impact toward solving the problem. Out of the hundreds that we could put in that category, we will deal with only a relative handful that were particularly effective as examples of what Hollywood can contribute to society – other than chewing gum for the eyes (to use television critic John Crosby's description of that medium). Some of the films that are discussed in the following chapters had significant impact at the time, actually changing official or unofficial practices and in some cases even leading to legislation or local, state, or national agency rules and regulations. Some of these films continued to have impact long after their release, insofar as the problems the films addressed continued with little abatement or reappeared in subsequent years.

For example, a 1979 film, *Norma Rae*, was a dramatized account of a true story of an attempt to organize a union in a fabric mill in the American South, with a woman playing a key organizing role. The concepts of resistance to cruel exploitation and the virtues of solidarity among workers made the workers victorious. The film reflected the struggle of labor against management and provided strong motivation for workers who weren't sure of the benefits of a union in their non-union workplaces or who were afraid to speak out because they felt they were standing alone. The labor movement continues, to this day, to show *Norma Rae* at union organizing meetings as a motivation for employees who feel they are being exploited by the companies and bosses they work for. Of course, not all "content" films have been so successful over a long period of time in achieving their purposes. Some that seemingly had no impact when they were made, years later became political cult movies when the time appeared to be more conducive to dealing with the particular issue. Most of the films of protest, given the specific nature of the subject matter addressed, were dramas. Some, however, in order to be released by the Hollywood mogul gatekeepers and to be accepted by a public that by and large did not and still does not want to sit in a theater being forced to think about serious issues, were produced as comedies or satires.

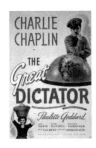

Figure 1.1
*The Great
Dictator
(Charlie
Chaplin, 1940)*

For example, two of the critical issues in the twentieth century were the Holocaust and the possibility of a nuclear war between the United States and the Soviet Union that could leave the entire Northern hemisphere radioactive.

The only Hollywood movie that dealt with the plight of the Jews and with concentration camps – although it was made before the death camps of the "final solution" – was Charlie Chaplin's *The Great Dictator* (1940). Chaplin had a difficult time making the film and getting it distributed. That he was able to do so at all was principally due to his reputation as the world's most popular and creative performer of the time and because he used satire to present a serious subject. Some critics have argued that the use of humor limits the seriousness of a message. Despite the studios' fears and the overt objections to the release of *The Great Dictator*, the use of humor – satire – and Chaplin's own beloved comic techniques made both the release and its success possible.

During the entire period of Nazi horror, the favorite and most honored Hollywood films, as designated by Academy Awards for Best Pictures, barely acknowledged what the Nazis were doing throughout Europe, no less the genocide going on in German concentration camps. Beginning in the first year of Hitler's chancellorship, 1933, we find the Oscar going to *Cavalcade*, a pageant of the twentieth century up to that time. In 1934 it went to *It Happened One Night*, a romantic escapist comedy. In 1935 it was *Mutiny on the Bounty*, in 1936 *The Great Ziegfeld*, and in 1937 *The Life of Emile Zola*, which did touch on anti-Semitism in terms of Zola's opposition to the persecution of Captain Alfred Dreyfus in France. In 1938 the comedy, *You Can't Take It With You*, won, in 1939 it was *Gone With the Wind*, in 1940 *Rebecca*, a period piece, and in 1941, *How Green Was My Valley*, about coal-mining life in Wales. In 1942 the war's impact on England was the subject of Academy Award-winner *Mrs. Miniver*, which did not, however, acknowledge concentration camps and genocide. In 1943, *Casablanca* showed the opposition to Nazism by the Free French and alluded to concentration camps, but not to genocide. *Going My Way*, about a young priest saving his parish church, won the best picture award in 1944, and *The Lost Weekend*, a picture of protest against alcoholism, won in 1945, the year the Third Reich was defeated and the war ended.

Subsequent films about the Holocaust – made well after the time when their release might have had enough impact on viewers everywhere to launch protests that might have saved many lives – have been accused of trivializing the message by the very nature of the Hollywood economic system – censorship and Hollywood's standards of filmmaking that pander to the largest audiences possible. Some after-the-fact films have dealt effectively with some of the practices of the Holocaust, films such as *Schindler's List*, *The Pianist*, and the *The Pawnbroker*. Whether they have had the kind of impact to energize their viewers to take actions to combat current genocides or to prevent future ones is problematical. One criticism of the post-Holocaust Holocaust films is that most end on an upbeat note – the liberation of the people on Schindler's list, the survival of the pianist. Hollywood "can't claim to make a

Holocaust movie if an audience leaves its seat feeling hopeful about humanity. The impulse to honor the good in man is noble, but disingenuous and misapplied when depicting an atrocity."[3]

Researcher Danielle Randall wrote:

Had Hollywood taken the strides to produce feature films about the Holocaust, during the Holocaust, the way in which this dark portion of history is regarded in film today would have been altered drastically. While today's Hollywood pictures have evolved greatly over the past sixty years and the popularity of films that address current events, however unpleasant, has grown immensely, it does not change the fact that such an important part of history came and went virtually unrecognized by the feature film industry.[4]

Nostalgia and sympathy frequently are used to convince the audience that it is emotionally involved while the intellectual realism of the subject may be subverted, in effect allowing the audience to go home without the burden of examining its own attitudes and its own role in a society that permits genocides of greater or lesser natures to occur and reoccur throughout one's lifetime. Critic Henrik Broder, commenting on the reduction of the real message in films, stated:

This is particularly true of Holocaust films, specifically commercial films, where such reductions or miniaturizations serve the function of diversion from the gigantic cataclysm of the Nazi genocide. By condensing and displacing the massive rupture in our history, such films often write around precisely the most problematical aspects of both the event itself and representation of the event.[5]

Dr. Strangelove: or, How I Learned to Stop Worrying and Love the Bomb (1963) dealt with the ultimate possible atrocity of the Cold War between the United States and Russia – atomic warfare. The film revealed the stupidity, ineptness, and inherent evil of American and Russian leaders in even considering the possibility of using a weapon that could destroy a considerable part of humankind. A leading character was a thinly disguised characterization of an American government official who was a principal proponent of atomic warfare. As with *The Great Dictator*, it used satire as its base, in some scenes reminiscent of some of Chaplin's films and of some other early movies with political satire, such as the Marx Brothers' *Duck Soup* (1933). But here's the rub: Considered one of the strongest protests against the United States starting an atomic war, *Dr. Strangelove* was a British production.

When Hollywood wants to affect the world for the better, it can do so. Unfortunately, most of the time the bottom line – the hundreds of millions in gross receipts possible from even the most innocuous movie – rules the content. But sometimes those hundreds of millions are paid to see films that attempt to right a wrong by protesting that wrong. We will examine some of these films as examples of what Hollywood can do when and if it wants to, even in an atmosphere of political and social repression and the fear of not making as many of those millions as might be possible.

This book is oriented to Hollywood entertainment films. Many pictures of protest have been made in other countries, including pseudo-documentaries aimed at achieving a specific political goal, as with the British film, *Jew Suss*, later made as a German film, *Jüd Süss* (1940), a purported revelation of how the Jews were destroying the German culture and economy and must be gotten rid of to save society. Hollywood, despite increasingly lagging behind some other countries, such as India, in the number of films produced each year, produces the "blockbuster" entertainment films that have the most impact not only on American audiences but on audiences all over the world. The Hollywood entertainment films discussed here that can be labeled pictures of protest are offered as examples of what Hollywood has done, can do, and could do to forward the ideals of freedom, equality, and justice within our interconnected global community.

A quote attributed to Andy Warhol – "They always say time changes things, but you actually have to change them yourself" – seems to be true of Hollywood. Almost every film of protest required foresight, courage, and a dedication to change things. Many if not most of these films were dependent on the few people willing to stick their necks out, risk their reputations, and who weren't afraid to alienate movie moguls who were responsible for their employment, in order to stimulate the audience to think. On occasion, it was a lone producer or director or performer or writer who moved from push to shove to get a film out.

Sometimes the times are right. That is, when the public – despite the steadfast alliance of virtually all of the media to maintain the status quo and not make waves for the media moguls controlling the press, television, radio, and cyberspace as well as Hollywood entertainment films – was willing to support issues that were either not common themes or were disturbing to owners, financiers, distributors, and others needed to get a movie produced and into circulation.

The first decade of the twenty-first century saw an upturn in the production of protest films. Increasing numbers of the public protested an increasing number of situations. Many people protested the invasion of Iraq because they thought it was not the way to catch the perpetrators of 9/11, who were in Afghanistan, or because they thought the weapons of mass-destruction excuse was not credible, or because they believed the attack was a thinly disguised motive to control foreign oil. Other protests focused on a wide range of social, economic, and environmental issues such as increased global warming, tax breaks for the rich, the costs of health care and the lack of health insurance, corporate malfeasance scandals, the continuing dangers of smoking, the lack of institutional response for the victims of hurricane Katrina, and the Patriot Act's goal of tracking potential terrorists becoming a tool for the invasion of personal privacy and the loss of civil liberties, among other issues. (The American Civil Liberties union stated that the Patriot Act "expands the ability of law enforcement to conduct searches, gives them wide powers of phone and Internet surveillance, and access to highly personal medical, financial, mental health, and student records with minimal judicial oversight" and "permits non-citizens to be jailed based on mere suspicion and to be denied re-admission to the United States for engaging in free speech."[6])

Americans were angry and protested "business as usual," giving Hollywood permission and, from a profit point of view, motivation to make pictures of protest. The result has been a number of films protesting oil and pharmaceutical industry practices, continuing racism and homophobia, the dangers of tobacco and its industry's machinations, and, despite some government attempts to stifle democratic dissent, the war on Iraq. More and more people wanted the media, including Hollywood, to warn the public about what they believed were dangerous inroads on democracy, and more and more artists, including filmmakers, wanted the opportunity to do so.

Protest films appear to be emerging in greater numbers than in the recent past. Back in the 1930s, the Great Depression affected all but the wealthiest Americans and even destroyed the fortunes of some of the economic elite. Comedies with name players could draw audiences and Hollywood writers who cared about the common weal created scripts that dealt with some aspect of economic inequality, but put it into gentle satire to convince producers that audiences would come and money would be made. For example, *My Man Godfrey* (1936 – remade and updated in 1957), starring fan favorites William Powell and Carole Lombard, satirized the upper economic class's supercilious and stereotyped attitudes toward the rest of the public, those who suffered most during the Great Depression. Other films satirized the insensitiveness and frivolousness of the rich while much of the rest of America was starving and homeless. Some films, such as *One Third of a Nation* (1939), dealt head-on with the inequities of wealth; an agitprop (agitational propaganda, applied to politically oriented artistic work) film, it took a hard and tragic look at the plight into which the economic system had thrust one-third of the United States. *Dead End* (1937) was one of the better of the genre that showed the hopelessness and crime that economic inequities had spawned.

Possibly because artists, including Hollywood creators, are, by the nature of their artistic environment, more sensitive and more open to individual and group feelings than the general population, in the latter years of the twentieth and early years of the twenty-first century Hollywood has produced a number of films protesting homophobia. Beginning with *Philadelphia* (1993), which dealt with AIDS, but carefully avoided showing actual love and or physical tenderness between the principal character and his male partner, to *Boys Don't Cry* (1999), which dealt openly with the brutality of homophobic violence, to *Brokeback Mountain* (2005), which depicted both the emotional and physical relationship between two otherwise-appearing macho males, pictures of protest against homophobic bigotry moved closer to the reality of the issue with each passing year.

Another continuing issue has been the role of big oil, particularly in the first decade of the twenty-first century in regard to the invasion of Iraq. Massive protests against the war before and continuing after the invasion featured signs such as "no blood for oil." This was not only pooh-poohed by the government and the media, but was characterized as a gross exaggeration fomented by a politically radical minority. However, as all the other reasons given for invading Iraq were proven to be false, the "no blood for oil" protests became increasingly valid to more and more Americans. Hollywood, at least in one film, attempted to deal with that issue; *Syriana* (2005) protested the United States' involvement in the Middle East for the purpose of controlling more and more oil sources in order to gain greater and greater profits for the US oil industry, even if it took a war and the lives of thousands of Americans and hundreds of thousands of others to get those profits.

Author Ron Kovic, whose memoir, *Born On the Fourth of July*, became one of the strongest condemnations of the Vietnam War on film, has stated that the invasion of and continuing war on Iraq had corporate profit as its sole motive – the control of Iraqi oil, and that he didn't think the United States

> will ever allow a democratic government because a democratic government would be a direct threat to the very reason they [the United States] went over there to begin with, and that is to dominate the oil, to control the region, and to literally steal the resources of that region for this administration, for the corporations and the businesses of our country."[7]

Commenting on *Syriana*, Mark Levine wrote in *Mother Jones* that

> Given the increasing numbers of Americans who believe the Bush administration deliberately misled the country to justify the Iraq invasion, many film-goers will no doubt be willing to accept the film's argument that America's thirst for oil – not the threat of terrorism and certainly not a concern for human rights – drives the country's policies in the Middle East, even when those policies violate our core ideals."[8]

Sometimes Hollywood has been in the vanguard of protesting practices harmful to society. For years the mainstream media ignored the dangers – and deaths – imposed on people in many countries by pharmaceutical companies that were willing to sell products that were harmful, in order to increase their profit margins. Alternative media and alternative newspapers occasionally carried such revelations – such as the deaths caused by a leading food company in Third World countries by distributing contaminated infant-formula products. But the mainstream media's ignoring of drug-company practices made it possible for them to continue with little public outcry. Ostensibly based on an adventure novel by John le Carré, Hollywood produced *The Constant Gardener* in 2005 as a clear protest not only against the practice of pharmaceutical companies, but about the cooperation of the companies and various governments to silence protesters and restrict information about the drug firms' activities.

Over the years Hollywood turned out a number of excellent films relating to the labor movement and to union-management issues. A few, such as *Norma Rae* (1979), are considered pro-union classics; others, such as *On the Waterfront* (1954), are considered anti-union icons. During the early postwar years, during the McCarthy era of political repression, unions were considered by many to be left-wing sympathizers with communism. It was only after the decline of McCarthyism that pro-union films were given credence in Hollywood as a means of addressing legitimate concerns of workers.

Ironically, Cold War fears prompted Hollywood to undertake an anti-union effort that significantly contributed to the pervasiveness of McCarthyism. In 1949 the Hollywood moguls were concerned that the formation of a film writers' union would infringe on their then virtually unlimited powers and cost them money. It was at a time when the Cold War between the United States and the Soviet Union appeared to be heating up. Congress's House Committee on Un-American Activities (HUAC) was established to root out communists, wherever they happened to be. The movie moguls met in New York at the Waldorf-Astoria Hotel in what became known as the Waldorf Conference, and decided that because some members of the writers' union were known to be or were rumored to be former or current members of the US Communist Party (it had been a legal party, despite media condemnation, with over one million acknowledged members and, at one, time, an elected member of Congress), they would use this to break the union. The movie moguls called in HUAC to hold hearings on the alleged infiltration of communists in the film industry. The members of the Committee were eager to do so, gaining headlines for themselves through the appearance of movie-star witnesses. Many Hollywood personalities, such as leading men Robert Taylor and Ronald Reagan, fearful for their own livelihood and in many cases out of political conviction, eagerly cooperated with the Committee and destroyed the careers of many friends and acquaintances by "naming names," alleging without necessarily any proof that they were communist supporters or sympathizers. The tenor of the times supported this anti-communist nationalism. What resulted was a blacklist in film, radio, and television, and a "red under every bed" climate of fear, in which the rubric was guilt by accusation. A senator from Wisconsin, Joseph McCarthy, censured by the Senate some years later, capitalized on the public's fears, giving the name McCarthyism to that era.

Many people – in all professions – lost their jobs through false and unwarranted accusations. Individual and national civil liberties were under siege. This applied to unions as well. An accusation that any given union had members who were communists or were influenced by communist ideology could bust that union. One prominent radio personality, John Henry Faulk, was a board member of the radio performers' union, the American Federation of Radio Artists (AFRA). To weaken the union and frighten other union members from seeking fair negotiations with management, Faulk was falsely accused of being a red. He was blacklisted. He eventually won a lawsuit against his accusers, but as with others, the accusation alone destroyed his career, and he worked only sparsely after that and was forced to return to Texas, his home state, where he became a chicken farmer. Many other performers had the same fate; some went into other fields; some, unable to support their families any longer, committed suicide.

Long after the fact, Hollywood did make some powerful movies protesting the blacklist, including *Fear on Trial* (the John Henry Faulk story) in 1975, *The Front* (1976), about blacklisted writers, and the more recent *Good Night and Good Luck* (2006), about journalist Edward R. Murrow's and his writer-producer Fred Friendly's exposure of Senator McCarthy. *Good Night and Good Luck* is interpreted by many as an analogous protest against what was happening politically in the 2000s, at the time it was made. Writer Howard Good stated that "new films are nostalgic for outrage . . . perhaps they are saying that we have to look to the past for people who represent individualism and conscience, like Edward R. Murrow in *Good Night and Good Luck*."[9] These films are discussed more fully in other chapters. It is noteworthy that Hollywood had never produced a movie about Hollywood's role in facilitating McCarthyism. A radio docudrama, *The Waldorf Conference*, has for several decades served as the only major dramatic production about that role. An independent 1976 film documentary, *Hollywood on Trial*, summarizes the HUAC hearings.

In his book, *Here's Looking At You: Hollywood Film and Production*, Ernest Giglio wrote:

> The [Hollywood] industry remained silent rather than attack the committee [HUAC] for violation of fundamental American rights and

liberties. Instead, Hollywood knuckled under and contributed to the red scare through motion pictures like *Big Jim McClain, My Son John,* and *The Red Menace,* which lent credence to the mass hysteria of an imminent communist conspiracy to take over the world.[10]

The media industries never fully recovered from the McCarthy-era repression. The blacklist became the gray list, then the strong influence of conservative advertisers and the consolidation of the media into fewer and fewer conservative hands, and the country's political swing to the right, including the ascendancy of elements of the radical right, resulted in, with few exceptions, right-wing content and the eschewing of "liberal-issue" protests. But by the mid-2000s Hollywood took the lead in addressing protest issues while television turned further and further away from meaningful content with innocuous so-called reality shows and inane sitcoms.

The impact of films is undeniable. Richard Corliss wrote in *Time* that

> Every movie is propaganda. Every character is a walking placard – for capitalism or idealism or monogamy or the status quo. Every shot, by its placement and rhythm and duration, is one more Pavlovian command to the viewer. A narrative movie is usually successful to the extent that it obscures these facts, transforms the thesis into entertainment and the placards into persuasive semblances of human beings.[11]

Perhaps the most memorable and effective seminal film of protest – in this instance protesting the principles of equality and freedom – was D. S. Griffith's *The Birth of a Nation* (1915), which portrayed African-Americans following the Civil War as ignorant, scheming, and bestial, and promoted the saving of purported American principles, culture, and white society through the actions of the Ku Klux Klan (KKK). Although the Civil War had been over for some time and the KKK had been in existence for an appreciable time, the first significant stirrings for equal rights in decades began to be heard during World War I, and this Hollywood movie not only protested the possibility of rights for all, but had a great impact on a large part of the American public in fighting against such rights. Gerald Clarke wrote in *Time* that "Movies and TV are probably the most effective means of persuasion ever devised. D. W. Griffith's 'The Birth of a Nation' was the history of the Civil War for many moviegoers." He added a more contemporary example, from television, of comparable impact: "So far as millions of TV viewers are concerned, *Roots*, in 1977, told them all they need to know about slavery."[12]

Hollywood content, with rare exceptions, reflects the attitudes of the times. For example, when Charlie Chaplin made *The Great Dictator*, a satire on Nazi leaders and a poignant plea against the plight of the Jews in Germany, it was still peacetime in the United States (the film was produced during much of 1939 and released in 1940). The United States maintained a semblance of neutrality with the promise from President Franklin D. Roosevelt that "our boys" would not be sent to fight on foreign soil. In addition, anti-Semitism continued to be pervasive throughout the country. Even though *The Great Dictator* was billed as a comedy, the public did not want to deal with controversial issues during peacetime and the movie received much prejudicial criticism.

Sometimes the imposed atmosphere of fear for the purpose of control has superseded public attitudes. During the counter-culture revolution of the late 1960s and early 1970s, public protests grew against the US military involvement in Southeast Asia. But Hollywood did not produce protest films concerning the Vietnam War. Stephen Farber wrote in the *New York Times* that Hollywood's "cowardice can ultimately be traced to the Vietnam War . . . [Hollywood] did not want to take a chance on alienating part of the audience by making either pro-war or anti-war movies . . . the studios' growing fear of controversy affected other subjects as well."[13]

In the 1980s, as a further example, the me-me-me-philosophy made it both easy for Hollywood to avoid producing films that might be considered controversial, and at the same time presented a target of protest to many filmmakers who matured during the previous decade's counter-culture revolution. Change continued into the 1990s, with the rise of independent filmmakers who began to break away from dependence on traditional Hollywood studios. Their work and its influence on Hollywood studios resulted in movies protesting many issues, perhaps the most prominent of which was politics itself. Films such as *Dave* (1993), *The American President* (1995), *Wag the Dog* (1997), *Primary Colors* (1998), and *Bulworth* (1998) took deep bites into the alleged hypocrisy of political leaders, parties, and practices.

Even the Academy Awards for Best Film appeared to shift from pure entertainment to social purpose. For example, *Million Dollar Baby*, a film that examined the controversial issue of assisted suicide, won the Oscar in 2004, and *Crash*, a film that dealt with bigotry and racism – albeit criticized by some critics as being too tame and oversimplified – won in 2005. Every once in a while a film will protest a practice that has been demonstrated to be harmful to society, but which continues to remain legal through the influence of powerful business and legislators who gain monetarily and politically from continuation of the practice. Cigarettes kill hundreds of thousands of people a year in the United States alone, but the selling of the poison continues to remain legal. So powerful are the tobacco lobbies that any protest against their products could be met with devastating retaliation. Yet, two Hollywood films of recent years, *The Insider* (1999) and *Thank You for Smoking* (2006), have confronted big tobacco head-on. Their impact: Possibly educating some people away from a practice that will likely eventually kill them, but no dent in the Congressional steel cover protecting cigarettes and the companies that make them.

In *Camera Politica: The Politics and Ideology of Contemporary Hollywood Film*, Michael Ryan and Douglas Kellner write about social commentary films:

> The susceptibility of the genre to political change was demonstrated in the fifties when, during a period of conservative ascendancy, the percentage of social problems films fell off markedly. The leftist revival of the sixties brought with it a renewal of interest in the genre. Indeed, one of the major generic transformations of the era is a revival of the social problem film in the seventies and eighties.[14]

While many filmmakers believe that films reflect society and should be responsive, not proactive, in regard to social issues, others take the opposite view. One of the former is George Clooney, whose films of protest include *Good Night and Good Luck* and *Syriana*. Clooney has said, "Film reflects society; it doesn't lead society. I don't think we're first responders. It takes us two years always."[15] On the other hand, Steven Spielberg said he made the film *Munich* (2005), a condemnation of how retribution diminishes all causes, in this case that of the Israelis, as a "wakeup call to all studios." Spielberg stated: "We need to stop worrying only about making the number one film for the July 4 weekend and realize we can all contribute something in terms of understanding the world and human rights issues."[16]

Whatever specific differences in their motivations, Hollywood producers, directors, or stars who make pictures of protest are subject to political and social criticism – especially if the content questions the actions of the establishment – whether government, corporate, religious, or otherwise. Clooney was vilified by many on the right for his for work with *Syriana* and *Good Night and Good Luck*. His response: "I was sick of the idea that any sort of dissent would be considered unpatriotic. To me, the most patriotic thing you could do was question your government."[17] Clooney reflects the point made by many that if you truly love your country, you will do what is necessary to make it better when you find it is wrong, even at the risk of approbation; this is the mark of true patriotism.

Another reason proposed by some critics for Hollywood's emergence in the early twenty-first century as a purveyor of protest relates to the increasing closure of controversy and, especially, dissenting ideas in other media. As noted above, consolidation or conglomeration has resulted in an emphasis on status-quo, conservative content in electronic media. The elimination of the Fairness Doctrine in 1987 has resulted in broadcast stations presenting only their side of a given issue without fear of having to present any of society's alternative viewpoints. With the print press falling into the same category, only the Internet remains a principal source for alternative ideas and beliefs. Concomitantly, the increasing rise of independent film production morphed into an increase in films designed to fill the information gap. To the surprise of many, some of these films not only achieved critical acclaim but made money as box-office hits. These hits spurred other filmmakers to take a chance on more protest films.

A look at the history of films reveals a much higher number of pictures of protest than common beliefs might imagine. Below are just some of them, selected at random to provide an overview of the kinds and issues that were generally popular enough to reach a large audience with their messages.[18] As mentioned earlier, *Birth of a Nation* was an early protest film, albeit the opposite in content to films that want to change society for the better and are frequently labeled "liberal."

Antiracism became a frequent film theme after World War II, with *Home of the Brave* (1949), *Bad Day at Black Rock* (1955), *The Defiant Ones* (1958), *Guess Who's Coming to Dinner* (1967), *In the Heat of the Night* (1967), *To Kill a Mockingbird* (1962), and *Do the Right Thing* (1989). Issues were presented that were critical in society at those times. To the extent that racism was and is a continuing practice in the United States – and, to varied extremes in the rest of the world – almost any contemporary film on racism would have an application to this contemporary problem. That paradigm doesn't necessarily apply to all other genres.

For example, in peacetime, films protesting the horrors of war might not appear to have an immediate and current application, despite the fact that in humanity's current limited state of evolution, murdering other people who disagree with you is still accepted as a right and duty of the social organization we label government, whether a village, a city, a state, or a country, and is occurring every day in many places on our planet. When *All Quiet on the Western Front* was produced in 1930, World War I was over and World War II had not yet started. Most of the world was not at war. Yet, this film, arguably the most powerful antiwar film ever made, appears to have had a profound effect on people who saw it and purportedly influenced many to take a moral and, when appropriate, active stand against war. The same might be said for an early Marx Brothers' film, *Duck Soup*, released in 1933 when no major wars were raging. Nevertheless, it satirized the nationalism and militarism that developed after World War I and that not only threatened but ultimately resulted in another war, World War II. As noted above, other films that dealt directly or indirectly with war or the threat of war included one of the most telling antiwar films of all time, *Dr. Strangelove: or, How I Stopped Worrying and Learned to Love the Bomb* (1964), released during the Cold War, when half the world went to sleep at night not knowing whether they would be annihilated by an atom bomb before they woke the next morning. As also noted above, but worth reemphasizing in terms of the orientation of this book, *Dr. Strangelove* was a British, not a Hollywood film. While Hollywood made many movies about the heroics of the Vietnam War, one is hard put to find any film echoing the ongoing protests of the vast majority of Americans against the war, similar to Hollywood's stance, until 2007, about the Iraq War.

The medical system, including hospital treatment, has been a frequent subject of protest by Hollywood and includes such films as *The Snake Pit* (1948) and *One Flew Over the Cuckoo's Nest* (1975), both condemning the treatment of people in mental institutions.

Anti-Semitism has not been a frequent subject of Hollywood movies, although, like racism, that bigotry also continues in the United States, although not as openly or as flagrantly as prejudice against people of color and, in the mid-2000s, against immigrants, particularly of Hispanic, Asian, or African origin. Yet, right after World War II, in 1947, two powerful films protesting anti-Semitism were made, *Gentleman's Agreement* (which won several Academy Awards, despite efforts by Hollywood moguls to prevent its being made) and *Crossfire*, set in the rubric of a crime story. Some Hollywood films, such as *Elephant Man* (1980), dealt with society's ongoing prejudice against people who look "different."

Poverty, as defined during America's Great Depression of the 1930s, has been directly confronted in a number of films, ranging from stark drama such as *Dead End* (1937) and *The Grapes of Wrath* (1940), to satire or comedy with a message, such as *My Man Godfrey* (1936) and *Sullivan's Travels* (1941).

The justice and prison system was also protested in many Hollywood films. Perhaps the most significant film was *I Am Fugitive from a Chain Gang* (1932), which was credited with forcing changes in the prison systems in a number of states. Other films dealing with various aspects of justice and prison, from the jury system to capital punishment – continuing issues in society – include *12 Angry Men* (1957), *I Want to Live* (1958), and *Dead Man Walking* (1995).

American politics, also a continuing target for criticism, too much of the time justifiably so, has been a subject of protest in many films, such as *Mr. Smith Goes to Washington* (1939), *The Candidate* (1972), and, as noted above, several key films in the 1990s.

Even the media, including Hollywood itself, have been subjects of sharp protest by Hollywood films. Examples are *All About Eve* (1950), a revealing stereotype of ego and cutthroat competition in theater; *The Bad and the Beautiful* (1952), a searing indictment of Hollywood practices; and *Network* (1976), a condemnation of the television industry.

People don't want to be preached at in movies. They want to be entertained. As befits Hollywood feature entertainment films, protest films that were generally most successful were the ones that held their audiences by being entertaining (whether comedy, satire, or drama) even while they protested.

The above are only some of the genres and subject areas, and only a sprinkling of sample films that could be categorized as pictures of protest. In this book only a representative selection of subject areas and an even smaller selection of films will be covered. Hopefully, the material presented will nevertheless provide a useful overview of

Hollywood's feature entertainment films that have been pictures of protest, their possible impact at the time they were released, and their relevance, where applicable, to films and issues in society today. The following subject areas will comprise the chapters that follow: war, racism, anti-Semitism, homophobia, sexism (women's rights), poverty, the prison and justice system, labor-management, politics, technology, and a final chapter, "Hide or Seek," a brief introduction to several other protest categories not covered in this volume.

Notes

1 Berger, John, "The Impact of *Fahrenheit 9/11*." www.countercurrents.com.
2 Lasky, Ed, "Hollywood: The Imperial City." www.americanthinker.com.
3 "Holocaust Movies," January 9, 2003; "The Third Reich," October 26, 2006. http:www.thirdreich.net/Holocaust_movies.
4 Randall, Danielle, "Hollywood and the Holocaust," unpublished paper, November 1, 2006.
5 Broder, Henrik, "Das Shoah-Business," *Der Spiegel*, 47, No. 16, 1993, pp. 248–56.
6 www.aclu.org. "Summary of the USA Patriot Act and Other Government Acts." Accessed April, 2006.
7 Gilmer, Tim, "Ron Kovic Reborn," *New Mobility*, June 20, 2003. http://www.vvawaii.org.
8 Levine, Mark, "*Syriana* and Iraq," *Mother Jones*, November 30, 2005. http://www.motherjones.com.
9 Howard Good, quoted in Neumaier, Joe, "Hollywood Again Rages at Injustice, Greed, Political Corruption" (Fort Myers, FL), *News-Press* (Lifestyles), November 24, 2005.
10 Giglio, Ernest, *Here's Looking At You: Hollywood, Film, and Production* (New York: Peter Lang, 2000), pp. 1–18, 207–18.
11 Corliss, Richard, "Persuasive Pictures," *Time*, February 15, 1982. www.time.com.
12 Clarke, Gerald, "Persuasive Pictures," *Time*, March 8, 1982. www.time.com.
13 Farber, Stephen, "Where Has All the Protest Gone?," *New York Times*, March 31, 1974, p. 127.
14 Ryan, Michael and Douglas Kellner, *Camera Politica: The Politics and Ideology of Contemporary Hollywood Film* (Indianapolis: Indiana University Press, 1988), pp. 87, 236.
15 Karger, Dave, "Luck Is on His Side," *Entertainment Weekly*, January 20, 2006, pp. 22–6.

16 Steven Spielberg, quoted in Thompson, Anne, "H'wood, Applied Liberally," *Hollywood Reporter*, February 1, 2006. www.allbusiness.com/services/motion-pictures/4904769-1.html.

17 Edwards, Gavin, "George Clooney Renegade of the Year," *Rolling Stone*, December 15, 2005. http://www.rollingstone.com.

18 Names and brief annotations include information provided by Mark Hilliard on "Heart of Oak" and "Drama Films." http://www.filmsite.org.

2
War

Hell for whom?

Is there any worse evil than war, the deliberate and systematic murder of human beings by other human beings? Of all the pestilences that can beset humankind, war is the most devastating. And it is the stupidest because, more than any other catastrophe, it can be avoided.

Not yet in our state of evolution have we learned how to control earthquakes, tsunamis, hurricanes, tornadoes, and other natural phenomena that destroy the equilibrium of our physical environment and, concomitantly, human lives. To some extent we have begun to learn to eradicate and prevent some diseases, but in our relatively still primitive state of scientific development we continue to be at the complete mercy of many others, such as pandemic flu, cancer, and AIDS, that periodically wipe out a substantial number of the earth's human population.

Ironically, resources such as money and the human talent of time, energy, and skills that might well be used to find cures for many of these pestilences are used instead to wage wars. The most important contribution that the media, including the Hollywood feature film, could make to the world in which it functions – a world which generously supports the media – would be to use its persuasive power to convince people to abhor and avoid wars; to bring unrelenting pressure against those who would initiate wars for economic and/or political gain for themselves and/or their friends and associates by shining the light of exposure on the war-makers' chicanery. Muck-raking protesting, when assiduously and relentlessly done, especially in relation to serious controversial issues, historically has shown significant moments of success. Is there any evil more deserving of protest by those who make the media than war?

Has Hollywood reflected this belief? No less and no more than other media. During the Vietnam War, when revelations such as those in the Pentagon Papers showed that American government leaders were deliberately lying to the American people in order to garner support for the war, Hollywood did not deal with the issue. While millions of Americans were marching in protest every week in cities large and small throughout the country, this overwhelming opposition to continued American military actions in southwest Asia was ignored by Hollywood, as well as by virtually all other mainstream media. It was only after the end of the war, at a safe distance from controversy and away from a time when it might have had an actual impact on stopping the war, that Hollywood and other media began to produce material reflecting the wartime issues. It is pertinent that *Variety* magazine, the voice of the industry, described the media's behavior during the Vietnam War as "no-guts journalism." This behavior was repeated several decades later when many Americans accused their American President and Vice-president of generating an unprovoked invasion of Iraq by giving the public false information about weapons of mass destruction, about atomic bomb materials, about ties to Al-Qaeda terrorists, and by falsely implying that Iraq had some connection with the 9/11 attack in 2001 on the World Trade Center and the Pentagon. Not a single Hollywood feature entertainment film addressed this situation, nor did any Hollywood film deal with the presumed true motivations for the war or the behind-the-scenes manipulations with private contractors and US oil companies. Now, that's the stuff that drama is made of, as exciting and convoluted as any fictional spy story. (Note the success of *All the President's Men*, about the Watergate scandal, albeit made after the immediate controversy was past.) Even after a period of war in Iraq longer than America's participation in World War II, Hollywood did nothing with the events and actions that were begging to be dramatized. As this is written, in early 2008, Hollywood has finally, tentatively begun to touch on aspects of the war, including the torture and murder of "enemy" combatants and civilians. A few films have emerged that can be considered protests against the war in Iraq. But, by and large, Hollywood continues to play what appears to be the role of supportive sycophant or, at best, continues to turn a blind eye, as it has done with previous wars.

This is not to say that Hollywood has never had the courage or taken the responsibility to deal with current or ongoing issues of war. Ironically, however, arguably the most effective anti-war movie ever made was produced during a period when no major or international

Figure 2.1
All Quiet on the Western Front (1930)

war was going on – between World War I and World War II. *All Quiet on the Western Front* was produced in 1930. It touched people throughout the world, despite – or because of – the fact that its protagonists, with whom we came to empathize as well as sympathize, were the enemy of most of the countries where the film was shown: German soldiers.

The film captured the universality of war, how its horrors equally affect combatants on all sides of a conflict. More than any other film until that time, it delineated the individual soldier's journey from patriotic euphoria through the confidence of youth, the myth of self-immortality, the trauma of initial combat, the suffering of battle, the depression and despair of continued combat, the cynicism accompanying a realization of the hypocrisy of war, and the inevitability of death. Reviving the physical and sense memories of those who had been in combat in World War I and imposing a fear as well as an understanding of combat for those who might participate in any future war, the realism of *All Quiet on the Western Front* was in no small part effective because Erich Maria Remarque, the author of the novel of the same title upon which the movie was based, himself had been a young soldier in the German army in World War I and had experienced much of what his protagonists underwent in the novel and the film. Although the director, Lewis Milestone, had not been in combat, he came to the film with an understanding of the military based on his work as a soldier in the US army during World War I, making war-training films.

The trench-warfare scenes in the film were brutal, combining the physicality of maiming and killing with the unrelenting fear of immediate death, the senselessness of the entire concept of war, and overwhelming individual hopelessness.

Reviews of the film were ecstatic, particularly focusing on its realism and describing it as the first true anti-war film. Critic Howard Barnes wrote that "with all preceding war stories brought to the stage and screen . . . there has always been an inevitable glamour attaching to the fighting . . . in *All Quiet* there is no glamour. It is courageously bitter."[1] *Variety* magazine's critic stated that "it is recommended that the League of Nations should distribute it in every language to be shown every year until the word War shall have been taken out of the dictionaries."[2] And the London *Times* critic observed that "realism reaches its zenith in this picture. I hate it. It brought back the war to me as nothing has ever done before or since."[3] In more recent years, critic Tim Dirks compared *All Quiet* to more contemporary films, none of which, either, were made as protests during a war or the obvious buildup to a war, but which, to much lesser degrees, served as protests against war in general.

> The film includes a series of vignettes and scenes that portray the senselessness and futility of war from the sympathetic view of the young German soldiers in the trenches in the Great War who found no glory on the battlefield, meeting only death and disillusionment. Recent-day war films, including *Platoon* (1986), *Full Metal Jacket* (1987), and *Saving Private Ryan* (1998), have similarly portrayed a perspective of war from the soldier's point of view.[4]

But perhaps more significant than its raw realism was its revelation of the kind of propaganda and emotional appeals that prompt people, particularly the young and naïve, to behave in what, objectively, appears to be an insane way: Supporting and volunteering in a war in order to kill other human beings and be killed themselves.

In *All Quiet on the Western Front* these young people are students in a secondary school in Germany during World War I. As new volunteer soldiers march past their school, their professor lectures them:

> It is not for me to suggest that any of you should stand up and offer to defend his country . . . I know that in one of the schools, the boys have risen up in the classroom and enlisted in a mass. If such a thing should happen here, you would not blame me for a feeling of pride.

And then, as the students react with the same nationalistic fervor and mixture of envy and stimulated testosterone, the professor adds:

> I believe it will be a quick war. There will be a few losses. But if losses there must be, then let us remember the Latin phrase which must have come to the lips of many a Roman when he stood in battle in a foreign land: Sweet and fitting it is to die for the Fatherland . . . Now our country calls.

In those brief segments of dialogue, *All Quiet on the Western Front* captures the rationale and approach used in all wars, past and future, and by all countries, to convince people to go to war, but revealed as travesty in very few films other than this one. Hitler's second-in-command, Hermann Goering, a war criminal convicted at the Nuremberg Trials, stated it this way:

> Of course, the people don't want war. But, after all, it's the leaders of the country who determine the policy, and it's always a simple matter to drag the people along whether it's a democracy, a fascist dictatorship, a parliament, or a communist dictatorship. Voice or not voice, the people can always be brought to the bidding of the leaders. That is easy. All you have to do is tell them that they are being attacked, and denounce the pacifists for lack of patriotism and exposing the country to greater danger.

In terms of the subject of this book, isn't this exactly what happened in the United States in the decades following World War II?: Hollywood (and other media) supporting – or, at least, not protesting – America's leaders applying Goering's dictum to gain support for several wars.

While the film became an icon for anti-war groups in many countries, it became a pariah in countries where nationalism and jingoism were keystones of governments that kept the prospect of war as a tool to maintain control of their peoples. Germany, where the film was shown shortly after its release in 1930, banned it shortly thereafter until it was reedited and later reedited again, and then banned it permanently. "In Germany, where the defeat of the war was still a bitter memory, screenings were stormed by Nazi party rabble-rousers who objected to its 'lies' about the glory of combat. Even in the United States it was boycotted by the American Legion."[5]

Some critics have suggested that Hitler himself kept a copy of the film for personal viewing, just as it has been suggested that *The Great Dictator*, which a decade later satirized Hitler and Nazism and was also banned in Germany, was also in Hitler's private collection and viewed with humor by him. As World War II loomed, some of the potentially combatant nations banned or censored the film, including France. *All Quiet on the Western Front* was perceived, accurately, as a powerful anti-war and even antimilitary film, and considered harmful to uncritical patriotism.

Film historian John Whiteclay Chambers II wrote that

Because of its strong ideological message, the film also contributed to the political debate both immediately and years after. Most dramatic, of course, was the role the film played in the already polarized political debate over Germany's past and future in the late Weimar Republic. So potent was the film's universal anti-war message that it was also quickly banned by fascist Italy and other authoritarian states, and allowed to be shown in a number of other countries only after the censor had reduced or eliminated some of the most powerful anti-war scenes.[6]

All Quiet on the Western Front won Academy Awards for Best Picture and Best Direction, was almost universally lauded by critics and was extremely popular at the box office, the public finding its anti-war message important to watch despite the painful scenes of the horrors of trench warfare. But even in the United States many in the military and government establishment joined their brethren in authoritarian countries in attempting to ban or censor the film. One example was a Major Frank Pease, director of the Hollywood Technical Directors Institute, who denounced the movie as an effort to "undermine belief in . . . authority."[7] Also in the United States, the American Legion, an association of veterans, boycotted the film. Even today, in the first decade of the twenty-first century, a number of countries continue to ban any showing of *All Quiet on the Western Front* because of the fear that it may undermine military and governmental authority and potential jingoism.

Although not made during World War I, when it might have discouraged public support of and participation – including that of Americans – in the war, its continued existence as a classic film, frequently shown in college courses and at citizen associations, influences at least some members of the generation involved in that war's senselessness and futility. In fact, the young star of *All Quiet on the Western Front*, Lew Ayres, was so affected by his participation in the film that a decade later, when the United States entered World War II, he was a conscientious objector, refusing to serve in a position where he might have to kill another human being, and instead he served in the war as an unarmed medical aide. Nationalistic fervor resulted in his being blacklisted in Hollywood for many years.

In the same category, but entirely opposite in form and approach, is the 1933 Marx Brothers film, *Duck Soup*. A farce-comedy-satire

(Marx Brothers movies were generally regarded as farce-comedies, but invariably contained sharp social and/or political satire, usually ignored by audience and critics alike, who viewed the madcap content as an escape from the economic depression of the 1930s), *Duck Soup*, like *All Quiet on the Western Front*, "showed the propaganda involved in creating a certain pride in your country, which then makes you believe the war is being fought for a good cause."[8] Preposterous insanity of characters and actions, with Groucho Marx as the leader of a country bent on making war against another country, combined with war-inciting musical numbers, marked *Duck Soup*. It was a "short but brilliant satire and lampooning of blundering dictatorial leaders, fascism, and authoritarian government."[9]

"Duck Soup" was, at the time of its release, marginal at the box office and even less so in critical reviews. Film historian Tim Dirks stated that "audiences were taken aback by such preposterous political disrespect, buffoonery and cynicism at a time of political and economic crisis, with [US President Franklin D.] Roosevelt's struggle against depression in the U.S. amidst the rising power of Hitler in Germany." Not only did Hitler take umbrage, but Mussolini took insult at characterizations that purportedly could be likened to himself, and *Duck Soup* was banned in Italy.[10] The film's essence was that a gullible population can be propagandized into doing whatever its leaders want, including self-destruction in a war. One explanation for the title put it this way: "The film's title uses a familiar American phrase that means anything simple or easy, or alternately, a gullible sucker or pushover. Under the opening credits, four quacking ducks (the four Marx Brothers) are seen swimming and cooking in a kettle over a fire."[11]

Many entertainment-feature war films have been made during wartime. But with very few exceptions these have been films stressing the heroes and heroics of war, supporting whatever war the given country that made the film was in at the time. Among those made during World War II were films that featured performers who, in the public mind, became war heroes even though they may not have actually served in the military.

Films, as television did later, created perceptions of reality in the public mind. Many Americans thought of John Wayne as an American war hero in World War II because of his roles in many war movies. And Ronald Reagan, who also did not fight in World War II, at least at one point during his presidency referred to his personal participation in World War II, confusing reality with his movie roles. It is possible, course, that the Alzheimer's disease that later afflicted him may have already been in its early stages.

While many films made during the war included scenes and/or concepts that indicated the horrors of war, the films as a whole were not oriented to protesting war itself or any part of the particular ongoing war. Movies like *The Flying Tigers* and *Wake Island* in 1942, *Action in the North Atlantic*, *Crash Dive*, *Destination Tokyo*, *Guadalcanal Diary*, and *A Guy Named Joe* in 1943, and *The Fighting Seabees*, *The Fighting Sullivans*, and *Thirty Seconds Over Tokyo* in 1944 were action-filled with valor, designed to bolster public morale. Although most would agree that World War II, unlike almost all other wars, was a "necessary" war, the representation of war as something difficult but glorious did nothing to prompt viewer antipathy, resistance, or protest when, in the future, unprincipled or misguided leaders attempted to convince the public to participate in another war.

Following World War II, a number of films were made that more strongly showed the futility and horror of war. Hollywood took pride in such films, but one cannot help but take that pride with a grain of salt. Had they produced some similar films during the preparation for and/or existence of an actual war – think of Vietnam, Panama, the Gulf War, Somalia, and Iraq, all seriously questioned as to necessity and motive – one might take a less critical view of Hollywood. *The Best Years of Our Lives*, in 1946, dealt in a timely manner with the impact of war on individual participants and their families and friends as the former returned from war and tried to readjust to civilian life. *A Walk in the Sun* (1946) and *Battleground* (1949) attempted to show the reality of war, as opposed to the glamorous heroics that dominated most war movies during and after the war. Their content would have been more meaningful several years earlier. *Home of the Brave*, also after the war, in 1949, was a postwar protest against racial prejudice, showing the behavior toward an African-American veteran, and although not about war itself, reflected attitudes the belied the so-called democratic purpose of fighting World War II. A similar film, oriented toward disabled veterans, paraplegics, was *The Men*, in 1950.

One of the most potent anti-war films of protest was *Paths of Glory*, released in 1957. Like some other anti-war films, it s impact was peripheral – hopefully educating the generation watching it to recall its emotion and message when another war loomed on the horizon. For some, it did just that. *Paths of Glory* is a bitter, biting indictment of a deceitful military and political hierarchy that has no compunction about lying to the public and to the soldiers who fight and suffer from a war – in this instance, World War I – while the military commanders and the political elite sit safely far removed from the scenes of battle. A key segment of the film shows the military commanders sending men on a suicide mission, knowing that few, if any, are likely to survive, while assuring the men that they can make it back alive. "We don't have to tell the people the truth," one of the leaders says, "let's just tell them what they want to hear, but make it plausible."[12] The general who orders the disastrous mission puts the blame on three of the soldiers who return, protecting his own incompetence by ordering that the soldiers be executed for cowardice, the film stressing even further the chicanery of the leaders of war. It was a "devastating denunciation of the hierarchical structure of military organizations wherein the elite officers [were] detached from the brutal realities of the soldiers who [were doing] the actual fighting and dying."[13]

Although *Paths of Glory* did not reach popularity at the box office when it was released, it became a classic anti-war film for anti-war individuals and groups during the early years of the US–Soviet Cold War that followed the end of World War II. It was shown in small theaters to reinforce what appeared to be the opposition of a small minority to the saber-rattling – in mid-twentieth-century terms, atom-bomb juggling – that infected both sides. Not long afterward the United States was in a war in Vietnam, strongly opposed by the American people and ultimately brought to an end by massive protests and the revelations that the Pentagon and the government had consistently lied to the public about what was happening in Vietnam, revealed in what became known as the Pentagon Papers. Hollywood, not surprisingly, made no films that reflected the public opposition to the war or controversies surrounding the justification and implementation of the war. For many who remembered the release of *Paths of Glory* a decade earlier, the film became a metaphor for what was happening in Vietnam. Film historian David Cook wrote that director Stanley Kubrick's "classic anti-war statement, *Paths of Glory*, relentlessly exposed the type of military stupidity and callousness that would lead us into Vietnam."[14] Perhaps the concept and practice of warfare that marked both world wars had become too outdated by the time the United States invaded Iraq almost half a century later because, although the attack on Iraq was patently built on lies under the guise of plausibility, *Paths of Glory* was not resurrected as a rallying vehicle for the vast majority of those opposed to the US action in the Middle East.

Early in the Vietnam War, however, in 1964, two of the most dramatic anti-war films were made. Ostensibly dealing solely with the Cold War between the United States and the Soviet Union, *Dr. Strangelove: or, How I Learned to Stop Worrying and Love the Bomb* and *Fail-Safe* clearly showed the planetary disaster of mutual destruction that could take place if the Vietnam War were to get even more out of hand. At the time, however, the Vietnam War had not yet generated the massive protest movements that finally brought the war to an end. More pertinently, these films reminded the public of an event of just two years earlier, the Cuban missile crisis, in which the United States and the USSR came to the brink of worldwide nuclear destruction. Both films, adapted from the same novel, emphasized the insanity of even considering nuclear war as an option. *Dr. Strangelove*, made by the director of *Paths of Glory*, Stanley Kubrick, was a dark comedy, an unrelenting, biting satire that showed the idiotic beliefs and behavior of those with the power to initiate and conduct a nuclear war: The leaders of the United States and the Soviet Union. A deranged, delusional American officer, convinced that the Soviet Union must be destroyed, orders planes loaded with nuclear bombs to attack. The President and his cabinet and advisors meet to discuss how to stop the attack, given that the Soviet Union has a doomsday device that will destroy the entire world if it is attacked. The American leaders are revealed as fanatics, not concerned about the destruction of millions of Soviets, but only of the retaliation. The characters are larger than life, especially Dr. Strangelove, whose Nazi-like thinking and posture are thinly veiled disguises for US President Richard Nixon's chief foreign policy adviser at the time, Henry Kissinger.

The satire is so strong and the characters' representation of US people and policies carried to such lengths of *reductio ad absurdum* in this world of film representation that we laugh even while realizing that atomic disaster could literally occur in our real world at any moment as long as these characters' counterparts and their policies exist in reality. Because of the fallibility of American policy and the incompetence of its leaders, as delineated by satire in the film, one US plane gets through to the Soviet Union and the mindless, "bring-it-on" cowboy attitude has the plane's pilot riding the bomb down as it approaches what will be the end of the human race as we know it. Even the music satirizes the hypocrisy of the atom-bomb policy, the film ending on the notes of the World War II song, "We'll Meet Again": "We'll meet again, don't know where, don't know when / But I know we'll meet again, some sunny day."

The portrayal of the US as well as the Russian leadership as crazed and/or unbalanced ideologues prompted condemnation from many of those who supported the Cold War and US nationalism. Lewis Mumford countered these supporters, noting in an article that

> It is not this film that is sick; what is sick is our supposedly moral, democratic country, which allowed the policy of nuclear extermination to be formulated and implemented without even the pretense of open public debate. This film is the first break in the catatonic cold war trance that has so long held our country in its rigid grip.[15]

Did the film, as strongly entertaining and intellectually stimulating as it was, have an effect on either the public's thinking or the leadership's actions? Critic Roger Ebert wrote:

> The bomb overshadowed global politics. It was a kind of ultimate hole card in a game where the stakes were life on earth. Then Kubrick's film opened with the force of a bucketful of cold water, right in the face. What Kubrick's Cold War satire showed was not men at the mercy of machines, but machines at the mercy of men.[16]

Along the same lines, critic Jonathan Kirshner wrote:

> Made at a time when anti-communism pervaded American society, and people could still get in trouble by saying the wrong thing [*Dr. Strangelove*] subverted the very idea of the Cold War itself. Rather than switching, as much scholarship did, from an ideological position that blamed the U.S.S.R. to one that accused the U.S. . . . they did not take sides, but instead ridiculed both and trivialized their conflict, asserting that the differences between them were meaningless.[17]

Director Sidney Lumet's *Fail-Safe*, essentially the same plot-line, was a straightforward, serious telling of the story. The film portrays the US President as sincere and cautious, and intent on avoiding a nuclear war. However, when the errant plane cannot be recalled and it is clear that Moscow will be atomized, in order to avoid a wider war the

President arranges with the Soviet President to achieve retaliation through a similar atom bombing of New York City – despite the fact that the President's family is there and will be annihilated with the rest of the seven million residents. While *Fail-Safe*, a Hollywood film, did not receive nearly the praise or publicity of "Dr. Strangelove," did its realism and objective identification and empathy with the characters by the audience more effectively reach people's minds and emotions?

Should these anti-war – or more precisely, anti-atomic war – movies count as pictures of protest, inasmuch as no hot war involving the United States was in progress at the time, given that at that point relatively few troops had been sent to Vietnam and not too many people saw it as our descent into the "big muddy"? The media and the public in general, fooled by the government with false information, by and large supported the US venture into Southeast Asia at that time. These films, one British, the other US, more than other entertainment feature films up to that time, protested the Cold War that could have led to mutual annihilation, and because they were used as a metaphor by those protesting the US presence in Vietnam, they certainly can be considered pictures of protest. They ran counter to Hollywood's unrelenting promotion to turn the Cold War into a hot war through a series of anti-Communist, anti-Soviet spy thrillers designed to frighten the American public into a perceived self-protective war action. Hollywood was emulating the role of film producers and other media in virtually every country that attempted to propagandize the public into acquiescence to war by intensifying their fear of the designated enemy. The greater the fear imposed on the public, the greater the power the public cedes to its government. For the present generation of moviegoers and the general public, Hollywood acquiesces to the government's continuing manipulation of fear of attack by anyone, even unnamed, that the government labels as terrorists.

*M*A*S*H* is an excellent example of a proxy film; that is, a film that protests a war taking place at the time the film is released without referring to that war. In 1970 the Vietnam War had already galvanized a majority of Americans into massive protests in Washington and throughout the country. As had already become the norm for America's "no-guts" media, Hollywood eschewed any scripts representing opposition to the Vietnam War. However, the Korean War – about which no films criticizing it or war in general were produced during its 1950–3 duration – was sufficiently in the past. Based on a novel that had been rejected by some thirty publishers before it was accepted – possibly reflecting the timidity and establishment brown-nosing of the publishing industry as part of the media – M*A*S*H was a human comedy set in the indignity of war, showing through its well-defined characters the stupidity of war and its military supporters. That it was an analogy, in fact, a parallel for the Vietnam War, was not lost on anyone except those who did not want to acknowledge it. M*A*S*H makes a mockery of both the concept and practice of war, at the same time not sparing the audience from the pain of war's destruction and death. It was banned from being shown in military movie houses, presumably because it would undermine the unthinking, unquestioning obedience the military demanded from its personnel, and the film emphasized through its principal empathetic characters a mocking disrespect for military protocol. It ridiculed the pro-military, pro-war officers while emphasizing the humanity of the non-career officers opposed to the conflict. Critic Jan Dawson wrote that "one suspects the real source of official displeasure with the film is the way its enlisted characters obdurately persist in behaving like civilians . . . no one salutes anyone, doctors and nurses devote all their extra-curricular energy to getting into one another's pants."[18]

Based also on a book, Catch-22, the film of the same name was released the same year as M*A*S*H, 1970. Set in World War II, it deals less with the concept of war, per se, than with what it presents as the hypocritical, inane structure and practice of the military itself. The vignettes that dominate the film include representations of corrupt military, government, and private-sector opportunists; sadistic top brass, including generals; and non-sequitur military rules and regulations that literally drive personnel insane. In a larger sense, one can see the application of the content of Catch-22 to society as whole.

The most effective and artistically highly praised anti-Vietnam War films were made well after the end of American hostilities in Southeast Asia. Among them were such movies as The Deer Hunter (1978), Apocalypse Now (1979), Platoon (1986), and Born on the Fourth of July (1989). Each, in its own and different way brilliantly criticized America's role in that war. While these films supported anti-war activists in general and those who protested against the Vietnam War in particular, whether they had an appreciable impact on preventing or ameliorating subsequent wars is unclear. These films are still used as reference points, however, in opposing wars, including the one in progress in Iraq as this is being written, and the one appearing to be built up against Iran with the same rhetoric used to invade Iraq.

Somewhat different than other anti-war movies and, in a more acerbic sense somewhat reminiscent of *The Best Years of Our Lives*, about homecoming veterans and their families after World War II, *The Deer Hunter* examines the tragedy of a group of men from the same small town who are sent to Vietnam to fight and its subsequent effect on their families and their town. *Apocalypse Now* delineated the brutality of the war, including the actions of some of the American soldiers that resembled the persona of homicidal maniacs. One aspect of the film deals with American soldiers who have formed their own society in the jungle because they cannot fathom adjusting to a return to their so-called civilized lives back home after the horrors they experienced and perpetrated in the war. Marlon Brando's role as an American who defects to become the ruler – in effect, a god – in a native village emphasizes the greedy, power-hungry insanity that is a basic ingredient of war. And yet, this man whom the American forces feel has lost his senses and must be eliminated may be, in his assessment of right and wrong, saner than the others who support the conventional view of war and society. The others include the helicopter pilot blaring Wagner's *Die Walküre* as he swoops down on a schoolyard full of children with his guns blazing; and the epitome of the gung-ho soldier who has lost all sense of humanity as he is trapped in a war that, by its very nature, denudes him of humanity, and who utters the pervasive line: "I love the smell of napalm in the morning."

Platoon is considered by many critics to be one of the best films ever made about the trauma suffered by individual soldiers in a war, the unrelenting fear, degradation, deprivation, suffering, and death endured by the individual soldier on the battle line. Some have compared this film about the Vietnam War with the content and impact of *All Quiet on the Western Front*. Director Oliver Stone took the audience into battle with the characters in the movie. Critic Roger Ebert wrote that *Platoon* "was written and directed by Oliver Stone, who fought in Vietnam and who has tried to make a movie about a war that is not fantasy, not legend, not metaphor, not message, but simply a memory of what it seemed like at the time to him."[19]

Figure 2.2
Platoon (Oliver Stone, 1986)

That *Platoon* was clearly an anti-war film rather than an adventure film set in a war was emphasized by Ebert:

> It was François Truffaut who said that it's not possible to make an anti-war movie because all war movies, with their energy and sense of adventure, end up making combat look like fun. If Truffaut had lived to see *Platoon*, the best film of 1986, he might have wanted to modify his opinion. Here is a movie that regards combat from ground level, from the infantryman's point of view, and it does not make war look like fun.[20]

Another overview of *Platoon* reinforced its impact: "A savage yet moving look at the Vietnam war ... one of the most powerful war [anti-war] movies ever made ... a series of blistering, messy images of war – a war where there is no Hollywood hero but instead just a patriotic boy who slowly becomes disillusioned with all he believed he was fighting for."[21]

Figure 2.3
Born on the Fourth of July (Oliver Stone, 1989)

Similar in many ways to *All Quiet on the Western Front* and *Platoon*, but going beyond them in terms of the postwar impact of the war on the human participant, is *Born on the Fourth of July*, also directed by Oliver Stone. Researcher Ana Aragon Tello describes the film as follows:

> *Born on the Fourth of July* creates a visceral impact on audiences with its direct anti-war message. By portraying a soldier whose body, mind, spirit and society have been wounded by a war, the movie is able to convey the heavy toll of war even outside of combat. The movie's themes emphasize the consequences of war, as opposed to other movies, like *All Quiet on the Western Front*, in which the focus is primarily the military training and the battlefield. *Born on the Fourth of July* addresses the theme of a soldier's physical wounds as a consequence of combat by illustrating how these afflictions disturb a soldier's return to civilian life, and it also addresses the theme of a soldier's psychological trauma after witnessing and taking part in violence and horror ... Another theme the movie explores is the toll war has on society. The movie begins by portraying an idealized community during peacetime, which later develops into a society

of turmoil, a society shattered by war. The progression of the disintegration of society is a parallel to the disintegration of the film's real-life subject, Ron Kovic. He is portrayed as an all-American boy who decides to fulfill his patriotic duty and serve his country at war by enlisting as soon as recruiters visit his high school – a direct real-life parallel to the volunteering students in *All Quiet on the Western Front*. Further, the movie deals with the brainwashing on both the level of an individual and of society. It portrays how both were tricked into believing the emergency need for war and combat and believing in the hypocrisy of idealized heroism and patriotism.[22]

The impact of the war and the nationalism, jingoism, and hypocrisy of much of the United States when he returned home with the war still going on turned Ron Kovic into a leading anti-war protester. After saving himself from the depths of physical and mental degradation, Kovic, confined for the rest of his life to a wheelchair, not only fought against the continuation of the Vietnam War, but became an anti-war organizer, speaker and icon as the United States planned and initiated future wars. As this is written, Kovic is one of the many Vietnam war veterans who have taken leading roles in the continuing and growing protest marches and rallies against the continuation of the war in Iraq and the manipulation of public opinion for a war on Iran. And the film about his life, "Born on the Fourth of July," while too late for the Vietnam War, has helped make it possible for him to motivate thousands of his "Nam" buddies for current anti-war action.

One film made shortly after an ostensible war action was *Black Hawk Down*, an adventure movie on America's ineptly conducted and too-obviously staged raid on Mogadishu, Somalia, in 2001. The film concentrates on the graphic delineation of war's brutalities. In that respect, it is somewhat similar to the opening sequences of *Saving Private Ryan* (1998), with its remorseless, merciless, raw representation of the carnage of D-Day in World War II. And, like *Private Ryan*, *Black Hawk Down* is only anti-war to the extent that it shows the horrors of war and its effect on individual soldiers, but at the same time lauds the valor of the American combatants and motivates pride in America's armed forces. Although *Black Hawk Down* does imply that the action was ill-defined and that men died for no clear reason, it – in the same way as *Private Ryan* – is not like some of the other films cited here, a clearly specified protest movie. It can be, in the broad sense, considered anti-war, but at the same time supportive of Americans fighting a war. In that sense, these films represent what appears to be a growing trend in the United States as the Iraq War drags on, longer than America's participation in World War II: Support the troops, but end the war.

Some critics have suggested that the film, *Jarhead*, which received neither the popularity nor the artistic acclaim of some of the other films, should be considered an anti-war film directly pertinent to the war in Iraq, which was in progress when the film was made in 2005. *Jarhead* deals with the first war in the desert, the Gulf War of 1991. The final words of the film, "We are still in the desert," refer to the fact that the participants – in this case, the Marines – will always carry a part of that war with them. But those words could also have a political connotation, reminding the audiences who saw the film in 2005 and later that we still have troops in that same desert.[23]

Jarhead does not deal with the combat experience of war and does not show the impact of battle on the participant. It concentrates on the tedium of preparing for war, on the boredom of the traditional military mantra, "hurry up and wait." Yet, there are some sections of the film that appear to touch on anti-war concepts. The principal character says at one point that "the man fires the rifle for many years, he goes to war, and afterward . . . he believes he's finished with the rifle. But no matter what else he may do with his hands – love a woman, build a house, change his son's diaper – his hands remember the rifle."[24] For all its faults and, in the opinion of most critics, clearly missing the boat if, in fact, it attempted to be an anti-war movie, *Jarhead* did include the question of how the United States got pulled into the quicksand of the first Gulf War and, by extension, into the current Iraq nightmare. Even obliquely, it is a rare protest in film against a war currently being fought.[25]

By the beginning of 2007, public opinion, including the attitudes of movie-going audiences, had turned overwhelmingly against the Iraq War, and Hollywood felt less uncomfortable about joining the vast majority of Americans in protesting the war. In 2007 several films were released that were critical of the two-front wars that the United States was engaged in and a third, against Iran, that US policymakers were trying to convince the public would be necessary. Anti-war critics were pleased that there were any films at all questioning the US war policy in the Middle East. But they were not so sanguine about the quality of the films themselves. A. O. Scott wrote in the *New York Times*:

> Brian De Palma's *Redacted*, a prizewinner . . . and a polarizing selection at film festivals . . . is one of a slew of American movies that try to deal with the war in Iraq and related matters. Their moods and methods vary widely. *Redacted* is furious and confrontational; Robert Redford's *Lions for Lambs* is pedagogical and talky; Paul Haggis's *In the Valley of Elah* is mournful and unsettled – but I find myself drawn, in each case, to more or less the same conclusion. I am glad the movie was made, and I wish it were better.[26]

Redacted dramatizes some of the most sordid, real events of the Iraq War, as seen through the camera lens of an American soldier fighting there, who plans to use his filming as a way to break into Hollywood movie-making. We see the behavior, boredom, and belligerence of GIs, of American soldiers raping a teenage girl and murdering her family, beheadings, and bombing of civilian targets – all of which actually occurred.

Critic Scott is concerned that although the ideas and emotions in the movie are confused and unpleasant, as they are in real life, they are also too familiar to the 2007 audience. He wishes the film had more clarity and freshness to make a greater impact.[27]

The Valley of Elah is about the efforts of the father of a GI who is just back from Iraq and has gone AWOL and been found dead, to determine how and why his son was killed. Ultimately, he links it "to the culture of war, to the hardening of young men to death, even of their own kind."[28] "Underneath its deceptively quiet surface is a raw, angry, earnest attempt to grasp the moral consequences of the war in Iraq and to stare without blinking into the chasm that divides those who are fighting it from their families, their fellow citizens, and one another."[29] The message of *In the Valley of Elah* is not "ambiguous or unclear. The message is that the war in Iraq has damaged this country in ways we have only begun to grasp."[30] That the criticism of the Iraq War is arrived at through an indirect device and that it doesn't deal with the political chicanery that launched the war and the military incompetence that conducted it, and which have lost America a host of its friends and gained America a host of enemies, is not surprising. If there is a surprise, it is, at a time when Hollywood and the other media are acquiescing to the government's propaganda wishes, that it contains any criticism of the Iraq War in any form or shape.

Lions for Lambs is divided into three parts and pulls no punches in criticizing "the wars [in Afghanistan and Iraq], the politicians who manufacture them, the media's pandering, complacent college kids not out rioting and protesting."[31] In one part, a Republican senator wants to start a new war that can be won easily; in another part, two young American soldiers are trapped behind enemy lines in Afghanistan; the third part deals with a professor trying to get his students to take a stand on the Iraq War. Critic Wesley Morris felt that much of the film was too preachy, more like a series of lectures rather than convincing drama. He wrote:

> When the wars in Iraq and Afghanistan started, I was naively eager that Hollywood would find ways to dramatize the conflict's political complexities and personal toll. We're probably too close to get any real artistic perspective. "The great movies about Vietnam either were not about the war or were made once it was over . . . Hollywood had time, distance, and money on its side to process the many tentacles of this imbroglio into compelling entertainment."[32]

A late 2007 film, *Grace Is Gone*, uses the background of the Iraq War to dramatize a personal family tragedy in which a father has to find a way to tell his young daughters that their mother, serving in the military, has been killed in Iraq. Actor John Cusack, who plays the father, said, "I just wanted to do something that just told the human side of it . . . I wanted to explore the reality of grief and loss, so that the war didn't become another abstraction that's on television."[33] One reviewer, noting that the film is "based on the foundation of a serious contemporary issue," stated that it "makes a case against the war in Iraq."[34]

A new film, scheduled to open weeks after this is being written and, therefore, without any critical commentary or reviews available, appears to be a protest against at least one aspect of the Iraq War. *Stop-Loss* is directed by Kimberley Peirce (director of *Boys Don't Cry*), the title referring to the military practice of extending a tour of duty beyond the contracted-for period. The film's promotion website describes the plot thus: "Decorated war hero . . . makes a celebrated return to his . . . hometown following his tour of duty." He attempts to make peace with civilian life when, against his will, "the Army orders him back to Iraq, which upends his world. The conflict tests everything he believes in: the bond of family, the loyalty of friends, the limits of love and the value of honor."[35]

Other films about the Iraq War that emerged in 2007 were relatively unsuccessful at the box office. Coincidentally, *Time* magazine and *U.S. News & World Report* had stories on this lack of box-office success in the same week in late 2007. The *U.S. News & World Report* headlined its story: "War: the Box Office Bomb," and stated, "Most Americans are unhappy with Bush's handling of the war on terrorism, particularly in Iraq. So why aren't people attracted to films that generally support their dissatisfaction? The simple answer is that people don't want to think about the subject."[36] *Time* magazine's story headline was: "This Means War. Why audiences aren't packing the cineplex to see Hollywood's take on the Iraq conflict," and said that audiences want war movies to be "edifying entertainment" and that "it's hard to make a feel-good war movie when a country's reputation falls as its body count rises."[37] Both made the point that successful movies about wars are made after the wars are ended. Jay Tolson wrote in *U.S. News*, "The success of Vietnam War movies . . . is that they came out after the war. But since Vietnam remained a divisive issue, those films still had a problem."[38] Richard Corliss wrote in *Time*, "Politicians and pundits were noisy enough during the first four years of the U.S. occupation of Iraq, but . . . Hollywood was quiet. Precious few films appeared on the Middle East wars . . . But that's the way the movie industry works. In the decade that the U.S. military spent in Vietnam, only a few films surfaced."[39] A review of *Grace Is Gone* stated that "the war is the preeminent issue across the USA, yet movies that explore politically sensitive topics have been suffocating at the box office . . . [the] consensus in Hollywood is that ticket buyers would rather escape reality."[40] The *New York Times* review of 2007's *Charlie Wilson's War* (about how the United States built up the Taliban in Afghanistan in order to oppose the Soviet Union) added the following consideration: "You can make a movie that is relevant and intelligent – and palatable to a mass audience – if its polit-ical pills are sugar-coated . . . Hollywood has long found it tricky to find a balance between being taken seriously on geopolitics without falling short on what movies are supposed to do: entertain."[41]

Have films of protest against war had any real effect? They appear to have had little in respect to stopping or preventing wars. Their con-tributions to strengthen the anti-war movements may have had some impact on ending wars, principally by helping generate and galvanize political opinion that forced politicians who were responsible for a given war in the first place to protect their voting base by ameliorating and even withdrawing from a war. Some of these films make it clear that we are being led into war by people who we should not trust, and *Dr. Strangelove* and *Fail-Safe*, among other non-wartime earlier films, played such roles in helping to finally force an end to America's participation in Vietnam.

The US government has over the years become more and more sophisticated about the impact of media, including that of Hollywood films. American political leadership has strengthened attempts to obtain, buy, intimidate, or otherwise persuade Hollywood to support its war, as well as other, policies. David Robb, author of *Operation Hollywood: How the Pentagon Shapes and Censors the Movies*, states that this relationship is blinding Hollywood into whitewashing the Iraq conflict.[42] It is not accidental. Pulitzer Prize-winning journalist Susan Faludi notes that during the Iraq War, Karl Rove, reportedly a principal architect of President George W. Bush's policies, "met repeatedly with Hollywood executives to get them to make pro-American movies, which were heavy on John Wayne themes."[43] David Robb further stated that "in many ways Hollywood is imbedded with the military" and that the military "know when positive images are portrayed in movies and television shows, they see huge spikes in recruitment. The military is really pressing to get into these pictures ... these films [that receive Pentagon assistance] should have a disclaimer: 'This film has been shaped and censored by the military.'"[44]

We have learned from history that the lack of an independent media willing to protest or at least reflect the protest side of any given controversial issue contributes significantly to the demise of democratic thought and practice in the given society. If war is indeed the greatest of evils, should not Hollywood, as a key medium, show more courage in reflecting the controversies of that evil?

Notes

1 Movie diva, *All Quiet on the Western Front*, 2001. www.moviediva.com/ MD_root/reviewpages/MDAAllQuietWesternFront.htm.
2 *Ibid.*

3   *Ibid.*
4   Dirks, Tim, *All Quiet on the Western Front*, Greatest Films. 1996. www.filmsite.org/allq.html.
5   Russel, Jamie, "BBC1Films." *All Quiet on the Western Front.* www.bbc.co.uk/films/2003/11/03all_quiet_on_the_western_front_1930_review.shtml.
6   Chambers II, John Whiteclay, "*All Quiet on the Western Front* (1930): The Anti-War Film and the Image of the First World War," *Historical Journal of Film, Radio & Television*, Vol. 14, No. 4, 1994, p. 13.
7   www.selu.edu/kslu/allquiet.html.
8   McCray, Patrick, Review of *Duck Soup*. www.film.u-net.com/Movies/reviews/DuckSop2.html.
9   Dirks, Tim, *Duck Soup*, Greatest Films. 1996. www.filmsite.org/duck.html.
10 *Ibid.*
11 *Ibid.*
12 Gee, Rick, "The Great Anti-War Films: *Paths of Glory*." www.lewrockwell.com/orig/gee6.html.
13 *Ibid.*
14 Cook, David A., *A History of Narrative Film* (New York: W.W. Norton, 1996), p. 928.
15 Mumford, Lewis, "*Strangelove* Reactions," March 1, 1964.
16 www.suntimes.com/ebertreviews/1994/10/947940.html.
17 Kirshner, Jonathan, "Subverting the Cold War in the 1960s," *Film and History*, Vol. 31, No. 12, 2001, pp. 40–4.
18 Dawson, Jan, Review of *M*A*S*H*, *Sight and Sound*, Vol. 30, No. 3, Summer, 1970, pp. 161–2.
19 Ebert, Roger, "Current Reviews: *Platoon*," *Chicago Sun-Times*, December 30, 1986. www.suntimes.com/ebert/ebert_reviews/1986/12/125248.html.
20 *Ibid.*
21 Schneider, Steven Jay, ed., *1001 Movies You Must See Before You Die* (New York: Quintet Publishing/Barron's, 2003), p. 740.
22 Aragon-Tello, Ana, "Anti-War Movies," a paper written for a course, "Pictures of Protest," at Emerson College, April 29, 2006.
23 Kaufman, Anthony, "Marines on the Big Screen," *Progressive*, Vol. 70, No. 1, January, 2006, p. 40.
24 *Ibid.*
25 Johnson, Brian, "The Looking-Glass War," *McLean's*, Vol. 118, No. 45, p. 64.
26 Scott, A. O., "Rage, Fear and Revulsion: At War With the War." http://movies.nytimes.com/2007/11/16/movies/16reda.html.
27 *Ibid.*
28 Hunter, Stephen, "*Valley of Elah* Spins An All-Too-Timeless Tale," *Washington Post*, September 14, 2007, p. C4.

29 Scott, A. O., "Seeking Clues to a Son's Death and a War's Meaning," Film Review, *New York Times*, September 14, 2007, p. B1.

30 *Ibid.*

31 Morris, Wesley, "Political drama feels more like a lecture," *Boston Globe*, November 9, 2007.

32 *Ibid.*

33 "John Cusack wanted to tell human side of Iraq War toll," *News-Press* (Fort Myers, FL), December 10, 2007, p. A2.

34 Puig, Claudia, "*Grace Is Gone*," *USA TODAY*, December 7, 2007, p. 6E.

35 www.stoplossmovie.com

36 Tolson, Jay, "War: the Box Office Bomb," *U.S. News & World Report*, November 26–December 3, 2007, p. 31.

37 Corliss, Richard, "This Means War. Why audiences aren't packing the Cineplex to see Hollywood's taken on the Iraq conflict," *Time*, November 26, 2007, p. 80.

38 Tolson, "War: the Box Office Bomb."

39 Corliss, "This Means War," pp. 80–1.

40 Quoted in a letter-to-the-editor by Mark Richard, *USA TODAY*, December 14, 2007, p. 21A.

41 Berke, Richard, "*Charlie Wilson's War*," review, *New York Times*, December 16, 2007. www.nytimes.com/2007/12/16/movies/16berk.html.

42 www.usatoday.com/life/movies/news/2005-02-07-military-projects_x.htm.

43 Kingbury, Alex, "Q&A: Susan Faludi; Post 9/11, a More Macho America," *U.S. News and World Report*, October 22, 2007, p. 30.

44 www.usatoday.com/life/movies/news/2005-02-07-military-projects_x.htm.

3

Anti-Semitism

Some of my best friends . . .

Given the endemic nature of anti-Semitism throughout the world, including the United States, virtually from the beginning of recorded Western history, coupled with the fact that many of the Hollywood moguls, from the beginning of that city's movie-making, have been Jewish, it is surprising that so few feature entertainment films have been made protesting anti-Semitism. Since the end of World War II a number of "Holocaust" movies have been produced, emphasizing the tragedy that occurred because of the lack of protest against anti-Semitism throughout the world. Prior to that, Hollywood produced several popular films based on historical events and personalities related to Jews in Europe, although, with few exceptions, the matter of anti-Semitism was largely deemphasized. Some of these films have been excellent, both in the sense of protest and in artistry. One that dealt directly with a real-life *cause célèbre* was *The Life of Emile Zola* (1937), Zola being the French author – not Jewish – who became a leading protester to the railroading of a Jewish army officer, Alfred Dreyfus, for treason. The Dreyfus Affair, in large part because of Zola, became and remained a popular worldwide example of anti-Semitic prejudice. Interestingly – and indicative of Hollywood's cowardice in directly confronting the subject of anti-Semitism – the film never refers to Dreyfus as Jewish or to the plot against him as government-directed anti-Semitism. *Disraeli* (1929), about the Prime Minister of England who was Jewish, dealt only gently with his struggles as a Jew in an anti-Semitic environment. Another popular Hollywood movie about Jews, *The House of Rothschild* (1934), traced the history of the Jewish banking family and was seen by many as reemphasizing the anti-Jewish stereotype of Jews as clever in money matters and in using questionable tactics to outwit authorities in amassing a fortune.

What about contemporary, ongoing anti-Semitism, particularly in the United States? Such films have been few. The conventional explanation is the one associated with *The Great Dictator* anomaly. During the entire period of the World War II Holocaust, in which the German government conducted the systematic extermination of at least six million Jews, not one Hollywood feature film was made protesting this action. Except for a brief, passing mention of concentration camps and Jews in one or two other films, Charlie Chaplin's *The Great Dictator* was the only film that even came close to protesting the Nazi's policies toward the Jews, and that film was made because of Chaplin's personal persistence in the face of opposition to its production by the Hollywood Establishment. It was distributed only because of Chaplin's reputation as the world's greatest performer at the time and because it was a satire that included Chaplin's comedy routines. It has been suggested – by some, concluded – that the reluctance of Jewish producers and studio heads in Hollywood to make films protesting the destruction of millions of Jews in Europe was because of their concern that the larger society would accuse them of self-interest in their films, of leaning over backward to support a Jewish agenda, thus harming their chances of entering the social and political life of southern California, largely otherwise closed to Jews. A further reason sometimes proposed is that for film executives of whatever religion, ethnicity, or persuasion, movies about social problems, especially about Nazi death camps, were not likely to do well at the box office – despite occasional surprises such as *All Quiet on the Western Front* and *The Grapes of Wrath*.

Even in the new twenty-first century, with virulent anti-Semitism growing globally because so many people and nations were associating all Jews with the United States' and Israel's repressive policies against Palestinians, Hollywood has made no movies protesting either anti-Semitism or the policies of the United States or Israel that provoked greater anti-Semitism. A notable exception is Steven Spielberg's *Munich* (2005), protesting the eye-for-an-eye, tooth-for-a-tooth philosophy that continues the deadly spiral of violence.

Anti-Semitism was rampant in the United States, as well as in other countries, prior to the Arab–Israeli conflict. New immigrant groups, including Jews, were scorned, labeled, deprived of job and housing opportunities, socially ostracized, physically attacked, and discriminated against in many other ways. That this has not changed much is evident from the rhetoric in the first decade of the twenty-first century against immigrants, legal as well as illegal. While it was easier for Jews to pass as part of the general population than many other immigrant groups who were easily identifiable by color or other non-Caucasian features, legally and by convention Jews were treated as second-class citizens. For example, many communities had legal codicils in real-estate agreements – restrictive covenants barring sales of homes in that community to Jews. Many restaurants refused entrance or service to anyone they knew or suspected to be Jewish. Private schools reserved the right not to admit Jews. Prep schools, colleges, universities, and professional schools had strict quotas for Jews (as well as for other minorities and for women). Jews were barred from social, sport, and other clubs and associations. (That's why we see today, in some areas, separate Jewish country clubs and social organizations.) Advertisements for most jobs, even for lower-level clerks, telephone operators, and secretaries, would have the notation that only "gentiles" or "Christians" need apply. Jews were barred from positions ranging from corporate white-collar jobs to jobs in factories. For example, Jews were rarely hired in the burgeoning auto industry in Detroit early in the twentieth century – in part due to the virulent anti-Semitism of Henry Ford. Many retail establishments wouldn't hire Jews because they felt their customers would object to being sold items by Jews. (That's why so many Jews were forced to go into business for themselves – no one else would hire them – or to go into professions where, although there was discrimination, they could work in large part independently, such as in the fields of medicine, law, and education.)

Some towns throughout the United Sates had signs posted at their city limits stating, in various versions: "No Jews or Dogs Allowed." In any given predominantly non-Jewish area, Jews were likely not to be accepted or included in social situations by neighbors or co-workers who were not Jewish. Self-protection and self-realization for Jews, as for other minority groups, resulted in self-ghettoizing, physically and socially. Ironically, how often have we heard the bigots say, "oh, they're so clannish" about Jews and others? At best, in many instances, Jews were condescended to. At worst they were beaten up, murdered, torched out of their homes, lynched on false accusations, and victimized in legal frame-ups. Jewish kids in non-Jewish neighborhoods were frequently taunted and beaten up with the accusation, "you killed Christ." Even today, where one or two Jewish families find themselves in a non-Jewish and, frequently, lower-education area, some of these things continue to occur. Even where a majority of society may have practiced tolerance and where there were no legal restrictions, "gentlemen's agreements" were adhered to.

Discriminatory actions against Jews that were highly prevalent during the Jewish migration from southern and eastern Europe in the late 1800s and early 1900s reflected similar discrimination against earlier migrations from Europe, such as against the Irish in the mid-nineteenth century, and continuous discrimination against more identifiable groups, such as Latinos and African-Americans.

While federal laws in the past several decades have made such discrimination illegal, it still goes on, not only against Jews, but to a greater extent for other minorities that have not yet integrated into the general society as well as have many Jews. Discrimination in many cases has become much more subtle, reflecting the Hank Greenberg syndrome. For non-baseball enthusiasts, Hank Greenberg was Jewish and a major league baseball player in the 1930s for the Detroit Tigers professional baseball team. He was a powerful home-run hitter. In 1938, as the season was coming to a close, it appeared certain that he would break what most considered the most venerated record in baseball, Babe Ruth's 60 home runs in a season. Not spoken publicly – at least in the media – a strong sentiment swept baseball that it would somehow be sacrilege if a Jew broke this record. During the last few weeks of the season, opposing pitchers, seemingly virtually en masse, appeared to be unable to control their pitches and Greenberg got few pitches that were hittable, even if it meant that he would draw a walk. He finished the season with 58 home runs. Movies such as *Pride of the Yankees* (1942), lamenting the loss to baseball through physical illness of one of its favorite players, and *Fear Strikes Out* (1957), showing how mental illness affected another big-league player, and many other films about baseball and football, many of them protesting something rotten within or without the game, have been made. But aside from a documentary, there have been no films about this dramatic event involving Hank Greenberg. The 2007 World Series raised an oblique question touching on the Hank Greenberg syndrome. The outstanding player on the Boston Red Sox team in winning the American League title series was Kevin Youkilis, who also is Jewish. His defensive play, home runs, runs batted in, and remarkable batting average of .500 for that series materially helped the Red Sox reach the World Series. Following the first two World Series games in an American League park, the teams moved to a National League park, where rules required the Red Sox to let the pitcher hit and to remove one of the offensive hitters from the lineup. Youkilis was left out of the starting lineup despite the fact that he could play several positions at which the players used had less effective records than he. Deliberate anti-Semitism? Not likely. But the action raises the question as to whether, subconsciously, if someone is to be left out of the game – like on playgrounds in many places in America – why not the "Jew-boy"?!

Before World War II very few Hollywood films even mentioned anti-Semitism, no less protested its existence. Jewish movie moguls stayed away from the subject for much of the same reasons they did not acknowledge the Holocaust in their films. Anti-Semitism was only "hinted at or passingly referred to, even when the film was about an act of anti-Semitism."[1] During World War II other media than Hollywood entertainment films brought to the attention of the American public the bitter fruits of anti-Semitic bigotry, reporting – albeit sparsely and usually buried on inside pages of newspapers – what was happening to European Jews (and gypsies, homosexuals, the elderly, the handicapped, political dissenters, and others) in Germany's death camps. Perforce, the public was made aware of anti-Semitism on a grand scale. It had little effect on US leaders, however, as President Franklin D. Roosevelt, the US State Department, and Congress made every effort to prevent Jews trying to escape from the Holocaust from entering the United States. In fact, in Congress some Representatives and Senators made openly anti-Semitic remarks. In one instance, where Representative John E. Rankin of Mississippi called a journalist he didn't like a "little Communist kike," the House rose and gave him prolonged applause. It was with this background that World War II ended, its ostensible purpose to preserve democracy auguring a new era. But, as writer Brian Webster noted: "Those who are too young to have lived amidst the post Second World War culture of the U.S. might be shocked to know that, in the aftermath of Hitler's defeat and when the Holocaust was fresh in everyone's mind, anti-Semitism was still widespread in America."[2]

It was in 1947 that two films were produced that reflected the hopes of some people for that new era. *Crossfire* and *Gentleman's Agreement* protested anti-Semitism without equivocation. The latter was produced by Darryl F. Zanuck, a leading Hollywood producer. Bigotry at the time was a taboo subject for films. But after World War II, when the horrors of the Holocaust became known worldwide, it seemed to non-Jew Darryl F. Zanuck that it was the right time to bring up the subject of Jewish discrimination in America, even though every other Hollywood studio had passed on it as too controversial.[3]

Gentleman's Agreement over the years became recognized as the seminal film protesting anti-Semitism in the United States. A few months before its release, however, another Hollywood film protesting anti-Semitism, *Crossfire*, made its debut. Made in black and white in film-noir style, this deals with a

> "weary Washington detective trying to get to the bottom of a seemingly motive-lacking murder, with the prime suspect a boozy soldier who can only vaguely recall the events of the night . . . the story really digs its heels into lots of postwar issues – how soldiers need a place to put all their violence once the war is over and the other problems of adjusting to civilian life."[4]

The plot of *Crossfire* has several soldiers on leave meeting a man at a bar, going to his apartment, with one of the soldiers staying after the others leave and killing the host. During the slaying the killer uses the slur, "Jew-boy," about his victim. A detective of Irish extraction is assigned to solve the murder:

> *Crossfire* becomes more of a film about anti-Semitism than it does a murder investigation, especially since there is no real mystery as to who did the killing. Finlay [the detective] tries to explain the killer's bias by saying "hate is like a gun". He goes on to give a history lesson about prejudice in this country, about how his Irish grandfather was lynched because he was Catholic.[5]

Ironically, the book that served as the basis for the film had a homosexual as the victim. But the Breen office, Hollywood's censor, and the movie studios themselves were afraid to deal with the topic of homosexuality at that time and the subject was changed to anti-Semitism. Even that was considered too controversial for Hollywood, but the impact of the revelations of the Holocaust and the persistence of the director and producer, Edward Dmytryk and Adrian Scott, allowed it to be made. It was nominated for five Academy Awards. However, as the McCarthy era of political suppression closed in on the United States, films about controversial subjects, such as *Crossfire*, were targets for anti-communist witch-hunters. Because the Communist Party officially opposed racism, anti-Semitism, and other widespread prejudices and inequities, anyone holding such views could be accused of being a communist. The investigation into perceived subversion in Hollywood by the HUAC, initiated by the movie moguls as a device to bust the film-industry unions, resulted in both Dmytryk and Scott being called to testify before HUAC. They refused to answer questions about their personal political beliefs, were blacklisted, found guilty of contempt of Congress, and served jail sentences as part of the "Hollywood Ten" – a group of writers who were principal Hollywood victims of McCarthyism.

Gentleman's Agreement was released shortly after *Crossfire* and shortly became the quintessential movie protesting contemporary anti-Semitism. But it was not easy. The subject matter, as noted above, was taboo in Hollywood. The script for the film was adapted from a bestselling book of the same name by Laura Z. Hobson. The title referred to the "unspoken agreement among gentiles to discriminate against Jews – a not so subtle form of the persecution prevalent in the years immediately following World War II."[6] The proposal for the film had been rejected by virtually every studio in Hollywood, including those run by Jews. It was at the insistence of a non-Jew, producer Darryl F. Zanuck, that the film was finally made. Zanuck hired a non-Jew, Elia Kazan, as director. The star of the film, Gregory Peck, was not Jewish. Almost all Hollywood pressured Zanuck not to make the film. Fear of linking Hollywood to such a controversial film prompted some executives, some sources have alleged, to try to buy and burn the finished print. Critic Dennis Schwartz wrote that "It might be difficult today to explain why the film was so daring back then, but it was because that sort of prejudice was kept under the radar and film executives, many of whom were Jewish, were nervous about how such a film would play to the public."[7]

Figure 3.1
Gentleman's Agreement (1947)

The main character in "Gentleman's Agreement" is Philip Green, a journalist who is seeking an angle for a story on anti-Semitism. He decides to approach it from the inside – that is, subjectively, rather than objectively, by pretending to be Jewish. Only his editor, his fiancée, his mother, and his young son know. As Phil Greenberg he encounters the usual litany of discrimination: social clubs, resort hotels, real-estate restrictions, job hiring and bias and, most distressing to him, physical attack on his son by classmates who believe he is Jewish. In other words, the everyday experiences of Jews of that era who had not isolated themselves in self-protective ghettos, isolation that minorities have been forced into from time immemorial for physical and psychological and sometimes economic survival. Green(berg)'s fiancée, portrayed at first as thoroughly unbiased and encouraging to his efforts, becomes alienated when she discovers the anti-Semitic bias she has to share in real life and not only in theoretical empathy. The film includes the difficulties of Green's army-officer friend, who is Jewish, with job and housing needs, and features a scene in which both are involved in an unprovoked anti-Semitic attack upon the friend.

While *Crossfire* dealt with a hate crime against Jews, *Gentleman's Agreement* was more subtle and, because of that, had more impact. It revealed not a dramatic instance of hate, but the everyday, unceasing prejudices against a designated group of people, particularly by those who otherwise one might consider intelligent, sensitive, and compassionate. The character of Phil Green learns that the people like him – friends he socializes with and even loves – are bigots just beneath the surface. One of the more striking moments in the film is when Phil Green's fiancée, intellectually completely supportive of what he is doing, reveals how unhappy she is when she realizes that her non-Jewish friends will think that her fiancé is Jewish. In one of the sequences, after he experiences what it is, at least for a short time, to be Jewish, Phil Green says:

> I've come to see that lots of nice people who aren't [anti-Semites], people who despise it and protest their own innocence, help it along and wonder why it grows. People who would never beat up a Jew or yell "kike" at a child, people who think that anti-Semitism is something that's way off in some dark crackpot place with low-class morons. That's the biggest discovery that I've made about this whole business – the good people, the nice people.

Critic Brian Webster described it this way:

What makes the film most effective isn't its criticism of those who are openly anti-Semitic, nor even those who keep their anti-Jewish feelings under wraps. Its real power comes when the film exposes those who cluck their tongues at anti-Semitism, but don't really do anything about it. The uncompromising moral stance of Phil, and the movie, makes it difficult for audience members to watch and not question their own day-to-day behavior.[8]

Gentleman's Agreement won several 1947 Academy Awards, including Best Picture and Best Director.

In a dramatic example of real life imitating art that has imitated real life, Gregory Peck, who played Phil Green and in the movie was banned from social clubs because he was believed to be Jewish, found himself blackballed by many social clubs around Hollywood and Los Angeles because they resented his role in a film that showed their barring of Jews in a negative light. After some years Peck was invited to rejoin these clubs, but turned most of them down.

In another bizarre twist, Elia Kazan, the director of this film extolling decency and attacking hypocrisy, took a totally opposite ethical stand outside of films. "It's ironic that Kazan would be honored for directing a film about taking a firm stand on principle, and then turn around five years later and rat on his friends before the U.S. House Un-American Activities Committee, but who says life must always imitate art?"[9]

Some critics now describe *Gentleman's Agreement* as too tame or too heavy-handed or, most damning, too irrelevant for lasting impact. They point out that the anti-Semitic issues presented then no longer are pertinent in current society. While some of those issues are no longer overt, having been addressed by federal anti-discrimination laws, those critics illustrate the very point of the film: If it's not blatant or obvious, then one pretends it doesn't exist. One survey in the first decade of the twenty-first century revealed that almost one-fifth of all Americans are overtly anti-Semitic, ranging from almost half of foreign-born Latinos to one-third of African-Americans to five percent of college and university faculty.[10] How many people do not consider themselves anti-Semitic, but do not associate much, if at all, with Jews, who listen to anti-Jewish ethnic or religious jokes, who believe stereotypes (positive and negative) about Jews, who consider Jews strange or different?

In terms of prejudice per se, as this is written in 2008, the United States has been engulfed in a climate of fear, orchestrated by its own leaders in the White House, that generates suspicion and hate – through manufactured fear – against Middle Easterners, Arab-Americans and Muslims. We know from history that one way for a government to maintain and aggrandize power is to create an enemy for the people to fear and to turn to an authoritarian for protection. In this light, other critics point out that *Gentleman's Agreement*, more than 60 years later, is still, unfortunately, relevant.

> It's a shame *Gentleman's Agreement* doesn't have the kind of cultural response it once enjoyed. Today, more than ever, its message is necessary. For all the strides it prides itself on, America [2002] is not that distant from America 1947; our racism and xenophobia just wear a few more layers of lip gloss, that's all. We're getting better at attitude adjustment, but there still exists enough shame and prejudice for some groups – those with "Middle-eastern-colored skin" or "sexually disoriented types," for instance – to talk about themselves in whispers and murmurs in certain mixed company.[11]

The artistic, box-office, and public relations success of *Gentleman's Agreement* gave it an aura of being the quintessential film protesting anti-Semitism, a reputation which continues to this day, and prompted Hollywood to venture into more so-called "problem" films, principally in the area of racism. Civil rights, which for a long time had not even been given lip service, now began to come to the fore, prompted in part by the World War II exposure of millions of Americans, including African-Americans, to countries and practices that were more democratic and tolerant than the United States in their treatment of minorities. Concomitantly, many Americans had learned from the horrors of the Holocaust where continued hate and intolerance could eventually lead. But this aspect of Hollywood feature films, protests against racism, is the subject of another chapter in this book.

A later film protesting anti-Semitism is *School Ties*, released in 1992. It is favored by the younger generation – that is, students doing research on the subject or taking classes such as the one this writer taught, entitled "Pictures of Protest" – because the protagonist is a student. The student, David Greene (critics have noted the surname similarity with that of the principal character in *Gentleman's Agreement*), is a promising athlete and is recruited by an elite New England prep school to help build the fledgling football team. David is Jewish and is pleased to have the opportunity to study in such an elite institution. The school has had few, if any, Jewish students and, knowing the general attitude of the school and at least the latent anti-Semitism among its students, the recruiters tell David to hide the fact that he's a Jew. As critic Roger Ebert noted, "[David] is a terrific quarterback and the school alumni want a winning season so bad they'll do anything to get one."[12] David complies, becoming "one of the boys" and a popular football team leader with many friends. He hides his reactions to the many-anti-Semitic remarks he hears – which are not directed at him because the other boys don't know – yet – that he's Jewish. "He's not amused when anti-Semitic remarks casually pass their lips. Rather than expose himself to their barbs, David hides his Star of David necklace and tries to fit in."[13] Finally, a jealous, bigoted teammate learns his secret and "outs" him. Now, suddenly, he doesn't belong. Instead of being a hero, he is a target of torment and hazing and, as frequently happened then and occurs today in many schools, the door of his dormitory room is daubed with swastikas. David's situation reaches a crisis and the plot opens up the full onslaught of anti-Semitism in an educational setting when "one of the students cheats on a test and the students are empowered to deal with it under the school's ancient honor code. The guilty student tries to pass the blame to David, relying on anti-Semitism to help him get away with it."[14] Among other parallels to *Gentleman's Agreement* is the romantic subplot. Just as Phil Green's fiancée shies away from him when she realizes her friends will think her fiancé is Jewish, David's *School Ties* girlfriend avoids him when she learns he is Jewish because a continued relationship would make her social life and acceptance at the school too difficult. In that respect "School Ties" is more realistic than "Gentleman's Agreement," which has a reconciliatory happy ending. Roger Ebert stated that *School Ties*

is not simply about anti-Semitism, but also about the way that bigotry can do harm by inspiring dishonesty. One of David's friends tells him it would have been best for him to proudly proclaim his Jewishness on the first day of school, and of course that is right; to remain secretive is to grant the bigots the power of their hate.[15]

That *School Ties*, produced in 1992, is set in 1950 suggests that even forty-five years after *Gentleman's Agreement* Hollywood was still too timid to tackle the issue in contemporary terms. That kind of discrimination was still going on in 1992 on many campuses – prep, high school, college, and on the playgrounds of elementary schools. Without changing the script, *School Ties* could have been set in the 1990s. Putting it in 1950, Hollywood could say that it wasn't challenging the status quo or presenting something that was currently controversial – that it wasn't a picture of protest.

Over the years a number of other films have been considered protests against anti-Semitism, some with obvious references, others obliquely by inference. *American History X* (1998) falls into the former category, with graphic violence illustrating the effects of anti-Semitism in the United States. The film shocks and offends the viewer with the action of one of the anti-Semitic protagonists. It goes beneath the outward manifestation of the hate and attempts to get to the roots of the problem. It presents a clear message: Hate is learned and therefore can be prevented. Importantly, it can be viewed in a contemporary context – an unambiguous protest against what is, in real time, occurring in society. Unlike *Gentleman's Agreement* and *School Ties*, however, which present the bigots as ordinary, everyday people we know and socialize with, *American History X* presents them as members of organized hate groups. Critic Laura Finley perceptively wrote that "the film sends the message that hate crimes are committed by people who shave their heads and wear swastikas – or in the case of other films, wear white sheets. If a viewer knows that he does not do this, he can rest assured that he is a not a racist" or anti-Semite.[16]

Some critics cite Holocaust films such as *Schindler's List* (1993) and *The Pianist* (2002) as examples of Hollywood films protesting anti-Semitism. They would fall into the second category above, obliquely. They do, of course, graphically show the ravages of anti-Semitism. But can what the viewer experiences be applied directly to his or her contemporary society, and especially in the United States? For Holocaust films to be truly protests against the Holocaust, they should have been made during the Holocaust. That is not to say that they do not have a salutary impact on viewers today and provide ideas and feelings that may motivate opposition to contemporary manifestations of anti-Semitism. In a comparison of *Schindler's List* to the film about genocide in Africa, *Hotel Rwanda* (2004), one critic wrote that "If the present genocide in Sudan's Darfur region follows the same story arc, as is likely, it will be acknowledged years from now in a Hotel Sudan sequel. By which time, of course, it will be too late to do anything meaningful."[17]

It would not be appropriate to end this chapter without some reference to those Hollywood feature films that help create the negative attitudes and actions that cry out for subsequent films of protest. Just as there have been racist films, emphasizing the negative stereotypes of African-Americans, most infamously D. W. Griffith's 1916 artistic triumph, *Birth of a Nation*, so there have been anti-Semitic films that have compounded age-old canards about Jews. In recent years probably the most controversial of such films is Mel Gibson's *The Passion of the Christ*, released in 2004. Aside from Gibson having personally displayed his anti-Semitism, one must look at the film itself. *The Passion of the Christ* has been described by many as a protest film *against* Jews. The producer's view of the biblical story in the film emphasizes the age-old diatribe used as the principal reason for animosity toward the Jews: They killed Christ. In its portrayal of Jews as evil, bloodthirsty villains, *The Passion of the Christ* has been criticized for allegedly being historically inaccurate in many respects. The Anti-Defamation League expressed its concern:

> We fear the consequences of the film. There will be many people who are not so familiar with the Gospel narratives and might believe that everything they see in the film derives directly from the New Testament. Much of what is on the screen is Mr. Gibson's artistic vision and finds its genesis in extra-biblical sources. We are also concerned about those who already are disposed unfavorably toward Jews and will use this film to fan the flames of hatred.[18]

Either way, there is no question that Hollywood feature films play a significant role in influencing the minds, emotions, and behavior of people in tolerating and understanding people who appear to be different in any way from themselves.

Notes

1 www.allmovie.com/cg/aveg.d11?p=avg&sgl=A19402.
2 Webster, Brian, "Apollo Guide," September 22, 1999. http://apolloguide.com/mov_fullrev.asp?CID=1749.
3 Schwartz, Dennis, "Ozus World Movie Reviews," January 23, 2004. www.sover.net/~ozus/gentlemansagreement.htm.

4   Schwartz, Dennis, *Crossfire*, February 18, 2000. www.rottentomatoes.com/ click/movie-1004989/reviews.php?critic=columns&sortby=default&page= i&rid=a78927.

5   *Ibid.*

6   Taylor, Dawn, *"Gentleman's Agreement*: Fox Studio Classics." www. rottentomatoes.com/click/movie-1044865/reviews.php?critic=columns& sortby=default&page=1&rid=1241377.

7   Schwartz, "Ozus World Movie Reviews."

8   Webster, "Apollo Guide."

9   *Ibid.*

10 Foxman, Abraham, "Anti-Semitism on the Rise in America," press release, Anti-Defamation League, June 11, 2002. www.adl.org/PresRele/ASUS_12/ 4109_12.asp.

11 Abrahams, David, "I Was Jewish for 8 Weeks," January 21, 2003. www.culturedose.net/review.php?rid-10004452.

12 Ebert, Roger, *School Ties*. www.suntimes.com/ebert/ebert_reviews/ 1992/09/778428.html.

13 Cooper, Jeanne, *"School Ties," Washington Post*, September 18, 1992. www.washingtonpost.com.

14 *Ibid.*

15 *Ibid.*

16 Finley, Laura L., *"American History X," Contemporary Justice Review*, No. 6, 2003, pp. 81–4.

17 "Consciences Stirred Too Late," *USA Today*, February 28, 2005, p. A14.

18 "ADL and Mel Gibson's *The Passion of the Christ*: Frequently Asked Questions." Anti-Defamation League, 2004. www.adl.org/Interfaith/ gibson_qa.asp.

4

Prison and Justice Systems

Not separate but unequal

America's prison and justice systems have been frequent subjects of Hollywood pictures of protest, ranging from the death penalty to cruel executions to chain gangs and prison brutality, to inept and biased juries to incompetent police investigations and framed evidence. In many cases the writers, producers, and directors have denied that they sought to protest the conditions that they showed, but were just making a movie that had suspense and adventure. Their explanations should be taken at face value, for, indeed, the stories associated with prisons and justice, even or perhaps especially the everyday, sometimes mundane reflections of events in real life, do have the built-in elements of drama. Will the chain-gang prisoners survive the brutal guards? Will the prison escapees make it across the river before the dogs catch their scent? Will the prison revolt against brutal conditions succeed without the inmate leaders or the sympathetic guards being killed in the process? Will the innocent prisoner being escorted to the death chamber be reprieved by a last-second call from the governor? Will the good cop be able to convince the police chief that the dirty cop planted phony evidence and get the victim's long prison sentence overturned? Will the good juror be able to convince the biased jurors that the person being tried could not have committed the crime? Will the judge's law clerk have the courage and personal integrity to reveal to the press that the judge is being bribed by a defendant? Take a few moments and you'll easily come up with many more plot examples. And all – if implemented well by the producer and director – provide a suspenseful conflict, with continuing rising action and complications, leading to the climax: Who wins and who loses? Prison and justice themes lend themselves well to such dramatic situations.

That is not say that many of these pictures protesting the prison and justice system were not deliberate in their revelation of the situation or condition being condemned. Many were made at the time the issue was before the public, with greater or lesser controversy about what should be done about it. In the late 1990s and early 2000s a number of films dealt directly with the death penalty, an issue of growing debate in the United States. Three-quarters of a century earlier there was growing concern about the inhumane conditions in many prisons, and Hollywood responded with films about the "big house," as prisons were called (one of the key films was entitled *The Big House*, 1930), and the infamous chain gangs.

These comments on prison and justice films seem to be in conflict with one of the basic tenets in this book about the reluctance of Hollywood to deal with controversial issues that were significant at the times the films were made. The apparent dichotomy needs to be looked at in terms of the kinds of controversy. It appears that the vast majority of Americans were sympathetic to the public protests about the unfair aspects of the prison and justice systems, and many politicians were also speaking out against these conditions. Therefore, for the vast majority of Hollywood producers, the films they made at that time on these subjects would not run counter to the general public opinion and therefore would not alienate many, if any, potential customers or power brokers. On the other hand, with much of the country anti-Semitic, as noted in chapter 2, or nationalistic or jingoistic – although the word "patriotic" was universally used to discourage dissent – in regard to its support for a given war (as suggested in chapter 1, particularly in relation to Vietnam and Iraq), Hollywood didn't want to risk losing at the box office or in its relationships with the political leaders who initiated and supported the given war.

Early Hollywood films of this chapter's genres tended to show prison conditions that motivated revolts, sometimes by sympathetic protagonists with whom the audience could empathize and who, the audience was clearly informed, were innocent of the crimes for which they were convicted. While some early films, before sound, had prison backgrounds and showed prison scenes, the first film generally regarded as a protest against the system was a 1917 movie, *The Honor System*. Produced well before there was a national outcry for prison reform,

The Honor System deals with a prison run by corrupt administrators and the impact of this corruption on the prisoners, particularly one jailed for murder. To make it possible for the audience to empathize with this principal character, it is made clear that he was innocent of murder per se, but killed another person in self-defense. To make the movie experience authentic, the director, Raoul Walsh, incarcerated himself in a prison for a short while.[1]

The seminal prison protest film, however, was produced in 1930, after the advent of sound. *The Big House* established the basic approach, form, and content for all prison movies to follow. Even the language that we now associate with prison films came principally from *The Big House*, terms such as "screws" and "bulls" for guards, and "the hole" for solitary confinement.[2] The movie took full advantage of the then relatively new dimension of film-making: sound. For the first time audiences watched prison scenes with what are now standard sound effects: the marching feet of hundreds of prisoners, the clanging of steel cell doors being slammed shut, the rapid fire of machine guns to quell a riot, the screeching of sirens to signal prisoner uprisings or attempted escapes.[3]

The setting of *The Big House* is an overcrowded prison, with 3,000 inmates in a facility designed for 1,800. The film's plots include the prison revolt instigated by convict leaders who, in desperation, seek more decent treatment, with subplots involving those convict leaders whose motives are to better their conditions and those who revolt purely out of anger and hate and/or as an attempt to facilitate an escape. This is counterpointed with good and bad guards, specifically a warden who tries to be more humane but is frequently provoked into harsh rule to prevent total chaos.[4] The principal character is a man convicted of manslaughter. His relationships with other prisoners end in the climax, an attempt to escape, which results in a massacre. The film – and the motivation for the action – was described this way: "*The Big House*: prison of no hope – the last terminal for lost souls. Only the strong survive; the weak crack or are corrupted."[5] The film reflected high-profile prison riots in New York's Auburn prison the previous year, 1929, in which a number of people were killed.

For an early film and especially one in a genre not yet clearly defined, "The Big House" has nuances and depth of characters not found in many movies for some time afterward, as well as the feeling of raw realism not experienced by audiences prior to that time. The impact of *The Big House* can be seen in prison films that followed, which borrowed virtually all of the innovations in plot lines and in production techniques.

The following year, in 1931, producer Howard Hawks released a film entitled *Criminal Code* and, capitalizing on the critical and box-office success of the *The Big House*, there was the mandatory *Ladies of the Big House*, also in 1931. Despite the cloning, *Ladies of the Big House* was a breakthrough in its own way, for the first time showing women in ugly situations, behaving in ugly ways, expressing rage and actions not generally attributed – at least not in the movies – to women. A year later, in 1932, the first of a subsequent number of chain-gang films, *Hell's Highway*, was produced.[6] The conditions of prison chain gangs, as differentiated from usual incarceration, were seen as much worse and much more inhumane. But it took Hollywood films revealing their worst practices that prompted more and more people to condemn them and led to their abolition – at least for a period of time – or to changes in how they were administered and treated prisoners.

> The living conditions were often unsanitary, crowded, and poorly constructed. These bad conditions of the past have given the chain gang an extremely bad rap. The way people view chain gangs has changed several times throughout their history in the United States. The earliest history of chain gangs holds the cause for the bad views of them. The public sees chain gangs as a racist part of the Old South. The first chain gangs began in England and the northern part of the United States during the eighteenth century.[7]

The following sums up the conditions of this facet of the prison system: "The harsh conditions on chain gangs included starvation rations, regular whippings, and heavy iron chains that were soldered into place. Not surprisingly, the death rate among members of chain gangs in various states was estimated at between 10% and 50% from the 1880s to the 1920s."[8]

Racism may be the principal reason for the post-Civil War growth of the chain-gang prison system:

> When southern states needed to find new sources of labor after their slaves were freed, the chain gang system was the answer. These prisons, which came to be known as Industrial Prisons, were operated like factories and used the chain gang form of punishment. The chain gang comprised a group of prisoners, linked

together by iron chains, who were forced to work in coal mines and to rebuild roads and buildings. Only men were placed in chain gangs, and most of them were black males who had once been enslaved. These men were frequently engaged in petty crime because they could find no jobs and were trying to provide for themselves and their families.[9]

In the 1930s the chain-gang prison system was fairly prevalent throughout the United States, most particularly in the South. In 1929,[10] Georgia alone reputedly had 140 such prison camps. Intense, harsh physical labor, sometimes for its own sake, was their hallmark. Work was enforced by whips and rifle butts. Minor infractions resulted in harsh punishment. Escape was virtually impossible because prisoners were chained together at their feet – thus the term "chain gang." Many prisoners died because of the body-breaking labor and through some of the most severe punishments.

It was in this atmosphere that, in 1932, *Hell's Highway* and *I Am a Fugitive from a Chain Gang* were released, both ostensibly protests against a practice going on at the time the films were made. *Hell's Highway* opens with headlines from real newspapers pointing to the abuses in the chain-gang system. Its main character is a criminal, not a victim of circumstances, as is the main character of *I Am a Fugitive from a Chain Gang*. Although in a chain-gang setting, with some insights into the desperation of convicts suffering the horrors of the system, *Hell's Highway* is principally a melodrama emphasizing one criminal's sacrifice for his brother, also incarcerated. The realism of the chain gang seems subverted to the drama.

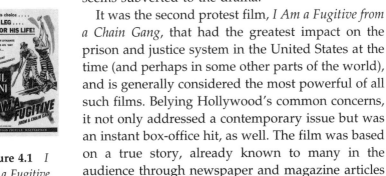

Figure 4.1 *I Am a Fugitive from a Chain Gang* (1932)

It was the second protest film, *I Am a Fugitive from a Chain Gang*, that had the greatest impact on the prison and justice system in the United States at the time (and perhaps in some other parts of the world), and is generally considered the most powerful of all such films. Belying Hollywood's common concerns, it not only addressed a contemporary issue but was an instant box-office hit, as well. The film was based on a true story, already known to many in the audience through newspaper and magazine articles and a novel, *I Am a Fugitive from a Georgia Chain Gang*, by the principal character's brother, the Reverend

Vincent Burns, who used the pseudonym Robert Elliott Burns for the first-person accounts.

The true story: A World War I veteran, Robert Burns, returned home to low-paying jobs, unable to make a decent living. He drifted around the country, seeking some way of earning money. Starving, he and two other destitute men robbed a grocery store in Atlanta, Georgia, of $5.80. He was arrested and sentenced to six to ten years on the Campbell County, Georgia, prison chain gang. After a few months, with the help of another inmate, he escaped and made his way to Chicago. During the next seven years, in Chicago, under an assumed name and persona, Burns became a respected public speaker, writer, and founding editor of *The Greater Chicago Magazine*. He married, but after several years of a purportedly unhappy marriage fell in love with someone else and asked his wife for a divorce. In angry retaliation, she informed the Georgia authorities who and where he was. The Governor of Illinois and other prominent people intervened on his behalf and the Georgia authorities promised that he would be given a full pardon if he voluntarily returned and served just 90 more days of his sentence. However, they didn't keep their promise and sent him to a prison chain gang in LaGrange, Georgia, to serve out the remainder of his six-to-ten-year sentence. His requests for an appeal to the Georgia Parole Board were ignored. After another year on the chain gang, he managed to escape again, in 1930. He reached New Jersey and became a tax consultant and wrote a series of magazine articles on his experiences on the chain gang. Warner Brothers bought his story, and shortly after the film, "I Am a Fugitive from a Chain Gang," came out, the Georgia authorities found him and arrested him. But the Governor of New Jersey – and two subsequent governors – refused to extradite him. Burns didn't return to Georgia until 1945, which had abolished chain gangs in 1937, largely due to the impact of Burns's story and the film. The reformist Governor of Georgia in 1945, Ellis Arnall, said he would represent Burns if the latter returned to the state. Burns did, and the Georgia Pardon and Parole Board commuted his sentence to time served. But because he had admitted committing the robbery, he did not receive a full pardon.[11]

Now, how was this true story represented in the movie, inasmuch as film dramaturgy by necessity must create drama that is larger and more intense than the too-often mundane aspects of real life in order to hold an audience? "I Am a Fugitive from a Chain Gang" held remarkably close to the true-life story, perhaps because this true-life drama was so dramatic in itself. In the film, Burns's name is changed to James Allen and his World War I service in the Army Engineers provides him with technical training that motivates him to want to work in construction when he returns home. His family wants him to return to his secure job as a clerk in a shoe factory, but Allen [Burns] wants to build bridges. "The Army changes a fellow," he says. "It kinda makes you think different. I don't want to be spending the rest of my life answering a factory whistle instead of a bugle call. I'll be cooped up in the shipping room all day. I want to do something worthwhile."[12]

At his family's continuing urging, he accepts the job in the shoe factory, but can't help taking long breaks to watch the work on a new bridge being constructed nearby. He decides to leave the shipping-room job and seek work closer to what he wants to do elsewhere in the country. Unable to find a decent job, he finally finds himself riding the rails as a penniless bum, ending up hungry in an unnamed Southern town. Another drifter tells him there's a diner where they can get a free hand-out, but when they get there his companion pulls a gun, gets $5 from the register and puts it into Allen's pocket. The police catch them as they try to flee and, although Allen is an innocent victim, the police find the money on him. He is sentenced to prison at hard labor. He gets an African-American inmate with whom he's working on a road gang breaking stones to loosen his shackles with his sledgehammer (actually, it was the way the real Robert Burns escaped the first time from the Georgia chain gang). Allen becomes a respected member of a northern community as a construction worker, engineer, and builder. As in real life, he falls in love with another woman while in a painful, unhappy marriage and his wife informs the Georgia authorities of his where-abouts when he asks for a divorce. And, also as in real life, he returns to the chain gang with a promise of an early release that he doesn't get. The film makes his second escape more dramatic as, with another inmate, he steals a truck and eludes a posse of cars chasing him, with the other escaped inmate dying. In real life his second escape was arranged by a nearby shop-owner. The film's ending, unlike the happy one in real life, is dramatized to make the protest against the system more intense. He is on the run now, hiding by day, furtively moving by night, hungry and disheveled. The final scene has him meeting the woman he had fallen in love with. After telling her what has happened, he tells her he is afraid to stay any longer and has to go. "I can't let you go like this," she says. He says, "I've got to." She asks, "Can't you tell me where you're going?" He shakes his head, says "no," and stares wildly at her. She asks, "Do you need any money?" He shakes his head, "no" again. "But you must, Jim," she says. "How do you live?" He retreats into the shadows. At that moment in the filming of the scene, the lights in the studio reportedly failed and thrust the set into total darkness, Allen vanishing into the blackness. His final line, unseen but heard, is "I steal."[13]

With the usual Hollywood hedging, despite the clear protest message of the film, the title of the movie, ostensibly the title of the book on which it was based, omitted the word "Georgia" and there were no references to Georgia in the film. It was clear, however, that the chain gang was in a Southern state and, having been aware of the book and magazine articles, the public knew that the film setting was in Georgia. The National Board of Review named *I Am a Fugitive from a Chain Gang* the best film of the year. This award made Georgia's authorities and its press, as well as its public, even angrier over the film's release, and many of the newspapers in the state headlined that anger with such words as "Yankee Lies." Two prison wardens even sued the producers, Warner Brothers, for libel, but their suit was dismissed. The film, as one might expect, was banned in Georgia.[14]

The film's impact was powerful. As noted earlier, it played a key role in the elimination of chain gangs in Georgia and in other states. The critics, then and since, reflected the public's reaction to the film. John O'Connor wrote in 1997 that

> Since the time of its release in 1932, *Chain Gang* [*I Am a Fugitive from a Chain Gang*] has earned a reputation as one of the few Hollywood products that can be directly associated with social change – not only a shift in popular attitudes, but a revision of government policy. The reform of the southern chain gang system can be attributed to public outrage generated by this movie.[15]

Another critic stated that the film's revelations of chain-gang conditions "almost single-handedly led to the elimination of chain gangs from the South."[16] And another said, "The film fueled a storm of protest from the general public that resulted in the reform of the prison chain gang system in the American South."[17] In fact, the impact of the film extended even further into the prison system and is credited with helping eliminate the forced-labor aspect of America's general prison system.[18]

That Hollywood can help change social and political wrongs is clear. That it cannot rest on its occasional laurels on any given issue is also clear. While it subsequently made many more films over the years dealing with various prison and justice issues, it appears to have determined that its remarkable success with *I Am a Fugitive from a Chain Gang* could not be duplicated with any subsequent film about chain gangs, despite the fact that the elimination of chain gangs turned out not to be a permanent change. In 1995 the state of Alabama revived the chain gang, not only imposing forced convict labor as a form of punishment, but requiring prisoners to pay for their own incarceration costs.[19]

> The reappearance of road gangs in Alabama revived painful images of the state and the South as a backward and racist region. National media prominently reported "a story smacking of bigotry of the old segregationist South" in articles highlighting the nostalgia with which some Alabamians greeted the system. The same media accounts recognized, however, that the chain-gang program of 1995 was not a continuation of the old system, but the result of political posturing by Governor Fob James, who tapped into the popular perception that tougher, public punishment would deter crime.[20]

Shortly after Alabama's lead, the states of Arizona, Florida, Iowa, and Wisconsin reestablished chain gangs for use on their highways – reminiscent of the original "road gangs." Although these new chain gangs were nowhere as harsh as those of sixty and more years before, protests, especially from civil rights organizations such as the Southern Poverty Law Center, shone new light on the practice, and by 1999 the chain-gang concept was abolished once again, although road gangs continue to exist today. No pictures of protest were made concerning the revived chain gangs. In 1987 an adaptation of *I Am a Fugitive from a Chain Gang* was released, under the title of *The Man Who Broke 1,000 Chains*, but it had nowhere near the critical or box-office success of the original, and as it came years before the chain-gang system was revived it was not a contemporary picture of protest.

One might raise the question as to whether a new film on the mistreatment of prisoners is appropriate in the middle and latter years of the first decade of the twenty-first century, given the official support of torture by the US government with regard to prisoners, including civilians, incarcerated as a consequence of the wars in Iraq and Afghanistan. As noted in chapter 2, Hollywood is not likely to touch anything that controversial and/or critical of the ruling establishment.

However, Hollywood has not been shy in recent years about making feature films on prison and justice topics that reflected (and reflect) growing protests among the American public, including the harsh, dehumanizing prison system. Some, like the early *Hell's Highway*, appear to be principally oriented toward presenting melodramatic in-prison violence to a young audience more interested in the blood and gore than in the issue. Other films were more disposed into looking into the specific injustices and the causes of the violence depicted in most of these movies. All, to greater or lesser degrees, protested greater or lesser facets of the prison system. One might say, of course, that since these factors were ongoing, any Hollywood film with prison characters and plot cannot help but at least touch on them. Nevertheless, a look at some of these films shows that Hollywood has, indeed, produced a number of movies that can be considered clear and unequivocal protests. Following an examination of some dealing with the prison system, we'll segue to the justice system and the death penalty, both key current issues.

In all of these films a common thread is almost always present: the dehumanizing system that makes inmates into machines, into the equivalent of a faceless number. This is punctuated by the depicted monotony of unchanging regulations. We see this shown by the prisoners' seemingly choreographed, highly structured movements as they trudge along steel landings, climb up and down staircases, go in and out of cells to the sounds of clanging bells and doors, and march into exercise yards.[21] Establishing the prison as a machine from which the prisoners fight to escape, internally through psychological trauma or externally through violence and riots, is a basic concept in these films.[22] Despite the success of *I Am a Fugitive from a Chain Gang*, there were relatively few similar protest films in the years immediately following its release.

A 1938 movie, *Each Dawn I Die*, reflected in its title the feeling of the inmates each morning when they face another day in prison. Like many prison films, it combines a protest against the justice system – in this one, as in many others, an innocent person is sent to jail – with a protest against the prison system. In 1947, a prison film entitled *Brute Force* reflected in some of its characters the kind of brutality attributed to the Nazis during World War II, which ended just two years before. The system in the particular prison is shown as hopelessly corrupt, with inmates trying to survive against the chief prison guard, "a petty dictator who glories in absolute power."[23] The violence is extreme, in many instances psychopathic. A stool pigeon is cornered with a blowtorch and pushed into a huge press; another informer is strapped to the front of a railroad car as it speeds toward blazing machine guns; the prison captain tortures an inmate with a rubber hose while the music of Wagner blares from a phonograph.[24] (Similarly, in the later film, *Apocalypse Now*, an American officer hears loud Wagnerian music as he machine-guns innocent children from his helicopter.) In *Brute Force* no one wins. Although the inmates kill the evil captain, they are all either killed trying to escape or are returned to their cells. The prison doctor sums it up by saying, "nobody escapes, nobody ever escapes."[25] Critic Marc Frankel summarized *Brute Force*: "Though ostensibly an indictment of a corrupt prison system, what emerges most clearly from the film is the sense of utter hopelessness."[26] Critic Travis Hoover called *Brute Force* "a no-holds-barred plea for prison reform, depicting the sorry lot of prisoners under impossible conditions trying to cope."[27]

A 1954 "B" picture, *Riot in Cell Block 11*, takes a surprisingly in-depth look at the prison system. In this case a group of prisoners select one of their own to lead a protest against the terrible food, enforced idleness, mixing of severely mentally ill prisoners with the others, intolerable overcrowding, and other poor conditions. The warden understands the prisoners' demands, but when a riot occurs he has to suppress it. While a protest against key aspects of the prison system, the movie tries to explore the difficulties of both the prisoners and those incarcerating them, eschewing stereotypes and showing even minor characters as complex individuals.[28] In 1962 Hollywood released a film that deals not with the sadism or violence of the prison system, but with its insensitivity. *Bird Man of Alcatraz* starred Burt Lancaster, who was the principal character in *Brute Force*, in a different kind of convict role. He portrayed a real-life person, Robert Stroud, as a humane and mild-mannered person, sent to Alcatraz after creating problems as a presumed unbalanced and dangerous inmate at other penitentiaries. Sentenced to a life term for murder, Stroud began to breed canaries while at Leavenworth prison. He studied their diseases and developed medicines to treat them. He became, reputedly, one of the country's experts in the care of canaries. At the end, when he is quite old, the prison authorities forbid him to continue his work with canaries, depriving him of his will to live and depriving society of the fruits of his work.

One of the most effective protest films against the prison system, which has since become a classic, was 1967's *Cool Hand Luke*. Paul Newman stars as a chain-gang convict sent to prison for robbing parking meters in order to survive during an economic depression. The film is based on a book by former inmate Donn Pearce about life on a 1940s chain gang, which was based on a real-life convicted felon, Donald Graham Garrisons.[29] Luke is a hero to the other prisoners, a nonconformist who rebels against authority even though he knows it will result in great personal harm to himself. This theme is emphasized in one of the posters advertising the movie: "The man . . . and the motion picture that simply do not conform."[30] Given the time of its production in the 1960s – although it was set in the 1940s – when much of America was nonconformist as it attempted to create a counter-culture revolution, the film held a contemporary message and identification for many Americans. The film not only deals with the horrors of the prison system, but the tragedies that befall anyone who has the courage to stand up against it. Whether deliberate or not, there are striking parallels between the lauded chain-gang movie of the 1960s, *Cool Hand Luke* and its lauded predecessor, *I Am a Fugitive from a Chain Gang*. Both leading characters are guilty of minor crimes in an attempt to survive. Both are war veterans. Both make multiple escape attempts, running through woods and streams; in a final escape attempt they use the same kind of truck, raising the rear to deflect bullets from the guards chasing them; an older mentor inmate jumps on the truck with each of them as they try to escape; in both films the strain of the work is illustrated by having an inmate faint from the heat and exhaustion; and there are similar routines in the prison block and cells, although the latter similarities may be attributed to both films representing the realities of chain gangs at the time of the events depicted.

Cool Hand Luke not only is a clear and unequivocal protest against the prison system, albeit a generic one set decades before the film was made, but it is also an in-depth character study of a rebel fighting the establishment and ultimately, himself. Luke is a "victim not only of the brutality and sadistic discipline of his captors, but also . . . of the indirect cruelty that comes from idolization in the eyes of prisoners and finally of himself."[31]

In 1980 the film *Brubaker* used a different approach to protest the prison system, presented from the point of view of a real-life prison warden who had tried to reform the system or, at least, the Arkansas prison he headed. Tom Merton, to better understand the situation in the prison he was assigned to, posed as an inmate, obtaining information on the operation, personnel, and inmate concerns that he wouldn't have been able to get as warden. He experienced the deplorable conditions in the prison, saw systematic abuse of the prisoners, including the unceremonious burial of prisoners in unmarked graves, and uncovered corruption among the guards and administrators, including fraud and graft in the work-release program. His revelations resulted in a number of reforms in the Arkansas prison system. But the system's establishment doesn't like reforms, and ultimately he was fired.[32]

As the prison systems throughout the country gradually reformed, in great part due to the revelations in and impact of the Hollywood feature films protesting prison conditions, the genre moved more toward a protest of the justice system per se, previously, for the most part, only one facet of the prison-system film. Still a classic, not matched by subsequent films, is the 1957 release, *12 Angry Men*. Based on a highly successful play, the movie is set in a jury room, exploring the prejudices and motives of each juror as the jury debates whether the accused is guilty or not. Conviction seems cut and dried for the young Puerto Rican man accused of killing his father, except for the holdout of one juror, who slowly and reasonably begins to convince others to consider the evidence – and their personal prejudices – more carefully. It becomes a powerful commentary on the rush to judgment that may condemn an innocent person and raises the question of how often the jury system results in a miscarriage of justice. Critic Tom Dirks describes it thus:

> The compelling, provocative film examines the twelve men's deep-seated personal prejudices, perceptual biases and weaknesses, indifference, anger, personalities, unreliable judgments, cultural differences, ignorance and fears, that threaten to taint their decision-making abilities, cause them to ignore the real issues in the case, and potentially lead them to a miscarriage of justice.[33]

. . . *And Justice for All*, a 1979 film, has a lawyer defending a judge accused of rape whom he knows is guilty. Critic Brian Webster noted that the movie is "an effective commentary on a justice system that favors the rich and powerful and places zero value on others."[34]

The Shawshank Redemption, a 1994 release, deals with a banker, Andy Dufresne, unjustly convicted of murder. Sentenced to two life terms, he attempts to survive in Shawshank prison by making the most of whatever positive opportunities exist for him. He organizes the prison library, teaches inmates how to read, and convinces the warden of his financial talents, earning an assignment in the warden's office as a financial bookkeeper. The plot includes the arrival at the prison of an inmate who knows who actually committed the murders. The warden refuses to follow up on the new evidence, ostensibly because he does not want to lose Andy's services. The new convict is killed in the prison shortly afterward, depriving Andy of the chance for freedom. Rather than sink into the hopeless depression that marks most prisoners in his situation, he tries to figure out new ways to ultimately get his redemption. He earns the respect of fellow-prisoners and of many of the prison staff. He develops a money-laundering scheme within the corrupt structure of the prison that enables him to siphon off considerable amounts of money. At the end Andy is redeemed, managing to beat the prison system and, with another inmate who helped him, is ready to resume a free, affluent life. It is a feel-good movie, the good guys winning out over the bad guys, played out like a chess game, emphasizing patience, friendship, hope, survival, and, finally, redemption. Advertising posters for the film summed up its theme: "Fear Can Hold You Prisoner . . . Hope Can Set You Free."[35]

Another film that protests a justice system that convicts and incarcerates an innocent person is the 1999 production, *The Hurricane*. It tells the story of Reuben Carter, a world-class boxer nicknamed in the ring as "Hurricane." Framed for three murders he did not commit, he served eighteen years in prison based on planted false police evidence, contrived perjured testimony, and intimidated witnesses who did not speak out. But, like most Hollywood films protesting some injustice, *The Hurricane* was made after many years of protests by groups and individuals seeking Carter's release and after it became clear that his conviction was based on a corrupt police frame-up. Carter's conviction came at a time when Black Power became a slogan for those attempting redress of grievances against racism and seeking institutional civil rights and equal opportunities. Boxer Hurricane Carter was considered a symbol of this protest and finding him guilty of a crime was part of an attempt by the Establishment, including the police, to discredit and stop the movement. The media had instilled fear into the general population about the civil rights movement, portraying Black men as dangerous would-be criminals. There were few protests from any sources when the FBI burst into a home where a number of leaders of the Black Panther group were sleeping and assassinated them. It was in this atmosphere that Carter was framed and convicted. Almost immediately protest groups were formed, pointing to the false and inconclusive evidence of his guilt. Protest marches, rallies, picketing, and other organizational efforts continued through the eighteen years Carter spent in prison. When Hollywood finally made the movie about this travesty of the justice system, it was too late to help Carter. Others had already done that. The question has to be raised about this and similar films. If they had been made while the given injustices were going on, would they – like *I Am a Fugitive from a Chain Gang* – have had an impact on rectifying the injustices?

Without polemics, Hollywood feature films from time to time over recent decades have protested capital punishment by showing the impact of the death penalty on individuals: The guilty, the innocent, and the observers. One of the earlier and most powerful films that is a clear protest against capital punishment is the 1958 release, *I Want to Live!* The movie has been described as "grim, almost unbearably intense,"[36] as it tells the story of a real-life woman, Barbara Graham, who is a prostitute, drug addict, liar, and perjurer who is convicted of murder and sentenced to death. She had attempted to live a clean, normal life, but her marriage falls apart and she returns to the streets, where she is involved in a murder. Actress Susan Hayward received an Academy Award for her "intense, shattering performance without one false note."[37] Although the real-life evidence suggests that Barbara Graham was indeed guilty, the film portrays her as the innocent victim of the criminal justice system. *New York Times* critic Bosley Crowther wrote:

> the death-house phase of this film is a harrowing synthesis of drama and cold documentary detail. As the minutes tick off and the tension of last-gasp appeals is sustained through the pacing of death-house formalities against the image of the near-by telephone, attendants go through the grisly business of preparing the gas chamber for its lethal role. Anyone who can sit through this ordeal without shivering and shuddering is made of stone.[38]

Another review states that "the final scenes, which lead up to Graham's execution, are exhausting in their emotional intensity as the audience is spared nothing of Graham's agony, despair and desperation when she finally loses the long battle to save her life."[39] Another critic wrote that "the final execution sequence is one that will stay with you for days."[40] The final ten minutes of the film have been characterized as "the most eloquent plea against the death penalty you will ever see."[41] *I Want to Live!* can be described as important to protesting capital punishment as *I Am a Fugitive from a Chain Gang* was to protesting the prison system. In more recent years two films especially are noted for their protest of the death penalty. *Dead Man Walking* was released in 1995 and *The Green Mile* in 1999. Both were made at a time of rising conservatism in the United States and a concomitant rise and acceptance by the American people of the death penalty. Radical right-wing hate groups were also growing and many elected officials tended to ignore the violence they engendered. In fact, when the legislature of the state of Texas, which has had the highest number of death-row executions in the country, was in the process of attempting to counter the violence by passing an anti-hate crimes law, the then-Governor of Texas, George W. Bush, saw to it that it was not enacted.

The Green Mile centers on a prisoner who appears as a gentle giant, on death row for rape and murder. We begin to empathize, if not sympathize with him, and we are shocked at the vivid cruelty of his execution. *Dead Man Walking* is more believable in its exploration of the implications of the death penalty. A Catholic nun, Sister Helen Prejean, had become a pen pal of a convicted killer on death row and, through their correspondence, became an activist opponent of the death penalty, not because her correspondent was innocent, but because of the unfair application of the death penalty and the nature of it as cruel punishment. She wrote a book about this experience, *Dead Man Walking*. About the death penalty, she stated:

> judges don't look at the other constitutional protections like a decent lawyer and jury of your peers. We have a mentality in the court that has legalized death and has cut off appeals. So that poor people – who are ninety-nine percent of the people on death row – do not have good attorneys. As a result, you cannot have an adversarial system of getting to the truth at trial.[42]

She was concerned that richer defendants and those whose victims were Black were less likely to be executed, that innocents were frequently put to death, and that the death penalty had not been shown to be a deterrent to crime.[43]

Her book came to the attention of producers-directors-performers Tim Robbins and Susan Sarandon, leaders among the Hollywood figures dedicated to human rights, liberties, and social justice. They decided to make a film that countered the prevailing right-wing domination of American thought in relation to the unfair system of capital punishment. However, rather than polemic, with the usual innocent-man-unjustly-convicted theme, the condemned man was guilty and they explored the meaning of the death penalty itself by in-depth exploration of the inner persons of the characters in the story. Not since *I Want to Live!* did a film have such impact on a justice system that included capital punishment. *Dead Man Walking* is considered by many critics to be the most powerful prison/justice film of recent years, affecting its viewers strongly enough to motivate new social attitudes toward capital punishment. "In the real world the film won space for a renewal of opposition to the death penalty and allowed a wide range of public figures to publicly associate themselves with the anti-death penalty cause."[44]

Today, in the latter part of 2000's first decade, it is difficult to know the extent to which a Hollywood film protesting state-sanctioned murder – as death-penalty opponents describe it – would have an effect. Have we Americans become desensitized to unjust violence and death? Over the years we have seen countless films depicting prison brutality, murder, and execution, and the corruption and miscarriage of justice. In real life we have become inured to government approved and conducted torture in the US-operated, subsidized, or controlled prisons throughout the world, such as that at Abu Ghraib. We have permitted the incarceration for years, without legal charges, trials, or convictions, of hundreds of people at Guantánamo prison. We have permitted the imposition of the Patriot Act, which has eliminated some of the traditional American civil liberty safeguards against arbitrary incarceration and physical violence against alien and citizen alike. Given the acceptance of these injustices by a substantial part of the American people, one must question whether any Hollywood protest film at this time could sensitize many Americans to the continuing injustices of the domestic prison and justice systems. Given

Hollywood's history on matters of political controversy, is it too idealistic to expect Hollywood to make protest films on these controversial actions that belie most Americans' commitment to judicial fairness and compassion?

Notes

1   All Movie web site. www.allmovie.com/cg/avg.dll.
2   www.turnerclassicmovies.com/ThisMonth/Article/0.218744%7C21845% 7C21848.00.html.
3   *Ibid.*
4   Prison Flicks web site. www.prisonflicks.com/bighouse.htm.
5   *The Big House.* www.imdb.com/title/tt0020686/.
6   *I Am A Fugitive From A Chain Gang.* www.filmsite.org/iama.html.
7   www.free-essays.us/dbase/d4/lvw51.shtml.
8   *Harvard Law Review*, Vol. 109, No. 4, February, 1996, p. 876.
9   Owens, Lois Smith, "History and Debate: Prisons," *Think About Prisons and the Criminal Justice System*, 1992, pp. 43–8.
10   "About Chain Gangs." www.jailmuseum.com/aboutchaingangs.htm.
11   www.filmsite.org/iama.html.
12   *Ibid.*
13   *Ibid.*
14   *Ibid.*
15   O'Connor, John E., "Introduction: Warners Finds Its Social Conscience," *I Am a Fugitive from a Chain Gang*, 1997, pp. 9–10.
16   Minchew, Kaye Lanning, "How Hollywood Reformed the Georgia Prison System," 1992. www.trouparchives.org/burns.html.
17   McGee Scott, *I Am a Fugitive from a Chain Gang.* www.turnerclassicmovies. com/ThisMonth/Article/0,1126,00.html.
18   *I Am a Fugitive from a Chain Gang.* www.answers.com/topic/i-am-a-fugitive-from-a-chain-gang.
19   www.prisonactivist.org/crisis/labor-of-doing-time.html.
20   Dodge, Timothy, "State Convict Road Gangs in Alabama," *Alabama Review*, October, 2000. www.findarticles.com/p/articles/mi_qa3880/is_200010/ ai_n8908409.
21   Mason, Paul, "System and Process: The Prison in Cinema." www.imagesjournal.com/issue06/features/prison2.htm.
22   *Ibid.*
23   Crawford, Ron, "Plot Summary For *Brute Force*." www.imdb.com/title/ tt0039224/plotsummary.
24   www.turnerclassicmovies, 0.440.00.

25 *Ibid.*
26 Frankel, Marc, "October Cult Movie Picks – *Brute Force.*" www. turnerclassicmovies.com/ThisMonth/Srticle/0,,440.00.html.
27 Hoover, Travis, "*Brute Force.*" www.daysofthunder.net/bruteforce.htm.
28 http://movies.yahoo.com/shop?d=hv&id=1800111995&cf=info&intl=us.
29 www.filmsite.org/cool.html.
30 *Ibid.*
31 Crowther, Bosley, "The Screen," *New York Times,* November 2, 1967. www.proquest.
32 www.criminology.fsu.edu/crimemedia/lecture10.html.
33 Dirks, Tom, "*12 Angry Men.*" www.filmsite.org/twelve.html.
34 Webster, Brian, . . . *And Justice For All.* http://apolloguide.com/mov_fullrev. asp?CID=2841&RID=763.
35 www.filmsite.org/shaw.html.
36 Rasmussen, Linda, summary review of *I Want To Live!* http://movies. nytimes.com/movie/24154/I-Want-To-Live-/overview.
37 *Ibid.*
38 Crowther, Bosley, *I Want to Live!* movie review, *New York Times,* November 19, 1958. http://movies.nytimes.com/movie/review?_r=2&res.
39 Rasmussen, summary review of *I Want To Live!*
40 "*I Want to Live!* Review." www.channel4.com/film/reviews/film.jsp?id= 104483.
41 *I Want to Live!* http://en.wikipedia.org/wiki/I_Want_to_Live%21.
42 "The Social Edge Interview: Author of *Dead Man Walking,* Sr. Helen Prejean," *Social Justice and Faith.* www.socialedge.com/archives/gerrymccarthy/ 1articles-may2003.htm.
43 Shapiro, Laura, "I Would Not Want My Murderer Executed," *New York Times,* July 4, 1993, p. BR10.
44 O'Sullivan, Sean, "Representing 'The Killing State': The Death Penalty in Nineties Hollywood Cinema," *The Howard Journal,* Vol. 41, No. 5, December, 2003.

5
$\mathcal{L}abor-\mathcal{M}anagement$
Whose side are you on?

When one thinks of films dealing with the struggle between labor and management and with pro-union and anti-union activity, specifically those movies protesting the mistreatment of workers by insensitive or exploitative corporate or private businesses, three films invariably come to mind: *Salt of the Earth* (1954), *Norma Rae* (1979), and *Modern Times* (1936).

The latter is a Charlie Chaplin satire on how workers are treated and how the "little man" is abused by the public and private establishment both. It does not mention unions, but its message is clear: without common effort and organization there is little hope for fairness. *Modern Times* will be discussed under its principal rubric in the chapter on the tyranny of technology. The other two films are clear and unequivocal protests against anti-union forces. The workers joined together are the "good guys." Those opposing them are the "bad guys." Interestingly enough, these and many of the other feature films with the union as a focal theme have been based on true stories. Some of the films, like *The Molly Maguires* (1970), are rife with the real-life violence that saw not only corporations hiring strikebreakers, or "scabs," they are called, but also employing "goons" to beat up and, in many cases, to shoot and kill striking and picketing workers, with the police and national guard supporting the anti-union forces.

The union movement is the keystone of the history of labor in the United States. The first labor union in the United States was formed in Philadelphia by shoemakers in 1792. The modern labor movement began in Europe in the mid-1800s as result of industrialization that required many low-paid workers to put in endless hours each week to maximize profits. The term "sweatshop" arose from those businesses and factories where the workers labored under sometimes inhumane conditions, with no protections from physical, psychological, and monetary exploitation. Crowded, unsafe conditions resulted in much illness and death, with no compensation to the victims or their families. Those who complained were summarily fired.

It should be noted that it was not simply coincidental that the poorest paid, the last to be hired, and the first to be fired were minorities, most particularly African-Americans, and in the Southwest Latinos and on the west coast Asians. Racism, seemingly endemic in the American psyche, was and continues to be an integral part of discriminatory labor practices.

Even small children worked 12 to 16 hours every day. As industrialization grew in the United States, so did the sweatshops and the unsafe and oppressive conditions under which people were forced to work. There were more workers than jobs, and people took any kind of work and literally did anything in order to survive. Employers played off one worker against the other, and could bargain for lower and lower wages.

To protect themselves, workers began to cooperate with each other in seeking decent – or, at least, better – wages and conditions. They began to organize unions, which were vilified by management as subversive, communistic, anarchist, and in whatever other terms appeared to be the most denigrating to the general public. In many countries unions were outlawed and in others union leaders were framed for a perceived crime and put in jail so that they couldn't influence their fellow-workers. In 1842 a US court ruled that workers had a right to organize, but that didn't stop management, with the complicity of other courts, the military, and the police, from stopping strikes, most often with violence, and from firing organizers or other employees showing partiality toward unions. In some cases organizers were beaten up, maimed, and murdered. Perhaps the most notorious case was the framing for murder and the subsequent execution in 1927 of Nicola Sacco and Bartolomeo Vanzetti, Italian immigrants, a fish-peddler and a shoemaker, respectively, who were active in promoting and organizing unions.

Through solidarity and the willingness to strike, causing management to lose money, union members could effectively negotiate. While the bosses could easily fire one or a few dissident workers, they couldn't fire the entire workforce. The strike was the workers' weapon of last resort and the most effective one.

Unions gave labor bargaining power. At first many courts ruled that unions were illegal and they were heavily prosecuted and persecuted, both as a group and as individuals. But workers and unions persisted under the most trying circumstances, and in 1913 the Department of Labor was established and a year later, in 1914, the Clayton Act legalized boycotts, strikes, and peaceful picketing, all key resources for labor in negotiating contracts with management. The establishment of the National Labor Relations Board (NLRB) under the Wagner Act in 1934 gave unions more equal legal standing in disputes with management. In 1947 the Taft–Hartley Act was passed in an attempt to undermine unions once again by allowing employers to hire non-union employees in union shops. In recent decades the power of the unions to protect workers and obtain decent working conditions (such as the 40-hour week, a minimum wage, paid vacations, safe working environments, health and life insurance, maternity leave, protection from dismissal without legitimate cause) has diminished: In part, because of the corruption found in some unions, in part because of the rise of anti-union political and social attitudes and supportive politicians, and in part because much of American media have demeaned unions to the general public.

Although neither a dramatic commentary nor a satire on sports teams and scabs, a 2000 comedy, *Replacements*, is the story of how the players on one professional football team go on strike and the team's owner brings in a new coach and scab replacement players to finish out the season. (In fact, this happened some years before with the National Football League, when one of the most popular professional football players scabbed against his friends and colleagues.)

The decline of the power of unions in the United States is reflected also by the growing outsourcing of jobs to other countries, particularly in the past decade. Companies that want to have their goods produced in foreign countries, where they can pay considerably lower wages in environments that reflect some of the worst pre-union conditions, are not intimidated by the threat of a strike. They don't need American union workers. We have all read and heard recent revelations of child labor, dangerous working conditions, and general exploitation of workers making goods abroad for American companies. Even workplaces that are frequently labeled as bastions of liberal thought – such as colleges and universities – have in recent years turned against unions. Federal case law established several decades ago that faculty members were management and not labor, and therefore college administrations did not have to recognize or bargain with faculty unions. In some colleges where administrators hypocritically aver that they are not anti-union and support labor, they nevertheless attempt to nullify the impact of a union and, when they do agree to a contract with, say, an American Association of University Professors faculty group, it almost always eliminates any faculty governance or policy participation, resulting in what, in all fields of endeavor, is called a "company union." That is, a union in name only, with little if any prerogatives. Academics are notorious for saying one thing theoretically (the stereotype is true in this case), but not having the courage or integrity to act on it. Falling back on the excuse that they don't want to interrupt their students' education, they almost invariably refuse to call a strike, which could in many cases achieve their demands.

Hollywood has not been remiss in making films protesting the conditions of labor and, directly or by implication, the need for unions. And because the labor-management struggle is a continuing one, many of these movies fall into the protest pictures category. They vary in the types of approach they take to the subject. For example, two of the early Hollywood films, *Modern Times* (1936) and *The Grapes of Wrath* (1940), concentrated on worker exploitation, one through satire, the other through biting drama, but neither directly uses unions as key elements. *The Grapes of Wrath* does show the exploitation of workers by farm owners. A key example in the film: During America's great economic depression in the 1930s, with more than twenty percent of Americans without jobs, especially in the drought-ridden Southwest, farm owners distributed flyers throughout the region making it appear that there were plenty of jobs available in the California fields. Considerably more workers showed up than there were jobs, with the owners then pitting the destitute workers against each other in working for the lowest wage. *The Grapes of Wrath* is, essentially, a film protesting poverty and the treatment of the impoverished, and won't be discussed in this chapter again, but will be featured in the chapter on films protesting poverty.

The Garment Jungle (1957) and *F.I.S.T.* (1978), on the other hand, make the "goons," the people hired by management to beat up strikers and destroy the unions, the good guys. A 1980 film, *Nine to Five*, uses comedy to show three female secretaries uniting to throw off corporate patriarchy. *Silkwood* (1983), based on a true story, tacitly suggests that a company killed one of its employees who was about to deliver damning documents about safety issues to the authorities. *Matewan* (1987), also based on a true story, emphasizes a brutal confrontation between striking workers and mine operators. Even Arnold Schwarzenegger, in *Total Recall* (1990), portrayed a hero who stopped a corporate fascist government from exploiting workers on Mars. And even a "toon" – *Antz* (1998) – shows workers winning out over unjust rulers by organizing. One of the best-made films of all times, *On the Waterfront* (1957), is an anti-union film, in which the hero becomes a hero by revealing the corruption in his union. Some labor-management films did not necessarily take a polemic pro-labor or pro-management stand, but simply revealed the feet of clay in one or the other. There are, basically, the pro-union/anti-management film, the anti-union/pro-management film, and the pro- and anti-union film and the pro- and anti-management film, without necessarily condemning or praising the opposite number. There are films that deal with worker and management issues that do not directly make unions a key element.

The pertinence of these films is current. Although covered up or minimized by the media, labor-management struggles continue in the new millennium. For example, one of the most dramatic and nationally known union struggles was the success of the United Farm Workers (UFW), led by César Chávez, in obtaining union contracts in the 1970s and 1980s, due in large part to consumer boycotts of the exploiting companies. But as companies were bought and sold in recent years, union contracts and protections changed or disappeared. In 2006 a letter to the public from the United Farm Workers included the following description of a labor–management situation:

> Dear Friend of Farm Workers,
> I need your help today because the new owners of Pacific Coast Mushrooms want to go back to "the good old days." Back to the days when they paid their workers poorly, gave them no benefits, and were free to treat them like dirt.
> As you can imagine, the workers are not so nostalgic. Twenty-five years ago, the workers voted to form a union and be represented by the United Farm Workers. Their employer at the time, Pacific Mushroom Farm, agreed to a contract. For a quarter of a century, he workers lived a better life – a whole generation. Then, early last year, the company, by then known as Money's Mushrooms, suddenly announced it was closing down. Going out of business.
> The workers were crushed.

To understand the depths of their despair, you have to know that at Money's Mushrooms they felt they had a chance. Management couldn't abuse them. It couldn't steal their wages. It couldn't ignore their safety. All of this added up to the opportunity to work hard and give their children a better life than they had. That's all they ever asked for. When they learned the company was going out of business, all the workers could imagine was getting a job at one of the many mushroom, vegetable, fruit, and flower farms where workers don't have contracts.

Martín Álvarez knows what that's like.

"I started working in a rose nursery. The working conditions were the worst you can imagine. The foreman harassed us the whole day, making us run back and forth. He didn't want us to go the restroom. At times, we had no water to drink. Sometimes, we suffered dehydration because it was very hot in the plastic buildings. The foreman didn't give us the tools we needed to do the work. Or if he did, he deducted it from our paycheck. We had to pay for the tools ourselves. He made us apply pesticides without protection. At lunch time, he didn't let us talk to each other. He said he would fire us if we did."

Sadly, this is what life is like for tens of thousands of workers on the farms of our nation. Some of the worst abuses take place in the mushroom industry.

... a few months after Money's Mushrooms closed its doors, the farm reopened, with a new name, Pacific Coast Mushrooms. The founders, who included most of the supervisors at Money's Mushrooms, insisted it was a new company, and therefore not bound by the previous contact. But Pacific Coast Mushrooms operates in the same buildings, with the same machinery, the same supervisors . . .

Last November, Pacific Coast Mushrooms sent out a letter to all the previous employees of Money's Mushrooms [offering] all the workers their jobs back. The letter didn't mention anything about the workers' union, or the contract negotiated with the UFW. Many of the workers, assuming they would still have their union contract, were happy to go back. Others went back because they have no other option. They have families to feed. Bills to pay. And very few opportunities for jobs.

But once the workers had returned to their old jobs, they quickly discovered that everything had changed. Their pay had been cut by more than twenty percent! They no longer had any benefits. And they no longer had any union protection from harassment and abuse.

As far as management was concerned, "the good old days" of greed were back.[1]

In 2001 the US government enacted four bills that (1) revoked a "project labor" agreement that required that union contractors be hired for federally financed projects; (2) ended retention policies for low-level employees on federal building projects, giving contractors the right to decide who to retain or fire; (3) abolished the National Partnership Council, a government group designed to resolve labor-management issues; and (4) authorized workers to withhold any part of their union dues not used directly for collective bargaining.[2]

At this time of writing, some of the country's largest companies, such as Wal-Mart, have consistently resisted unionization of their employees. Wal-Mart, for example, has been found to have required employees to work overtime without overtime pay compensation. The company has also been accused of gender bias in pay scales and job opportunities.[3] But rather than deal with a union, Wal-Mart has simply paid applicable fines and continued as a non-union shop, strengthening control over its workers.

Unions have come upon hard times in recent decades. "Workers who tried to form unions often found their workplaces had become hostile environments, with managers making thinly veiled threats of shutdowns, layoffs, or pay cuts."[4] A bipartisan Commission on the Future of Labor-Management Relations reported in 1994 that "The United States is the only major democratic country in which the choice of whether or not workers are to be represented by a union is subject to such a confrontational process."[5] It has not been easy to either form or be a union member in recent years. "Workers who try to organize unions often find that their jobs become a living hell. This puts a lie to the glib generalization that union membership has declined because workers no longer want to join unions."[6] (This writer can confirm from personal experience in an educational institution what appeared to be retaliation for union activity.)

The two arguably most effective pro-labor protest films of all time both deal with unions: *Salt of the Earth* (1954) and *Norma Rae* (1979). We will examine these and other films protesting some facet of labor vs. management.

Although not the first to deal with labor-management issues, *Salt of the Earth* is considered by many to be the seminal and perhaps most important film in this genre. Made in 1954, the movie represented a myriad of controversial issues at the time. It was, as noted earlier, the time of the McCarthy era, and a number of blacklisted writers, directors, and actors formed their own production company and, in looking for a film subject, decided to make a movie based on a 1950 strike by a local of the Mine, Mill, and Smelter Workers' union against the New Jersey Zinc Company in Silver City, New Mexico. Note, then, that this was not a Hollywood feature entertainment film, but a film by an independent group of artists who were considered communists or communist sympathizers by Hollywood and by much of the rest of country at the time. In addition, the film was about a Chicano community and Chicano workers. Then, as currently in 2008, hostility and prejudice toward immigrants, legal and illegal, was high, and there was a movement to close the borders between the United States and Mexico. The film, therefore, had two prejudicial strikes against it before production even began. A third strike, in the minds of generally sexist as well as racist America, was the emphasis in the film on feminism and women's rights. To put a stop to brutal exploitation by the mine owners, the workers go on strike. The film shows the effects of the strike on the families: male workers, their wives, and their children. It shows the organization and implementation of the strike, focusing on some workers who supported it and on some who opposed it, and on the subsequent picket line at the mine. It shows the collaboration of the civil authorities and police with the mine owners in trying to break the strike and the arrest of the picketers. After the mine owners get a legal injunction to stop the men from picketing, the women – wives, sisters, and mothers – take over the picket line. The traditional male–female roles are reversed, the women out front fighting for labor rights and the men taking over the household duties. In effect, it was one of the first and one of the strongest representations up to that time for what, in the 1960s, was to become the feminist movement.[7]

In this film about "a long hard strike in the mines of Silver City (New Mexico) in the early 1950s and the prejudice against the Mexican workers who sought to receive the same treatment as their white co-workers,"[8] "as the women find their voice, so the film finds its own, and the coda affirming perseverance, justice, and equality appears almost as radical and rousing today as it did in the dark days of McCarthyism."[9]

This potentially prejudicial third strike of feminism against the film was not the cause of its demise. The accusations of communist subversion had the strongest impact, particularly because the Communist Party strongly supported equal rights and opportunities for minorities and for women and the efforts of labor unions, hallmarks of the film's content and production. Leo Hockstader wrote in the *Washington Post*:

> It is doubtful that any other American movie ever inspired such official harassment and outright intimidation as *Salt of the Earth*, the saga of striking Mexican-American miners written and directed by blacklisted Hollywood filmmakers during the Red Scare. During the course of production in New Mexico in 1953, the trade press denounced it as a subversive plot, anti-Communist vigilantes fired rifle shots at the set, the film's leading lady was deported to Mexico, and from time to time a small airplane buzzed noisily overhead [to interfere with the soundtrack].[10]

Although the harassment brought the production to a halt, the movie was later completed, and was released in 1954. The *Hollywood Reporter* labeled the film as "commie propaganda" controlled by the Kremlin, and a Republican Congressman made a speech in the House of Representatives in which he promised to do anything he could to keep what he called a "communist-made" film out of movie theaters. The FBI sought but failed to find a communist connection in its financing. The American Legion asked for a national boycott of the film. Processing labs were told not to process it. Union projectionists were ordered not to show it. Major movie houses in the United States refused to show the film, but it was shown in Canada and in Mexico. The producers moved to Europe where *Salt of the Earth* became a big hit, and it played to enthusiastic audiences in other countries, including the Soviet Union and China.

In the 1960s the film was revived in the United States, in part because of the progressive political atmosphere of the time and in part because of the film's use by the UFW to energize its members during a long strike against grape growers.[11] The film was shown numerous times, for a period every Friday night, and was strong factor in boosting the morale of UFW strikers. In the last several decades *Salt of the Earth* has become a cult movie, a key part of many college film curricula, and a staple in union halls and among feminist and Latino groups, historians, and film buffs.[12] It has a present-day impact in the United States that appears to exceed that of the 1950s, when it was made. Two examples: A *Salt of the Earth* conference at the College of Santa Fe in 2003 had as its theme the proposition that the film's message of self-empowerment and the act of political dissent its production represented are as relevant in terror-obsessed twenty-first-century America as they were in communism-obsessed America of the McCarthy era.[13] The co-chair of the conference, Jonathan Wax, noted that "whether it's the broader issue of freedom of expression, or whether it's more specific issues relating to New Mexico . . . and labor history in the southwest, or just the history of Hollywood blacklist and whether that could happen again, I think all of those issues, people recognize, have become current again."[14] In 2004 *Salt of the Earth* was screened at a benefit and rally for striking grocery workers in California, some of whose health benefits had been cut by half and others who were locked out of their jobs and replaced by scabs when their employers decided to cut costs in order to compete with non-union Wal-Mart's plan to build forty supercenters in that region.[15]

The expertise in writing, production, performing, and post-production by the highly qualified – and blacklisted – professionals who made *Salt of the Earth* should not be overlooked, and should be a guide for any moviemaking. For instance, "the script was rewritten about sixteen times . . . to erase any stereotypes and to make it real, express [the strikers'] experience."[16] In addition, its sense of truth was enhanced by the casting of actual miners and strikers in most roles, with only two major roles played by professional actors, American Will Geer, who had been blacklisted, and Mexican Dolores Revueltas, who the authorities managed to deport to Mexico before the film was completed, on grounds of visa irregularities. *Salt of the Earth* is one of only 100 American films selected by the Library of Congress to be preserved for posterity, and has received a number of prestigious film awards.[17]

Although banned and boycotted in the United States in 1954 and for many years afterward, "Salt" had struck a chord with the conservative and right-wing elements in the country – a negative chord – and unions were even further vilified as communist, corrupt, or both. The atmosphere was right for an anti-union movie. One was produced that year, combining both vilifications. One, overt, was union corruption; the other, covert, justified the real-life informing by the film's director on his friends and associates, naming names as alleged or suspected communists to HUAC, destroying their careers to enhance his own. That film turned out to be one of the best written, directed, acted, and aesthetically produced films of all time: *On the Waterfront*, directed by Elia Kazan.

The story is based on a true story of an ex-prizefighter who, no longer able to fight successfully, becomes a longshoreman and, in a final burst of conscience, tries to expose his criminally corrupt union. He must turn against and expose his mentor, the union boss, and his co-workers and friends. (Certainly a purposeful metaphor and justification for Kazan's having turned against his mentors and friends.) The longshoreman, at the end, is brutally beaten up for becoming a turncoat, but bloodied and barely conscious, he confronts his fellow-workers and convinces them to turn against the union. Critic Roger Ebert wrote: "The film was based on the true story of a longshoreman who tried to overthrow a corrupt union. In life, he failed; in the film he succeeds, and today the ending of *On the Waterfront* feels too stagy and upbeat."[18] The role is brilliantly acted by Marlon Brando: "I coulda been a contender. I coulda been a somebody. Instead I'm a nobody. I'm a bum." Ebert wrote: "If there is a better performance by a man in the history of film in America, I don't know what it is."[19]

On the Waterfront remains one of the strongest anti-union movies ever made. Unlike many others, it is not anti-labor, but instead takes a pro-labor stance, making the enemy and exploiter the union, rather than, as in most labor-protest films, the employer. The film received twelve Academy Award nominations and won eight, and continues to be used by groups and companies for anti-union indoctrination.

Made twenty-five years after *Salt of the Earth*, in 1979, *Norma Rae* is arguably Hollywood's most important and influential pro-labor protest film. Indeed, the brutal opposition to *Salt* by Hollywood and continuing McCarthyism influence well into the 1960s and early 1970s frightened the self-protective Hollywood filmmakers, who abstained from seriously considering making a pro-labor movie, and those who did consider it were made to understand that even if it were made, there would be little, if any, chance of getting a Hollywood studio to distribute it. In 1979, after the anti-union Nixon administration and before the anti-union Reagan administration, a window of opportunity opened.

Martin Ritt, the director of *Norma Rae*, was blacklisted during the McCarthy era. When he was allowed to work again, one of his films, made in 1970, was *The Molly Maguires*, the story of a coal miners' secret union formed in Pennsylvania in the 1870s to protect themselves from and ultimately fight the violence against workers by the mine owners. This film will be discussed later in this chapter. *Norma Rae* far exceeded *The Molly Maguires* in critical acclaim, box-office popularity, and lasting impact.

Norma Rae is first and foremost a protest film against cruelty to workers, repressive management against labor, and the desperate need for unionization. The film also successfully protests racism, sexism, and even anti-Semitism . . . the film paints a realistic picture of what many workers have to undergo every day of their lives. The noise, dangerous ventilation conditions, low wages, short breaks, long hours, dangerous jobs, and harassment [as depicted in the textile-mill setting], are just a few of the many factors put up with by the obedient and brainwashed workers . . . Non-unionized companies often intimidate employees by threatening to take more away from them, or to fire them altogether. According to Harvard Professor Paul Weiler, "one out of twenty union supporters, an average of 10,000 workers a year, are fired by their employers during union organization campaigns."[20]

Figure 5.1
Norma Rae
(1979)

Jen Gagne has written that in times when the economy is bad, the threat of unemployment is easily used to intimidate workers. In *Norma Rae*, as with the real-life textile mill used as the basis for the *Norma Rae* story, this threat permits the "textile mill to push its workers to the limit . . . giving the textile mill the upper hand, allowing the company managers to mistreat their workers, ignoring basic human needs, such as those necessary to a safe working environment."[21]

Norma Rae is essentially a true story – with the necessary degree of Hollywood dramatization to make it a feature entertainment film rather than a documentary – of Crystal Lee's (her subsequent married surname was Sutton) employment, union organizing, and firing at a J. P. Stevens textile mill in North Carolina. Because the producers of the film couldn't get releases from everyone involved to use their real names, pseudonyms, such as Norma Rae, were substituted. Norma Rae is a poorly educated Southern woman who has worked hard in difficult, low-paying jobs from the age of 16, had several children, and is addicted to sex and alcohol, but whose strong will and personal courage belies her background. An organizer from the Textile Workers of America, who happens to be Jewish and from New York, arrives, and he recruits Norma Rae to work with him in getting a union into the mill. Management bribes her by promoting her, but realizing that the promotion jeopardizes her relationships with the other workers and her ability to influence them to join a union, she goes back to her old job. Norma Rae's father's death from a heart attack caused by pressure from management on his job at the plant, and her mother's deafness from the excess noise at the plant strengthen her determination to get it unionized. Her union work conflicts with her husband's views of the stereotyped traditional woman's role. One of the most telling scenes in the film is when Norma Rae is fired and she stands on a table, silently holding up a "Union" sign. The sheriff arrives and drags her off, but the other workers support her by turning off their machines in a show of solidarity. The film gets in its protests – through the actions of management, the townspeople, and the workers – of labor exploitation, anti-Semitism, and anti-feminism.

Finally, the workers, with Norma Rae having been fired, vote by a slim margin in favor of the union. The film ends on a hopeful note, with the organizer and Norma Rae, having flirted with but not, judging from the movie, consummated more than a close emotional and activist relationship, part as platonic friends, likely never to see each other again. Actress Sally Field won an Academy Award for her role of Norma Rae.

The future of the real Norma Rae, Crystal Lee, was not hopeful. She was forced to take what she later called the worst job she ever had, at a fast-food stand, after her firing for "subordination" by J. P. Stevens. Later she became a paid organizer for the Amalgamated Clothing and Textile Workers Union (ACTWU), with which the Textile Workers Union of America had merged. Further, even after she had become a celebrity after the release of the movie, she expressed concern that she had received no compensation from it. Ironically, although the workers voted for the union in 1974, J. P. Stevens continue to resist a union, and it wasn't until 1980, a year after the film was released, that the company finally signed a union contract. Many observers credit the film as a motivating factor.

The film became a powerful union tool.

The battle of the union and the company has become one of the epic sagas of union-versus-management history – one fought more with the modern tools of public relations than old-fashioned fists. It's been going since 1963, through the courts and National Labor Relations Board and the living rooms and meeting halls of the South, and there is no end in sight. *Norma Rae* is probably one of the most powerful tools the labor movement will ever have. Its moving saga of simple good and bad, of plain people winning against the bad-guy establishment, has inspired thousands.[22]

Professor Robert Kaufman wrote that "virtually no other American post-McCarthy labor film seems so effectively to have reached its intended potential audiences: namely, people currently experiencing, or likely to experience, organizing drives in their own workplaces," and that

Within a year of the film's release, the number of workers who began explicitly referring to or riffing off the film's story and dialogue (during union campaigns, all the way to the sort of National Labor Relations Board election portrayed in *Norma Rae*'s penultimate scene), was unprecedented – as again, countless participating workers, as well as union organizers, have noted.[23]

Martin Ritt's *The Molly Maguires* was a totally different kind of protest film, although dealing, as does *Norma Rae*, with the exploitation of labor and the role of unions. It was based on the true story of a group of Irish immigrant coal miners in Pennsylvania in the 1870s. These immigrants were already the target of extreme prejudice in America – it was the period of "no Irish need apply" employment signs and physical attacks on Irish immigrants. (America appears to have an ongoing phobia in which the descendants of immigrants, both legal and illegal, are vicious to new immigrants who wish to enter the United States in order to also find a better life for themselves and their children.) The Pennsylvania miners, in order to be kept in a condition of virtual servitude, were subjected to brutal violence by the mine owners. The miners' families, including small children, were in many cases starving. Many were dying from illnesses, some of which were the result of polluted environments and inadequate housing, with no medical care affordable or available. The owners refused to alleviate what was murderous exploitation. Finally, in desperation, the Irish miners formed a secret union, the Molly Maguires, to fight back using the owners' own violent tactics, including dynamiting trains and coal supplies. Fighting fire with fire, the Molly Maguires intimidated, beat, and even murdered mine owners, supervisors, police, and others who tried to do the same to them. Unlike the Gandhi model of passive resistance of many modern-day labor-management conflicts, the Molly Maguire period was one of mayhem, almost always originated by the union-busters and strike-breakers, but also making the Molly Maguires an anomaly in union history. In the film, re-creating the real-life scenario, the mine owners hire a Pinkerton detective to infiltrate the secret union and, after two years of working as a spy within the organization, he provides information to the authorities that results in the arrest, conviction, and hanging of the leaders of the Molly Maguires.

Although the film deals with an event that occurred a century before, the film does have current pertinence by showing what could happen when management is intransigent and forces labor to adopt management's own violent tactics. In the end, nobody really wins. Critic Shane Burridge wrote, after seeing *The Molly Maguires*, that "The most interesting element of the film is probably at what point viewers will decide which side deserves their sympathy."[24]

A year before *Norma Rae*, in 1978, two interesting protest films about labor management were released. Neither one received much lasting critical support or box-office acclaim. *F.I.S.T.* is sympathetic to labor, the story of a truck driver's efforts to organize a union despite a physical battle with the company's "goons." *Blue Collar* portrays union bureaucracies as just as corrupt as those of management. A plot assumption is that workers are considered essentially lazy and untrustworthy by both management and unions. Both, therefore, feel entitled to treat workers disdainfully, sometimes shamefully. Three factory workers, each desperately needing money and believing that their union has been dishonest with them, break into the union office, ostensibly to steal money to which they feel they are entitled. Once there, they discover evidence of union corruption and decide to blackmail the union boss. Predictably, they find themselves in trouble. "The film works well, as many Hollywood films do, in the way it exposes how workers as individuals lose out in the face of the corporate interests of companies and crime syndicates, but it plays up union bureaucracies as being just as bad."[25]

Labor-management protest films come with various genre approaches. In 1980, a comedy, *Nine to Five*, combined a pro-labor and a feminist theme. Three female secretaries unite to throw off the patriarchy of an evil, sexist, insensitive boss. Even a sci-fi series of films, *Aliens*, can be interpreted as taking an anti-corporate view.

An underlying message in this series, especially in *Aliens*, seems to be that that unrestrained capitalism is monopolistic, deceptive, and inhuman, often with horrifying consequences. The film's Company men want to bring back live specimens of Alien for use as biological weapons. There's a strong implication that the Company is ready to sacrifice individuals, whole communities, and ultimately civilization, to the profit motive.[26]

Another sci-fi movie, *Total Recall* (1990), can be considered pro-union. A corporate fascist government exploits workers on Mars. A nonconformist hero (played by Arnold Schwarzenegger) saves the day. Even "toons" fall into the labor-management protest category. *Antz* (1998) portrays a worker trying to win over a princess against all odds. He organizes other workers to help him. The story line becomes one of revolution and a celebration of individuality in the face of conformity. The film essentially says that people should fight unjust power, that workers, if organized, can obtain their basic rights. An interesting musical with a pro-labor, pro-union theme was *Newsies* (1992). Based on an actual event earlier in that century, it's the story of a group of young newspaper boys (in the not too distant past "newsies" sold newspapers on street corners and other locations around a town when many cities had a half-dozen or more daily papers) who go on strike after a price increase in the papers that they bought every day from the newspaper publishers made them unaffordable, costing them their livelihood.

Since *Norma Rae* the two Hollywood films that come closest to matching it and *Salt of the Earth* in artistry and impact are *Silkwood* (1983) and *Matewan* (1987). *Silkwood* is the story of Karen Silkwood, who is exposed to lethal radiation in the plutonium factory where she works as a chemical technician and is stricken with cancer. Because the company (in real life the Kerr–McGee corporation) has for years known of the dangers and has continued to cover them up, she attempts to get information that can be used for a public revelation of the company's chicanery. As a member of the Oil, Chemical and Atomic Workers' Union, Silkwood had been an active critic of the plant's safety. The events culminated with Silkwood's death in 1974. In the film Silkwood has obtained incriminating documents and is on the way to give them to a reporter. She never arrives and her car is found in a ditch, with her dead and the documents missing. The film raises the question of whether she even had the documents with her. The movie leaves it up in the air as to how she died, but presumably in a one-car accident. Although the final version of the film implicitly raises the question, given the continuing attempts of the company to stop her, of how she actually was killed, the ending and other parts of the movie were allegedly seriously influenced by pressure from Kerr–McGee. *Silkwood* is classic case of how even a fine movie is a victim of Hollywood caving in to the corporate powers-that-be. In real life, evidence and sworn testimony clearly showed that Silkwood was taking the documents to a *New York Times* reporter, that her car had been smashed into from behind, that Kerr–McGee officials, under the guise of checking Silkwood's car for radiation, retrieved the missing documents, and that the company not only had had her under illegal electronic surveillance, but had tried to poison her in her own home. A lawyer for the Karen Silkwood Fund later called the film "a watered-down version of reality."[27] But even in its self-censored version, *Silkwood* is strongly effective in revealing at least part of the viciousness management may resort to in covering up wrongdoing that might give labor and unions a bargaining advantage.

Matewan (1987), a John Sayles movie, is a feature fiction film using a documentary approach to tell the story of the massacre of twelve union coal miners in 1920 in Matewan, West Virginia. Like *Salt of the Earth* and some other strongly pro-union films, it was independently made and not a Hollywood protest film. This "historically accurate and dramatically tight and powerful"[28] movie shows the difficulties of the miners in trying to unionize for fair pay and safety standards, facing not only the company's guns and thugs, but the company's bringing in Black and Italian scabs to break the locked-out miners' picketing. Young miners, boys who raided coal cars for campfire fuel, were captured, tortured, and executed in cold blood.[29]

The scabs are caught between the two forces, with elements of racism and anti-immigrant phobia as factors. A union organizer tries to bring the miners and the scabs together in a common bond against the company's exploitation. At one point the organizer says, "You think this man is your enemy. This man is a worker. Any union that keeps this man out ain't a union, it's a club." The scabs see through the machinations of the company and, after a long and difficult time, become members of the union. The company owned the houses rented by the miners and paid the workers in scrip good only at the company store.

The strikers and their families were evicted from company-owned housing, arrested, beaten up by paid goons, and ambushed and gunned down at the railroad tracks, twelve of them killed.

In documentary style, the film opens with a narrator, a 15-year-old miner and preacher, who advocates the union cause from his pulpit: "The miners was tryin' to bring the union . . . and the coal operators and their goon thugs was set on keepin' them out." In another scene, he sums up the attitude of labor vs. management: "There ain't but two sides in the world – them that work and them that don't. That's all you got to know about the enemy." Like other protest films about a long-past event, this film had no impact on the event itself, but it makes the contemporary audience aware, in general, of the issues and practices involved in contemporary labor-management relations.

With growing attacks on labor and unions in the past decade, it is disconcerting that there have been very few movies dealing with the subject. One, *Coalition*, released in 2004, is about minority non-union labor working in construction in New York. "The story is based on the true inner workings of the police trying to infiltrate the corrupt coalition workers, the mob middle men setting up these coalition deals, the unions trying to organize against impending layoffs due to cheap and unskilled non-union labor."[30] *Bread and Roses* (2001) is based on the legendary 1912 textile workers' strike in Lawrence, Massachusetts and is somewhat similar to the *Norma Rae* plot, centering around an immigrant female worker in a non-union janitorial service whose personality resonates with her co-workers. A union organizer is assigned to win over the employees, who are subject to being fired at the whim of a foul-mouthed supervisor.[31] The largely female and immigrant workers use confrontational tactics to gain the attention of the company executives, not without difficulty and pain and not with overwhelming success. As reviewer A. O. Scott wrote in the *New York Times*, the strikers' gains are ambiguous, "no bread or roses without sweat and tears."[32] Neither film appears to have had much impact, either artistically or politically.

Hollywood has acquired the reputation of being a politically liberal town. Some pundits suggest that the need for creativity and understanding in creating characters for the screen who deal with and have to solve problems facing people anywhere and everywhere in the world and in all kinds of circumstances has resulted in greater sensitivity to the needs of people, and therefore a greater affinity and commitment to support politically progressive activity. That applies to labor management as well, on the part of arguably the majority of the creative workers in Hollywood, including writers, actors, and directors. They have been supportive of unions in general and their own unions in particular. In late 2007 the Writers Guild of America went on strike, seeking for their work a share of the income producers have been increasingly receiving from Internet distribution, which was not included in their previous contract. Their strike affects not only Hollywood films, but television shows and other media using scripts. They have been supported by many members of other unions, such as actors and directors. It is appropriate that Sally Field, who played Crystal Lee in *Norma Rae*, left the set of her television show to join the writers on the picket line.[33] As the real Crystal Lee (Sutton) has said, "I can only talk about what I know . . . the textile worker is an important worker. We didn't have any respect. We didn't have any decent working conditions. I just decided that if it was okay for other people to have unions, I didn't see why we couldn't."[34]

Notes

1   United Farm Workers letter, April, 2006. Received by the author.
2   http://salt.claretianpubs.org/washweek/2001/03/is0103b.html.
3   Bonamici, Kate, Corey Hajim, and Andy Serwer, "Bruised in Bentonville," *Fortune*, No. 151, 2005, pp. 84–8.
4   Kusnet, David, "The Case for Organized Labor and Democracy in the Workplace," *Union Advantage*, September 28, 2001.
5   *Ibid.*
6   *Ibid.*
7   These descriptions of *Salt of the Earth* were obtained in large part from www.library.csi.cuny.edu/dept/history/lavender/salt.html and from www.organa.com.salt.html.
8   *Salt of the Earth.* www.hollywood.com/movies/detail/movie/179004.
9   Keogh, Peter, "*Salt of the Earth*," *The Phoenix*. www.rottentomatoes.com/click/movie-1018110/reviews.php?critic=all&sortby=default&page=2&rid=761589.
10 Hockstader, Lee, "A Film Back from the Blacklist," *Washington Post*, March 3, 2003, pp. C1, 8.
11 *Ibid.*
12 *Ibid.*
13 Hockstader, "A Film Back from the Blacklist," p. C8.
14 *Ibid.*

15 *Ibid.*

16 "Lorenzo Torrez, production consultant for *Salt of the Earth,* on "Morning Edition," National Public Radio, February 27, 2003.

17 www.organa.com.salt.html.

18 Ebert, Roger, "Movie Reviews," *Chicago Sun Times.* www.suntimes.com/ebert/ebert-reviews/1999/01/water1118.html.

19 *Ibid.*

20 Rossini, Tom, "Unionization: Gender and Racial Equality in the Workplace," a paper prepared for the "Pictures of Protest" course, Emerson College, April 7, 2003. Source: Kusnet, "The Case for Organized Labor and Democracy in the Workplace."

21 *Ibid.* Source: Gagne, Jenn, "Exploration of Capitalism in *Norma Rae,*" Mount Holyoke College. www.mtholyoke.edu. October 1, 2000.

22 Rosenfeld, Megan, "Through the Mill with Crystal Lee and *Norma Rae,*" *Washington Post,* June 11, 1980. http://faculty.lagcc.cuny.edu/jselden/norma_rae.htm.

23 Kaufman, Robert (Stanford University), "Sociopolitical Difficulty in Modern Poetry and Aesthetics." www.rc.umd.edu.

24 Burridge, Shane, *"Molly Maguires."* www.rottentomatoes.com/click/movie-1014107/reviews.php?critic=all&sortby=default&page=1&rid=769683.

25 www.laborstart.org/lrd.shtml.

26 Hughes, J., "Films on labor and big business." www.changesurfer.com/Acad/Films/Labor.html.

27 *"Silkwood* – Was the Reality Uglier?," *L.A. Weekly,* January 6–12, 1984.

28 Chaw, Walter, *Matewan.* 1997. http://filmfreakcentral.net/screenreviews/filmsofjohnsayles.htm=matewan.

29 Smith, Gavin and John Sayles, *John Sayles on Sayles* (Boston: Faber & Faber, 1998).

30 *Coalition.* www.imdb.com/title/tt0398873/plotsummary.

31 *Bread and Roses.* www.imdb.com/title/tt0212826/plotsummary.

32 Scott, A. O., *Bread and Roses. New York Times,* June 1, 2001. www.nytimes.com/2001/06/01/ARTS/01ROSE.html.

33 *Boston Globe,* November 8, 2007, p. B10.

34 Rosenfeld, "Through the Mill with Crystal Lee and *Norma Rae.*"

6

Poverty

Anyone can play

One can sympathize with the impoverished, but cannot truly understand poverty unless one has experienced it. One doesn't know what hunger really is unless one has gone hungry to the point of virtual starvation. One cannot feel what the homeless feel unless one has lived on the streets without shelter, or been evicted from their home with their furnishings and possessions put out on the street for scavengers to steal, or been a member of a family crowded into an automobile night after night while seeking enough money to rent a place to live. One doesn't know what it is to be poor unless they've had to share one pair of shoes or a shirt or trousers with one or more brothers or sisters, able to leave their shelter and go to school only on the days when it is their turn to wear the shoes or clothing. One doesn't know what poverty is until a member of their family becomes ill and dies because there is not enough money to pay for a doctor or emergency care at a hospital. For most people in the United States and other nations who live at a standard infinitely higher than that of developing or Third World countries, even the concept of poverty is elusive. It is virtually impossible for most Americans and certainly for the vast majority of those reading this book to conceive of living without adequate food, housing, clothing, health care, sanitation, heat or air, education, or even a job. It is even more difficult for many Americans to realize that many millions of their own countrymen, women, and children are subsisting under such conditions. In the first decade of 2000 the situation in the United States was exacerbated with the government enacting a huge tax cut, eighty percent of it going to the ten percent wealthiest Americans, paid for by cutting food, housing, health, safety, education, and other services to the neediest Americans and plunging millions more into abject poverty. In the context of this book, it is important to note that the media – at least, the mainstream media – have done little or nothing to inform and energize the public to take electoral action against the political entities responsible for such a situation. One reason, as suggested frequently in this book, is that the media, by and large, are controlled by conservative forces that consistently appear to favor the rich at the expense of the poor.

The growing poverty in the United States in the latter part of the first decade of the twenty-first century has not yet, however, reached the depths that marked America's great economic Depression of the 1930s. Yet, there are parallels. Corporate consolidation in the 1920s was repeated in the 2000s, only more strongly through globalization. In the earlier time corporate America blossomed. In the period between 1919 and 1929, some 1,200 mergers swallowed up more than 6,000 previously independent companies. By 1929, some 200 corporations controlled almost half of all US industry.[1] (It is pertinent that in 2008 six companies controlled ninety percent of all media in the United States.) This concentration of wealth engendered greedy speculation in the stock market and resulted in the "Black Friday" stock market crash of 1929. "By 1932 industrial output had been cut in half. One-quarter of the labor force – about 15 million people – was out of work, and there was no such thing as unemployment insurance. Hourly wages had dropped by about fifty percent. Hundreds of banks had failed. More than 90,000 businesses failed completely.[2]

The 1930s Depression affected almost every family in America. Historian William Brinton wrote that

> there may have been enough food to feed those in need, but the system ... was itself not working. Landlords were used to getting their rent on time, but the growing number of unemployed ran out of money and were soon evicted. In agricultural areas, banks began to foreclose on unpaid loans and acquired the land itself in foreclosure proceedings.[3]

As this is written, in late 2007, the parallels are stark: foreclosures of homes resulting from the greedy lending practices of mortgage companies; increasing numbers of business and personal bankruptcies; wildly fluctuating stock-market declines; rapidly growing numbers of homeless families; reduced consumer monetary resources resulting in failing businesses and increased unemployment.

During the period of the Great Depression Hollywood established the Breen Office as a watchdog-censor to meet the increasing complaints from religious and other segments of society that films were too sexually suggestive and too full of violence and glorification of gangsters. The new production code dissuaded Hollywood from making films that dealt with virtually any controversial issue that might disturb any potential viewer. The Breen Office "encouraged movie-makers to avoid harsher realities of Depression-era life and to shun controversial political and moral issues."[4] From a bottom-line standpoint, Hollywood was eager to comply. Those people who had 10 cents to go to a movie (a double feature with toys or household items given away on designated days) wanted to escape from the somber realities of every day Depression life, and Hollywood met their desires with comedies and adventure stories.

Not that Hollywood had dealt to any significant extent with poverty previously. In some of the early silent films, principally the one-reelers, heroes or heroines were sometimes shown in situations of poverty from which they emerge, in most cases through personal enterprise such as an unexpected invention or artistic success, or through the intervention of a rich relative or benefactor. Some ended on a questionable note as to whether the protagonists would ever escape their life of poverty, with only a ray of hope on the horizon. When Hollywood movies did show poor people, it usually was with a negative or condescending stereotyping that continues to this day. Given the lifestyles of those who make films, Hollywood appears to have no concept of poverty – unless some of the filmmakers of a given movie experienced it before they made their way up the economic ladder. Today, as then, Hollywood usually associates poverty with a failing in those who are impoverished. For example, although poverty is a principal cause for crime – the basic instinct of humankind is to survive – Hollywood films invariably link the two disproportionately, just as it almost always portrays people in poverty as lazy or incompetent or scheming. The overwhelming majority of those in poverty are intelligent, hardworking, honest, capable people who are not in poverty because of their own doing: A single mother of a small child or children who cannot take a job because there is no one to look after her children – and has no other source of income; the chronically ill person who cannot maintain consistent work habits – and has no other source of income; the person who cannot reach a workplace because of the lack of adequate public transportation – and has no other income with which to buy a car; the elderly person who can no longer do the physical labor required in his or her field – and has no other source of income. Professor and writer Carla Johnston notes that the average American family is just two pay checks away from poverty. If a sudden, unexpected large family expense occurs, or a family member falls ill or dies or becomes unemployed, with the loss of the lone or one of the two family pay checks, that family is plunged into poverty. Hollywood has rarely, if ever, shown this in connection with any film about poverty or in which there are characters who are living in poverty.[5]

As the 1930s Depression developed and then hit America full-force, a complementary disaster was occurring in the country's farm belt. Farmers had plowed up the grasslands to plant wheat, a key survival crop. But a severe drought in the 1930s killed the wheat, and high winds scattered the topsoil, making much of the Great Plains of middle and southwest America – some 150,000 square miles – into what was called the Dust Bowl. Farmers were bereft of income, didn't even have crops upon which to personally subsist, couldn't pay their mortgages, and lost their land and their houses to the banks. The skies, black with dust, made it difficult for them to breathe, even through handkerchiefs. They choked and got ill, and some died. Thousands of these farm families, desperately seeking work, set out for the California fruit and vegetable farms where they heard there was work available for field pickers. Because many of these impoverished wandering families were from Oklahoma, all were called Okies. As dramatic and significant to the country as this was, Hollywood barely touched upon it. It wasn't until John Steinbeck won a Pulitzer Prize for his 1939 novel about these Okies, *The Grapes of Wrath*, that Hollywood became interested in the subject. Steinbeck provided the background in the novel:

And then the dispossessed were drawn west – from Kansas, Oklahoma, Texas, New Mexico, from Nevada and Arkansas, families, tribes, dusted out, tractored out. Carloads, caravans, homeless and hungry; twenty thousand and fifty thousand and a hundred thousand and two hundred thousand. They streamed over the mountains, hungry and restless – restless as ants, scurrying to find work to do – to lift, to push, to pull, to pick, to cut – anything, any burden to bear, for food. The kids are hungry. We got no place to live. Like ants hurrying for work, for food, and most of all for land.

Roger Ebert described Steinbeck's novel as "arguably the most effective social document of the 1930s."[6]

The film, *The Grapes of Wrath*, was directed by John Ford and released in 1940. It was not the first film to deal with the subject of poverty during the Great Depression. But it became the icon for such films. Some of the poverty films in the 1930s, such as *Dead End* (1937) and *One Third of a Nation* (1939), took a serious look at the subject. Most, such as *My Man Godfrey* (1936) and *Sullivan's Travels* (1941), were billed as comedies but had a clear layer of satire that brought the problem of poverty to the fore for any in the audience who were willing to listen. Those that weren't could simply concentrate on the comedy. But *The Grapes of Wrath* was a punch in the stomach that could not be marginalized. The film begins with Tom Joad (brilliantly portrayed by Henry Fonda) arriving and ends with Tom Joad leaving, and although the film is about him, it is about more than this one "everyman." His story becomes the story of the extended Joad family, which in turn becomes the story of tens of thousands of Okies and of hundreds of thousands of migrant workers seeking jobs and of millions of unemployed seeking survival – food and shelter – in a society whose economics dictate that from time to time only the affluent can survive. "Watching Ford's film pulls us momentarily into the Joads' pilgrimage through the wasteland of the Depression and lets us sample the diet or despair and injustice served up to those left behind by an indifferent economy."[7]

Critic Tim Dirks wrote:

> The plight of the Joad family is universalized as a microcosm of the thousands of other tenant farmers during the country's time of crisis, who suffered from oppressions imposed by the banks and big mechanized farm interests. The dispossessed, migrant family's departure from their windy and dusty land, and their slow disintegration provides insight into the thousands of Oklahoma, Colorado, Texas Panhandle, and Kansas families who were evicted and uprooted from their "Dust Bowl" farm land, and forced to search westward in the inhospitable Eden of California for jobs and survival with thousands of other migrant workers.[8]

Figure 6.1
The Grapes of Wrath (1940)

Dirks adds that the film used the "plight of the Joad family as a universal microcosm of thousands of other tenant farmers who suffered from oppression imposed by banks and big mechanized farm interests."[9]

Tom Joad returns to his family's farm in the Dust Bowl after several years in prison for killing a man in self-defense. He finds his friends' and neighbors' farms abandoned or in the process of being foreclosed, and his family's homestead, which it has occupied for generations, about to be. The land conditions have made it impossible for these families to pay their mortgages, and the banks have ruthlessly taken and in many cases bulldozed not only the land but the houses the people have lived in for many years, sometimes destroying their personal belongings if they've not vacated at a designated time. Resisting the bulldozers, as some try to do, is fruitless. One neighbor is about to shoot the bulldozer driver and the bank agent who are ready to demolish his house.

BULLDOZER DRIVER: Now don't go blaming me. It ain't my fault.
BOY: Whose fault is it?
BULLDOZER DRIVER: It ain't nobody. It's a company. He [bank agent] ain't anything but the manager . . .
MULEY: Then who do we shoot?
BULLDOZER DRIVER: Brother, I don't know.

The frustration deepens their despair.

Given no alternative to starvation, the Joad family and some neighbors and friends pile into an old jalopy truck and head west to California, where they hear from other migrants and see on flyers that there are plenty of jobs for fieldworkers. One typical flyer reads: "800 Pickers Wanted. Good Wages. Tents and Cabins Furnished Free. Store on Campground. Come At Once."[10] Thousands are made to believe there are jobs available for them. Despite intolerable difficulties, including hunger, illness, the breakdown of their vehicle, family defections, near-tragedies and tragedies along the way, the Joads – and other Okies – persevere. Hope leads them on: delusionary hope, as it turns out, as the audience knows from the beginning. As critic Frank Nugent wrote:

[The film is a] matchless description of the Joad family's trek from Oklahoma to California to find the promised land where work was plenty, wages were high and folk could live in little white houses beside an orange grove. [The film has not] blunted the fine indignation or diluted the bitterness of his [Steinbeck's] indictment of the cruel deception by which an empty stew-pot was substituted for the pot of gold at the rainbow's end.[11]

Along the way the Joads stop and seek work at transient camps where they've been led to believe there are jobs. Contractors who promised the jobs arrive at the camp with considerably fewer jobs than there are job seekers. They bargain down the amount they will pay per hour or per bushel, with the desperate workers forced to accept any wage in order to feed their starving families. In many cases, after the fruit is picked at an agreed-upon wage, the contractor gives the workers less: "Take it or leave it!" At the camps the company advances food and shelter, and after the work is done the migrants receive no pay, owing the company more than they earned. At one camp a migrant worker asks to see the contractor's credentials:

> Twice now I fell for that line. Maybe he needs a thousand men. So he gets five thousand there and he'll pay fifteen cents an hour. Then you guys will have to take it 'cause you'll be hungry. If he wants to hire men, let him ride it out and say what he's gonna pay. Ask to see the license. He ain't allowed by law to contract men without a license.

The labor practices concerning the Okies were reflective of the labor practices by management in capitalistic systems throughout the world.

> By ensuring an over-supply of labor and by keeping the laborers in poverty, they progressively drove wages down. If a desperate man has a wife and starving children to feed, he'll work no matter how low the wages, because if he doesn't, then someone else more desperate will. As long as there are more workers than work, this vicious system is self-enforcing, with lower wages driving more people into poverty and starvation.[12]

Needless to say, farm owners who employed migrant workers took great umbrage at the movie's revelations of the depraved conditions at their camps, as did law-enforcement authorities at the revelations of their conspiracy with the owners to keep the migrants in line. As *Variety* magazine noted in its review of the film, "There is nothing sunkist about the way state troopers and local constables push around the unwelcome visitors."[13]

The Joads also experience the animosity of the general public toward the migrant workers. "Okie" is used as a pejorative term. The Depression had affected all of America, and even in the comparatively benign atmosphere of California, the economic Depression made people fearful of any migration that brought in tens or hundreds of thousands vying for their jobs or seeking to share their resources. Even though the migrants expected resentment and opposition, what they encountered exceeded their fears. They were discriminated against, demeaned, vilified, run out of towns, jailed, beaten and, in some cases, even murdered. Writer Charles Todd quoted examples of the animosity:[14] "This isn't a migration, it's an invasion. They are worse than a plague of locusts"; "It stinks of Russia. Our women won't be safe on the streets. We never wanted this camp here. White men [Okies] are no good in our business. We like our Mexicans. They don't complain. They live where we put them and they aren't forever organizing." The children were not immune from the rancor: "Are you going to make it possible for more of these hobo brats to go to school with our children? This is another example of the evils of a paternalistic government."

Can readers today resent these kinds of attitudes toward the migrant workers in *The Grapes of Wrath* without resenting and trying to counter the exact same hate toward and treatment of immigrant migrant workers, illegal and legal, trying to keep their families alive, in twenty-first-century America?

A measure of hope, a little too obvious and gratuitous, invades the film. After a series of camps in which the Joads and other Okies are shamelessly exploited and subject to violence, the Joads arrive at a Department of Agriculture model camp, in which livable conditions, with facilities such as running water, clean quarters, and decent food are provided in an atmosphere of cooperation and care for the migrants. The mini-town even has a pleasurable social life. The camp director stands up to the bigots in the area who try to provoke a fight so that the authorities can arrest the camp residents. It all seems too good to be true. In reality, there were a number of such government camps, although perhaps not quite as ideal as the one depicted in the film. The question has to be raised as to whether pressures were put on the producer and director by the Hollywood moguls to insert a bright note in the treatment of poor people. *Variety* magazine commented that, despite the sympathy and kindness the Okies found in these camps, "a hundred such camps could not accommodate the army of refugees."[15] In real life, sources both in and out of government tried to shut down these Farm Security Administration camps. Not surprisingly, farm owners and contractors took leading roles in doing so, inasmuch as these camps, few as they were, reduced management's ability to exploit the farm workers at will. The Associated Farmers of California called for a boycott of all Twentieth Century-Fox films and the producers of *The Grapes of Wrath*.[16] Others were concerned – or pretended to be – that these camps were too reminiscent of the Soviet cooperatives and smacked of socialism.[17] Some quarters called for an end to the "red camps." In fact, with the advent of the Cold War and McCarthyism, the entire film, especially its pro-union, anti-management stance in presenting some of the causes of poverty, was put under suspicion, and novelist Steinbeck and director Ford were investigated for alleged pro-communist leanings.[18]

Before the Joads arrive at the Department of Agriculture camp, at a previous camp Tom Joad kills a lawman while trying to defend his family's close friend, a preacher, from the brutality of the lawman. The authorities track Tom down at the Department of Agriculture camp and Tom hurriedly says goodbye to his mother as he runs off in the middle of the night to escape. When his mother asks where he will go, Tom makes an impassioned promise in a long monologue that he will be where workers need him, where people are exploited, where the wrongs of poverty have to be put right. His mother looks to the future with hope and perseverance to survive, ending the film on a somewhat upbeat note – criticized by some critics as being inimical to the purpose and tone of the entire movie. Critic John Calhoun wrote:

> The film was meant by Ford [Director John] and Johnson [screenwriter Nunnally Johnson] to end with Tom's famous scene of leave-taking from Ma, a bittersweet moment if there ever was one. Zanuck [producer Daryll F.] imposed a slightly more upbeat ending, in which Ma delivers her "We keep a comin', we're the people that live" speech, but still the conclusion is fraught with uncertainty and no little amount of fear.[19]

Screenwriter Nunnally Johnson said that the only real change he made from the novel was in providing a less downbeat ending, "something that would keep the people who saw it from going out and getting so drunk in utter despondency that they couldn't tell other people that it was a good picture to see."[20]

The film was praised for its aesthetic and production qualities, as well as for its content. By 1940, when the film was released, America was beginning to pull out of the economic Depression, due in large part to the increase in production jobs for armaments and other goods being sent to Britain in its war against Germany, and the continuing growth of production to arm the United States for its certain future entry into the war. Some said a film on the subject should have been made earlier, during the height of the Dust Bowl and migrant poverty crisis. On the other hand, others said, "even if the script had been available [earlier], *The Grapes of Wrath* dealt with issues that were far too familiar and too painful to have been made during the early thirties."[21]

Its impact on American political, economic, and social thought has been great, if only in educating post-Depression viewers about conditions and practices that are harmful to human rights as well as to democratic principles. Whether it had a similar effect on Hollywood's future contributions to the issue through further pictures of protest is questionable. At the time, it was hopeful. *Variety* concluded its review of *The Grapes of Wrath* as follows: "*Grapes* is far removed from conventional film entertainment. It tackles one phase of the American social problem in a convincing manner. It possesses an adult viewpoint and its success may lead other producers to explore the rich field of contemporary life which films have long neglected and ignored."[22]

As noted earlier, *The Grapes of Wrath* was not the first Hollywood feature film to deal with poverty. Some of the early films showed the protagonists emerging from poverty, some not, but still hopeful. Most of these films showed a setting of poverty, with a protest implied or inferred, but not explicit. A few were explicit in their protest, with what might be considered an "agitprop" plea. ("Agitprop" was a term principally associated with drama, essentially stage plays, coming out of the 1930s social and political turmoil, and stood for "agitational propaganda.") *Our Daily Bread*, released in 1934, is one of Hollywood's early films in this category, made by Hollywood director King Vidor. The principals in this movie, disillusioned by the chicaneries of life in cities, with poverty exacerbated by corporate greed making the quality of life and even survival increasingly difficult, move to an abandoned farm in the countryside where they set up a cooperative farming community. More and more friends and acquaintances join them, and "then in a steady procession come the end products of the industrial collapse – plumber, carpenter, blacksmith, stonemason, barber, merchant, shoemaker, undertaker . . . ex-convict, lawyer, politician, cigar salesman, violinist, professor."[23] Their work in building a new community extols

the cooperative as opposed to the competitive system of human interaction and organization. Ultimately, the actions of the banks and corporate America, abetted by the law enforcement authorities, threaten
the existence of this new Eden. The selfless members of the new community overcome, for the moment at least, their oppressors, and there
is hope for the future. It is clearly a protest against the economic system
that was responsible for the widespread poverty that inundated most
Americans during the Great Depression.

Andre Sennwald's review in the *New York Times* stated that "Mr. Vidor's
attempt to dramatize the history of a subsistence farm for hungry
and desperate men [*sic*] from the cities of America would deserve the
attention and encouragement of intelligent film-goers" and described
Our Daily Bread as "a brilliant declaration of faith in the importance of
the cinema as a social instrument."[24]

When the usual Hollywood financial sources became aware of the
film's content, money was withheld. Director Vidor sought independent
funding, in addition to his own money, in order to complete the film.
He cut back on costs, including using a largely non-professional cast,
many of them unemployed people from the streets of Los Angeles. It
is important to note that, consistent with the protests against poverty
as well as various forms of social and political injustice in his films,
Charlie Chaplin's investment helped to save the film at the last minute.[25]
(Some of Chaplin's films are discussed elsewhere in this book.)

Another film in the "agitprop" category was *One Third of Nation*, produced in 1939. Based on a "living newspaper" stage play of the same
name, the film was a presentational showing of the tragedies that befall
a New York family forced into economic poverty, and purportedly
represented the third of the population that was ill-housed, ill-fed, and
ill-clothed during the economic Depression. The "living newspaper"
emanated principally from the Franklin D. Roosevelt "New Deal"
Federal Theater Project, which put to work thousands of unemployed
writers, directors, actors, and other theater people, akin to the jobs that
built roads, bridges, schools, and other buildings under the Works
Progress Administration (WPA). The Federal Theater Project presented
plays for free or for a nominal sum to poverty-stricken Americans all
over the country. It was eventually eliminated by Congress, which complained that it was communist-dominated – the rise of social protest
in America in the 1930s engendered much the same kind of national
paranoia that fueled the excesses of the McCarthy era over a decade

later. Such was the insanity of fear that one Congressman demanded to know in a congressional hearing on the Federal Theater to which communist cell Christopher Marlowe, one of whose plays was cited for communist influence, belonged. When the answer was that Marlowe was a great English playwright immediately preceding Shakespeare, the hearings were recessed, and when they were resumed the Federal Theater was abolished.

One Third of a Nation dealt directly with poor people living in horrendous slums. The plot itself is thin, virtually a boy-meets-girl situation set against the slum background. But it is that background that dominates the film, the working girl persuading a landlord to tear down his dangerous slums and build new, decent housing. Frank Nugent's review in the *New York Times* described the characters of the film as "a girl of the tenements, a handsome landowner who hadn't realized what pestilential buildings stood on his property, a slightly leftist young man and a kid brother who has been crippled in a fire and hates the malignant old building with a deep and personal hate."[26] (Film students will find it noteworthy that the young actor who played the crippled little brother later became one of Hollywood's leading directors of films that protested various conditions or attitudes in society: Sidney Lumet.) The landowner falls in love with the tenement girl and we are given hope that these tenements, at least and at last, will be replaced. The *New York Times* review adds that "it is the building itself that dominates the picture, gives it terror, pity and despair. It is more than a scabrous dwelling, pestilential, filthy and breeder of crime; it becomes the very symbol of reaction, of greed, oppression and human misery."[27]

The stark realism and searing protest of America's economic condition and system portrayed in films such as *Our Daily Bread* and *One Third of a Nation* did not engender much box office by people who wanted to escape from these same conditions that they were experiencing in their everyday life. A film that presented the same kinds of poverty conditions, but wrapped them in what was essentially a good-guy and bad-guy story and was character-driven rather than ideology-driven, was the 1937 film, *Dead End*. It was a huge hit. Set in a dead-end street in New York's East Side waterfront during the Depression, it presented the stark contrast between people living in the poverty-stricken slums – including the "Dead End Kids," who became key characters in a series of subsequent films, later called the "Bowery Boys" – which were literally looked down on by the adjacent Sutton Place luxury apartment buildings of the rich, who are untouched by the economic Depression. An imaginary but potent line separates the penthouses from the over-crowded, virtually uninhabitable flats, as it does the people living in them. The contrasts – and protests – are strikingly clear without the need for polemic. The film is "the story of the frustrations and rebellions of the underprivileged people"[28] living on the dead-end street. It concentrates on the people trying to escape from their poverty-stricken life in the slums. They try anything in desperation. One becomes a gangster, the bad guy; another becomes an architect, the good guy. The destructive effect of poverty on the lives of these people is potently clear.

Other films in the 1930s that protested poverty at a time when poverty was rife in America did so within a different dominant theme. For example, in 1932 *I Am a Fugitive from a Chain Gang* (discussed in chapter 4) showed poverty – that is, a Depression economy with no jobs available and people having to steal in order to eat – as a reason for being caught up in the justice and prison system.

Despite the successes of a few serious films such as *Dead End*, the public wanted an escape from the poverty of their daily lives and Hollywood gave them that escape through what some critics called "screwball comedies." In these films the audience could identify with protagonists who were seemingly not affected by the stench of poverty and who, with and without money, did unorthodox things that the average person would rarely if ever have the opportunity or the courage to do in a conformist society, things bordering on the "screwball." These occasional few hours of being transported away from reality into a world where one could empathize with carefree, even wild, behavior and adventure and where one could belong in that empathy to a sophisticated society translated into box-office success. Hollywood writers and producers who nevertheless were concerned with the state of the world in which they lived, but who would find it difficult if not impossible to make a serious movie on poverty, commented on and protested poverty within the genre of comedy.

One of the successful films of this kind was *My Man Godfrey* (1936). During the Depression, two sisters from an inane rich family seek a "homeless man" as part of a scavenger hunt. They find one living in a city dump among a group of unemployed and bring him home as part of their scavenger loot that includes a corset, a monkey, and a goat. The derelict appears to be remarkably suave, sophisticated, and know-ledgeable and they offer him a job as butler, which he accepts. This presumably inferior person who was living in poverty solves financial and other problems besetting the incompetent rich family. They do not know that he is a Harvard graduate, a lawyer, and was living as a homeless person while recovering from personal and professional setbacks. The insensitivity of the rich to the impoverished homeless is starkly presented. One reviewer stated that *My Man Godfrey* was "possibly the screwiest of all screwball comedies ... the ultimate Depression-era satire of the idle rich and tribute to the noble poor ... social satire at its broadest."[29]

Perhaps the most critically acclaimed film of this kind, then and now, was 1941's *Sullivan's Travels*, directed by a master of 1930s and 1940s screwball comedies with a sometimes subtle, sometimes obvious underlying message, Preston Sturges. "Sturges' films offered audiences a vision of a corrupt, ridiculous, but often vital people whose chief flaw was a profound lack of self-knowledge."[30]

The plot of *Sullivan's Travels* revolves around a fictional affluent Hollywood movie director named John Sullivan, famous for making successful frivolous films, who decides to make a serious film about conditions in Depression-era America. To do so, he travels through the United States, seeking out various situations in which poor people find themselves, in order to better understand what it is to be underprivileged. But *Sullivan's Travels* does not have the unrelenting tragedy that followed the travelers in *The Grapes of Wrath*, released just the year before. Sullivan fools himself into thinking he is seeing the real America, but he is not. It is part-comedy, part-satire about someone who is affluent trying to feel what the poor actually go through, and about the faux social significance of many Hollywood movies. At the end Sullivan is separated from the retinue of Hollywood PR people following him and ends up in a brutal prison camp where he finally learns about cruelty and poverty, and learns that laughter provides the only relief.[31] Critic Tim Dirks wrote that *Sullivan's Travels* "skillfully mixes every conceivable cinematic genre type and tone of film possible ... tragic melodrama, farce, prison film, serious drama, social documentary, slapstick, romance, comedy, action, and even musical, in about a dozen sequences."[32] Drawing people to it through laughter, the basic theme struck a chord for much of the audience. To the extent that people came in large numbers to see a comedy and came away with both smiles and a sense of concern about poverty, and a nagging feeling that they ought to do something about it, *Sullivan's Travels* was a successful picture of protest. As a movie of social comment, it is "one of the screen's more 'significant' films."[33]

Many critics were not as sanguine about sophisticated comedies being strong and deep enough to be pictures of protest that influenced people's hearts and minds. A European publication commented on such protest films thus:

> Glamour, a value introduced and perpetuated by Hollywood for the past 40 years has no place in these films about poor or maltreated people, the socially forgotten. These are not "good taste" films. Nor are they made with a sense of the exquisite, delicacy, and luxuriousness or with unlimited means. The best cinema about marginalism is something else entirely: a punch in the stomach for western society, for a Europe that increasingly manages to disguise its miseries.[34]

Somewhere between the two extremes of comedy and drama were movies by the filmmaker who arguably produced the most effective and largest body of films protesting social, economic, and political inequalities, Charlie Chaplin. Chaplin, from his early silent one-reel movies to his later and final films such as *Monsieur Verdoux* (1947) and *A King in New York* (1957), used pathos and comedy to get across his points of view. His early movie persona of the Little Tramp, the most acclaimed and known everyman in the world in all of film history, the person stricken by the inequities of a unfair society, never winning but somehow always surviving, morphed into the lead characters of his full-length films. It is difficult to categorize many of Chaplin's films with regard to a principal subject of protest, most of them addressing more than one issue extant in society when the films were made. Two of Chaplin's most honored films made during the depression that protested poverty, among other things, were *City Lights*, in 1931, and *Modern Times*, in 1936.

City Lights did so in a very subtle way, showing how people look at and treat other people who they think are poor as opposed to their attitude toward and treatment of people who they think are rich, or at least their economic peers. We see this through Chaplin's signature character, the Little Tramp. This impoverished everyman is beloved and lavished upon by a millionaire when the latter is drunk, but is not recognized and is avoided when the millionaire is sober and sees him as a symbol of poverty. The plot revolves around a blind flower girl for whom the penniless tramp tries to get money for an eye operation. The girl, unable to see him, is struck by his tenderness and envisages him as a well-to-do, handsome hero. The operation is a success. The tramp, having been accused by the millionaire – in a sober moment when he sees only the ragged hobo – of attempting to rob his home, when in fact the Chaplin character was trying to prevent a robbery, emerges from jail and sees the flower girl in her own flower shop. The flower girl sees him and laughs at the spectacle of poverty, not knowing he is her benefactor. Chaplin ends the film with a moment of pathos. From a touch of their hands the flower girl realizes who this disreputable-looking tramp is.

Modern Times is one of Hollywood's greatest contributions to the art of protest, if not the greatest. Essentially a satirical protest against what technology is doing to the essence of humanity in society (this will be discussed at length in chapter 10), it also protests labor exploitation by management, the police, the penal system, government insensitivity, and the treatment of the impoverished. Chaplin shows, through the Little Tramp and a homeless waif, what it is to try to exist without food, being homeless or living in a squalid shack, and being treated as a non-person with no rights by those who are not economically bereft. The *New York Times* called *Modern Times* a dramatization of the class struggle.[35]

The economic upturn during and following World War II and the subsequent decades of relatively good to excellent periods of economic conditions for most Americans lessened concern for those still remaining in poverty. The exponential rise in wealth of the richest ten percent of Americans and the growth of the middle class inured majority America to the plight of the third of the nation who were living under the poverty income threshold. There appeared to be not enough concern on the part of Americans to justify a film on poverty, one that would not likely draw at the box office, and Hollywood produced very little of what could be called protests against poverty. By the latter part of the first decade of 2000 the trickle-down economics theory – that is, funneling tax cuts and other economic favors to the wealthy in the belief that it will trickle down to the majority of Americans – proved once again a failure as the wealthy simply kept the money and divided it amongst themselves, in, for example, multi-million annual salaries and options and golden parachute retirements to corporate executives. As the rich got richer, the poor got poorer, and the middle class began to slide down the economic ladder, some observers speculated that Hollywood might once again consider making films reflecting the depressed status of an increasing number of Americans.

The title of a 1945 film, *A Tree Grows in Brooklyn*, has become a catchword even for millions who never saw the movie. Made from a partly autobiographical novel, the film is unpretentious and honest (like the novel's author, Betty Smith, who this author had the privilege of knowing) about a family struggling to survive in the grip of poverty. Unable to make a living, the father of the family turns to drink, which makes it even harder for him to find survival for his family. Like many of us, he is a dreamer, wanting to make something out of life and provide for his family, trying to rise out of poverty against all odds, like the now proverbial tree rising out the concrete pavement of a Brooklyn street. His alcoholism dooms him and his family. The film shows, with great human emotional impact, the effect poverty has on human beings, in this case on this one typical family with whom the viewer establishes tear-jerking empathy. For viewers, 1945 still had an identification with the previous decade, when many of them were in or close to the same predicament.

The counter-culture, equal and civil rights, and feminist revolutions of the 1960s and early 1970s created a new set of situations for protest films, focusing around discrimination against people of color, most particularly African-Americans and other races in America, women, and lifestyle nonconformists. Poverty was not a key issue, except where it was a factor in films dealing with these issues. One outstanding example is the film *Sounder* (1972), which dealt with poverty and racism in the rural South during the Depression. An African-American male head of a sharecropping family steals a ham to feed his starving children and is sent to a distant prison camp. The mother assumes the difficult burden of keeping the family alive and together. The movie makes it clear that, in that environment, being black equals a sentence of poverty. Critic Brian Koller wrote that "the social commentary of *Sounder* is obvious but never heavy-handed . . . Blacks are segregated and second-class, powerless facing a lifetime of poverty."[36]

A 1984 film, *Places in the Heart*, is another example of Depression-era poverty being protested at a much later time. Also set in a rural area, it too dealt with a woman, a widow, trying to support her children, and as in *The Grapes of Wrath*, trying to save her home and farm from foreclosure by the banks. What pertinence did it have, however, to the 1980s, a period of economic growth? However, the period wasn't growth for everyone. The rich and the upper middle class did well. Low-income families lost eighteen percent of their real income. Some people called the 1980s a "decade of greed."[37] "The 1980s brought a long period of uninterrupted economic growth, but . . . also ushered in persistent federal budget and trade deficits. The unprecedented financial developments on Wall Street, combined with supply side economic policies, created economic conditions that were not conducive to steady economic progress by all groups in our nation."[38]

Places in the Heart, unlike the story of most real-life families in the same circumstances, has a happy and hopeful ending. An African-American drifter offers to work on a farm in exchange for food and place to sleep. Working together, the family and drifter are able to pay the mortgage in time to prevent the bank from taking the farm. One reviewer stated that

In a day of computers, MTV, and frozen pizza, it's hard for us to imagine the hardships people faced during the early part of the 20th century. Having a can of beans and jug of milk was equivalent to us having a stocked fridge and pantry full of food. It is a rare movie that feels as if it has transplanted us from [the 2000s] to the 1930s with great ease – *Places in the Heart* is able to do that.[39]

Places in the Heart also had immediate relevance to farmers, who were having difficult times in the 1980s. While the government was providing huge subsidies to large corporate farms, small farmers were struggling to make ends meet. The large "factory farms" were – and still are – pushing small farmers into bankruptcy. This was exacerbated by the lack of help for small farmers who couldn't afford to employ large staffs, with more and more young people leaving the farms to seek their fortune in the cities. A year after the release of *Places in the Heart*, and perhaps in part due to the impact of the film, a number of musical artists, many originally from rural areas, formed "Farm Aid," annual concerts that raise money for family farmers' emergencies.[40]

The 1999 film, *Angela's Ashes*, was based on the Pulitzer Prize-winning memoir of the same name by Frank McCourt. It has been likened to *A Tree Grows in Brooklyn* in that both have an autobiographical base of presenting the effects of poverty through concentration on a particular family headed by an alcoholic father. Both are set during the pre-World War II economic Depression. The story is of the McCourt family's hard times in Brooklyn and their return to Limerick, Ireland, where life for them is even tougher. Reviews, however, took the film to task for tempering what real poverty feels like. As Janet Maslin wrote in her *New York Times* review, "the McCourt family wanted for food, coal, and decent housing . . . the actors radiate health even when made up to look pallid. Everybody has clean hair . . . [the film's] tidily controlled palette keeps any sense of real suffering at bay . . . The family's suffering, like the carefully mottled paint on supposedly run-down walls, is curiously unreal."[41] While the execution may have been faulty, Hollywood did produce a film that in essence was a protest against poverty.

A number of films in the past two decades contain settings of or comments on poverty, although their main thrusts are not protests against poverty. Some examples follow.

Spike Lee's *Do the Right Thing* (1989) is one of the strongest protests against racism in American movie-making. It dramatizes the environment, pressures, everyday life, exploitation, loves, hates, and fears of ghettoized Black America in the microcosm of one city block in Brooklyn. Unlike most American-issue films, it virtually replicates the police terrorism against minorities that led to the homicide by the police of an innocent youth and the reaction of the community to this killing. It is a panoply of the urban Black experience and, although it does not stress or dwell on economic conditions, the specter of being poor is in the background. As one reviewer noted,

> In a double-edged comment on the economic underpinnings of racism in our society, both Mookie and Sal view money as the solution to all problems – Sal thinks he can buy off trouble by slipping a few dollars to Da Mayor or Smiley or Mookie; and Mookie's a wage slave who doesn't seem to care about anything except "getting paid."[42]

Do the Right Thing is discussed at length in chapter 7.

In 1991 *Boyz N the Hood* painted a vivid picture of what racism, combined with poverty, does to the ambitions, hopes, and fears of young Black people in ghettoized Los Angeles in the 1990s.[43] "Drug use, teen pregnancy, broken homes, unemployment, hopelessness and violence between both black youths and authority and black youths among themselves are all a part of everyday life . . . [The film] addressed issues in

America that were being ignored." Roger Ebert's review of *Boyz N the Hood* further stated: "I realized I had seen . . . an American film of enormous importance."[44]

In America (2002) is another film in which poverty is a background factor, but not the principal theme. It tells the story of a young family trying to solve problems within the family while attempting to make a home in a "New York tenement populated by junkies and drag queens."[45]

Another 2002 film, *8 Mile*, is a dramatized biographical look at the life of rapper Eminem. It only peripherally suggests that there are issues in life other than music contests – if rap can be included in the definition of music – and what wannabe stars must do to succeed as rappers. Yet, in the background there is the struggle to succeed from a beginning that starts on the wrong side of the economic tracks, from poverty or near-poverty.

Do such films, most set in another time and place – *Do the Right Thing* is noted above as an exception – with many set in the 1930s Depression era, have any appreciable effect on viewers seeing them after the situation shown in the film has passed? Certainly, for most of us it's much too late to protest, no less do anything about the problem. Yet, as noted, in every time and place, there are still people impoverished, living in squalor, discriminated against, hopelessly shut out from the economic mainstream. To the extent that the concept of poverty and its impact reach the consciousness or remain in the subconscious of viewers, the viewers may be galvanized to understand those trying to eradicate poverty and support those trying to change the conditions of poverty when the media – rather if, given the control of the media by the wealthy and conservative – bring to their attention poverty situations in their own time and place.

Notes

1 Brinton, William M., *An Abridged History of the United States*, 1996, Chapter 5. www.einet.net/reviews/61862-477705/William_M_Brinton_s_Onine_History_Books.htm.
2 "Great Depression," *Encyclopedia Britannica Online*. www.search..eb.com/ebi/article?eu=296545.
3 Brinton, *An Abridged History of the United States*.

4 Mintz, S., "The Movies Meet the Great Depression." www.digitalhistory. uh.edu/historyonline/hollywood_history.cfm#depression.

5 Personal interview, November 25, 2007.

6 Ebert, Roger, "*The Grapes of Wrath,*" *Chicago Sun-Times*, March 21, 2002. www.suntimes.com/ebert/ebert_reviews/2002/03/033101.html.

7 McCormick, Patrick, "Two Thumbs Up for Social Justice," *U.S. Catholic*, Vol. 67, No. 9, 2002, p. 48.

8 Dirks, Tim, "*Grapes of Wrath,*" *The Greatest Films*. www.filmsite.org/grap. html.

9 *Ibid.*

10 Johnson, Nunnally, screenplay adaptation of Steinbeck's *The Grapes of Wrath*.

11 Nugent, Frank, "*The Grapes of Wrath,*" *New York Times*, January 23, 1940, p. 17.

12 www.nnbtv.dircon.co.uk/Books/2002/Grapes.html.

13 "*Grapes of Wrath*" (January 31, 1940), *Variety Film Reviews: 1907–1980* (New York: Garland, 1983).

14 Todd, Charles, "Voices From the Dust Bowl: The Okies Search For A Lost Frontier," *New York Times Magazine*, August 27, 1939, p. 6.

15 "*Grapes of Wrath,*" *Variety Film Reviews*.

16 "Trivia for *The Grapes of Wrath* (1940)." www.imbd.com/title/ttoo32551.

17 Todd, "Voices From the Dust Bowl."

18 "Trivia for *The Grapes of Wrath.*"

19 Calhoun, John, "*The Grapes of Wrath,*" *Cineaste*, Winter, 2004, Vol. 30, No. 1, pp. 51–2.

20 Van Gelder, Robert, "Who Wrote the Scenarios of *The Grapes of Wrath*?," This Business of Writing for the Movies, *New York Times*, September 1, 1940.

21 Pauly, Thomas, "*Gone With The Wind* and *The Grapes of Wrath* as Hollywood Histories of the Depression" (pp. 164–75), in *Movies as Artifacts*, ed. Sam Grogg, Michael Marsden, and John Nachbar (Chicago: Nelson Hall, 1982), p. 165.

22 "*Grapes of Wrath,*" *Variety Film Reviews*.

23 Sennwald, Andre, "*Our Daily Bread,*" *New York Times*, October 3, 1934. http://movies.nytimes.com/movie/review?res.

24 *Ibid.*

25 *Our Daily Bread.* www.rottentomatoes.com/m/OurDailyBread-1015722/ abot.php.

26 Nugent, Frank, "One Third of a Nation," *New York Times*, February 11, 1939. http://movies.nytimes.com/movie/review?_r=2&res.

27 *Ibid.*

28 McManus, John, "*Dead End,*" *New York Times*, August 25, 1937. http://movies.nytimes.com/movie/review?res.

29 Greydanus, Steven, "*My Man Godfrey*," *National Catholic Register*. http://decentfilms.com/sections/reviews/1646.

30 Cook, David, *A History of Narrative Film* (New York: W. W. Norton, 1996), p. 279.

31 Crowther, Bosley, "*Sullivan's Travels*," *New York Times*, January 29, 1942.

32 Dirks, Tim, "*Sullivan's Travels*," *The Greatest Films*. www.filmsite.org/sull.html.

33 Crowther, "*Sullivan's Travels*."

34 "The New Cinema," pp. 1–2. www.european-digest.com/ecd05/docs/digest15.htm.

35 Nugent, Frank, "*Modern Times*," *New York Times*, February 6, 1936. http://movies.nytimes.com/movie/review?_r=1&res.

36 Koller, Brian, *Sounder*. www.rottentomatoes.com/click/movie-1019463/reviews.php?critic.

37 Meegan, James, from a paper submitted in the "Pictures of Protest" course, Emerson College, February 2, 2004.

38 Anderson, Bernard, "Economic Growth." www.indiana.edu/~speaweb/perspectives/vol3/econ.html.

39 Nagle, Judge Patrick, *Places in the Heart*. www.dvdverdict.com/reviews/placesinheart.shtml.

40 Meegan, James, paper submitted in the "Pictures of Protest" course.

41 Maslin, Janet, "*Angela's Ashes*," *New York Times*, December 24, 1999. http://movies.nytimes.com/movie/review?_r=l&res.

42 Emerson, Jim, *Do the Right Thing*. www.cinepad.com/reviews/doright.html.

43 Powers, Jeremy, "*Boyz in the Hood*," from a paper submitted in the "Pictures of Protest" course, Emerson College, February 2, 2004.

44 Ebert, Roger, "*Boyz in the Hood*," *Chicago Sun-Times*. www.suntimes.com/ebert/ebert_reviews/1999/07/659469.html.

45 www.2.foxsearchlight.com/inamerica.

7

$\mathcal{R}$acism

Recipe for superiority

Mass media have played and will continue to play a crucial role in the way white Americans perceive African-Americans.[1]

Racism, usually in the form of stereotyped Black characters, has been a staple of Hollywood film since its beginning. The blackface minstrel, a favorite on the stage in the nineteenth century, both in the North and South, and in burlesque and vaudeville theaters of the early twentieth century, became a common figure in films as well. They were usually played by white men in black makeup. Frequently seen as servants and buffoons in silent films, the false stereotype carried over into early radio, where two white men acted the roles of the principal characters in America's favorite program for many years, *Amos 'n Andy*. Following World War II racist characters began to be frowned on as a consequence of American service personnel having seen the results of racial and ethnic prejudice, in China by the Japanese and in Europe by the Germans against Jews, gypsies, Blacks, and others. *Amos 'n Andy* didn't last long when it was adapted for television. However, it wasn't until the civil rights revolution of the 1960s that racist portrayals of Blacks as characters in "white" shows began to disappear from television. Nevertheless, to this day one still finds many racial as well as ethnic and gender negative stereotypes in television, including representations in African-American-oriented sitcoms.

Hollywood films seemed to follow the same pattern. Early silent movies and subsequent "talkies" were full of black characters in demeaning and/or stupidly comic roles. Except for performers such as Al Jolson – arguably America's favorite performer at the time, who made up in blackface as part of his act – African-Americans began to be hired to play those parts. Even the names of some of those actors were products of racism. Stepin Fetchit, for example, frequently played the oft-seen black character who is lazy, frightened, obtuse, and obedient. Hattie McDaniel, another example, earned an Academy Award for her performance as "Mammy" in the 1939 film, *Gone With the Wind*, but thereafter was thought of and sometimes labeled by many moviegoers and even by some critics as a "Mammy" character. Even the remarkable artistry and dignity of dancer Bill "Bojangles" Robinson, an African-American who was in a number of Shirley Temple movies, did not prevent his invariably being cast in subservient roles.

One of Hollywood's most artistic films and one that was a break-through for creative directing and technical effects was a protest movie. It was not against racism, however, but *for* racism. *The Birth of a Nation*, released in 1915, was an artistic triumph by director D. W. Griffith, even as it advocated not only racism against Blacks, but violence as well, and extolled the criminal actions of the Ku Klux Klan. As one critic wrote, Griffith "uses his narrative powers to humanize the white families, southern and northern, who are drawn into tragic combat [in the Civil War] . . . then watch how he uses these self-same powers to dehumanize his burnt-cork black characters."[2] The film deals with the purported evils unleashed upon the South during and after the Civil War in the form of ungrateful slaves who become monsters under the guidance of northern charlatans. Griffith praises the whites of the South, who organized the Ku Klux Klan to prevent Blacks, who he portrays as crazed and maniacal, from defiling white women and stealing and destroying what was left of Southern gentility. Writer V. J. Jerome described the movie as a "lying extravaganza glorifying slavery and vilifying the Negro people."[3] Jerome further notes that "the film, concretely, aimed to 'justify' the denial of civil rights and equal opportunities to Negroes, and to rationalize frame-ups, terror, and lynchings, as both 'necessary' and 'romantic'."[4] The reaction of many of Griffith's peers and many of the general public was so harsh that in 1916 Griffith produced a film entitled *Intolerance*, presumably an apology for the intolerance engendered by "Birth of a Nation." But with its overtones of anti-Semitism, it did little to assuage the harm already done. As for *Birth of the Nation*, it has had a dual existence in the near-century since its production – as a model for students studying directorial techniques and cinema history and as a pariah of content. In 2004, when a Los Angeles theater scheduled it, massive protesting crowds prevented its being shown.[5]

Racist portrayals, although not as vicious as in *Birth of a Nation*, continued in the rare instances that African-Americans appeared in Hollywood feature films. There were Black actors and actresses, but virtually no roles. And despite the desperation for jobs, many would not take roles that exacerbated racism. Just as in the music recording business, where so-called "race records" offered an opportunity for Black performers to make recordings in an industry that was essentially for "whites only," independent "race films" developed. In much of the country, especially in the South, not only were African-Americans banned from attending "whites-only" movie houses or confined to segregated upper-balcony areas, but they saw virtually no movies with positive characters with whom they could ethnically and racially identify. Enterprising Black producer-directors began to make independent films featuring Black casts in stories that were pertinent to Black life in America. The term "race films" was itself a protest against racism. Professor Carrie Golus wrote that "Many African-Americans sought to avoid the terms then in circulation, so instead of using 'Negro,' 'colored,' or worse, they used the word 'race', as in 'race men and women,' 'race causes,' 'race progress,' 'race records'."[6] The first race films reputedly were produced in 1910 by the Foster Photoplay Company, followed not long thereafter by the Lincoln Motion Picture Company and the Ebony Film Corporation. In the 1920s more than thirty independent production companies were producing race films.[7] Although most of these companies were owned or operated by African-Americans, the content of the films rarely included protests against racism, except by implication in the showing of some of the difficulties Blacks experienced. The purpose of these films almost always seemed to be solely for light entertainment, with many of the movies being slapstick versions of the Hollywood one-reelers. Nevertheless, the very fact of being able to identify with leading characters on the screen strengthened a sense of pride for many African-Americans. Perhaps the best known and most prolific of Black producer-directors was Oscar Micheaux, whose Micheaux Book and Film Company's *Within Our Gates* in 1918 is considered by some to be a groundbreaking serious anti-racist protest movie. One critic wrote that *Within Our Gates* is "the answer to the country's racism and the racism of Hollywood films like D. W. Griffith's 'The Birth of a Nation' . . . Micheaux films are about murder, racial injustice, and lynching."[8] Micheaux produced *Body and Soul* in 1924, starring the incomparable Paul Robeson in his film debut.

Micheaux produced the first Black "talkie," *The Exile*, in 1931, and some 59 more films before he retired in 1948.[9]

These "race films" were shown usually in makeshift screening spaces in segregated Black sections of communities and in the comparatively few movie theaters owned by Blacks. "These independent productions provided Black viewers with images of the African-American experience that were conspicuously absent from Hollywood films, including Black romance, urban migration, social upheaval, racial violence, alcoholism, and color prejudice within the Black community.[10]

These independent race films also gave Black viewers positive and respected characters who were doctors, lawyers, educators, business owners, and even cowboys – characters that they didn't find in Hollywood films. One critic wrote that "when actors like Paul Robeson, Lena Horne, Louise Beavers and Noble Johnson appear in race movies they perform in ways that acknowledge a predominantly African-American audience, and to some extent they move beyond stereotyping."[11] Although these were non-Hollywood independent films, they ultimately had an effect on Hollywood, as Professor Carrie Golus has written: "Race films by maverick African-American directors such as Oscar Micheaux and Spencer Williams laid the groundwork for later Black filmmaking, from the commercial successes of 1970s 'blaxploitation' films to the stylistic references and social commentaries of Charles Burnett, Julie Dash and Spike Lee."[12]

Many Black actors, performers, writers, artists, musicians, and others in the arts went to Europe, especially to Paris and London, to escape the restrictive racism of the United States, and many of them found not only much greater opportunity and tolerance, but artistic and financial success. It wasn't until the period following World War II that Hollywood began to provide non-stereotyped roles for African-Americans and – sometimes directly, sometimes by implication – protests against racism and racial injustice. As V. J. Jerome wrote in his 1950 book, *The Negro in Hollywood Films*,

It cannot be disputed that, in a formal sense, these films seem to leave behind the traditional Hollywood cliché Negro. Their central themes and characters do not seem to bear the mark of the Uncle Tom stereotype; or the viciously libelous subhuman brute type; or the comic relief calumny à la Stepin Fetchit; or the bucolic myth of laughing, singing, romping happy-all-the-day field hands possessed of the mentality of children and blessed with a natural contentment that makes the idea of freedom a rude, Northern interference.[13]

Ironically, it was the growing inclusion of African-Americans in Hollywood films in non-stereotyped roles that hastened the demise of the independent race movies.

We have dealt thus far in this chapter with racism as applied to African-Americans. Other races were treated with comparable prejudicial stereotypes. Asians (the so-called "yellow" race) were generally shown as inscrutable and devious and sometimes clever in a positive way; for example, a favorite of movie audiences was the *Charlie Chan* detective series. Chan was played by a series of Caucasian men in makeup – although his "Number One Son" was played by a Chinese-American actor. The so-called "brown" race, generally Mexicans, were stereotyped as untrustworthy, thieving, and drug-dealers. Native Americans, the so-called "red" race, were, with rare exceptions, portrayed as bloodthirsty savages in Western movies. There was much ethnic stereotyping, as well, with Eastern Europeans frequently stereotyped as uncouth, different, and unscrupulous. Even particular nationalities were stereotyped; for example, mobsters almost invariably had Italian names. This chapter – and book – will not, however, analyze these film stereotypes, inasmuch as there have been virtually no Hollywood films protesting these areas of racism, while there have been a plethora of Hollywood films protesting anti-Black racism.

In the 1930s there were occasional instances of screen situations that showed prejudice in a negative light, usually as a cameo-plot and sometimes as a legitimate sub-plot. A prime example of the latter was the 1936 film *Show Boat*, an adaptation of the 1927 now-venerable Broadway musical of the same name. A sub-plot shows the debilitating effects of racial prejudice on an interracial couple, the pathos of the drama, rather than polemics, serving as a protest against racism and a call for tolerance.

But it was in the post-World War II 1940s, as noted above, that Hollywood began to provide films that, through the principal plot and characters, dealt with and protested racism.[14] These films covered various aspects of the subject, from blatant prejudice to overcoming discrimination to escaping bias by passing as white. In 1949 and 1950, for example, several films opened up areas that not only paved the way for further films on racism, but whose box-office successes convinced

Hollywood that it was not only ethically possible but financially profitable to produce movies in that genre. Most of these films built the protest factors into individual-centered problems, sometimes showing the harshness of prejudice, sometimes putting prejudice into the background of a romantic or adventure story of someone who happened to be Black.

Even with Hollywood's postwar progress in the 1940s toward anti-racist sensitivity in some films, stereotyping of African-Americans continued in others, exacerbating if not directly promoting racism. One example is the 1946 Walt Disney production, *Song of the South*. It has "Uncle Remus" telling a young white child about his former life as a slave, the bucolic stories sugar-coating the truth about the antebellum South. It was criticized for "making slavery appear pleasant" and, in some of the stories, "pretending slavery never existed."[15] Protests against the film at the time resulted in limited distribution and, during the civil rights movement of the 1960s, it was withdrawn from distribution, and supposedly archived in 1970. But later in the 1970s and in the 1980s it was re-released for video and foreign distribution, its racist content notwithstanding.[16]

One of the first significant breakthrough anti-racist protest films was *Home of the Brave* in 1949. A young Black soldier in World War II is given psychological treatment for paralysis after returning from a mission. It is not only the shock of the mission and the death of his best buddy that have affected him, but the racist abuse he receives from most of the other soldiers on the mission. *New York Times* critic Bosley Crowther wrote:

> The urgent and delicate subject of anti-Negro prejudice, often remarked in Hollywood movies but never fully discussed in one of them, is finally advanced with thorough candor as the major theme of an entertainment film in Stanley Kramer's ingenious production of Arthur Laurents' play, *Home of the Brave* . . . [The] film shows the shattering damage which racial bias can do to one man. And it has not the slightest hesitation in using all the familiar, ugly words.[17]

A number of other breakthrough films protesting racism were released that same year. As Crowther noted, "*Home of the Brave* is a most propitious 'first' in the cycle of Negro-prejudice pictures which Hollywood now has in the works."[18] *Pinky* (1949) is another film in that cycle. Pinky,

the female protagonist of the film, described by the term used for iden-
tifying a Black person who is light-complexioned enough to pass for
white, is a nurse studying in the North who falls in love with a white
doctor. She returns home to the South because she does not want to
reveal to the doctor that she is African-American. He follows her and,
after learning the truth, still wants to marry her. She turns him down,
he goes back north, and she becomes a companion to an elderly woman
who dies and leaves her estate to Pinky. The rest of the film deals with
Pinky's difficulties, as an African-American, in inheriting white property, especially in the South.[19] A number of Pinky's experiences in the
film reveal the brutality of white racism. In one incident she is with an
African-American couple who are arrested by the police in an attempt
to protect Pinky from the couple, thinking she is white. They treat Pinky
with gallantry. When they learn that she, too, is Black, their attitude
toward her changes dramatically. "We see the white ruling-class justice
suddenly rip off its mask of chivalry to reveal itself as the racism we
know it to be."[20] In another scene two white men try to rape Pinky. This
"rare flash of truth on the American screen" of white rapists attacking Black women exposes "the 'rape' label used to frame-up [African-
Americans] as a bestial falsehood, devised to conceal the notorious
actuality of legally protected white ruling-class rapism."[21] While *Pinky*
was lauded for its forthright realism in some aspects, it was criticized
for its pandering in others, specifically the casting of a Caucasian,
rather than an African-American actress as Pinky (Hollywood felt the
American public would not yet accept Black and white performers
in a love relationship on the screen), the implied superiority of Pinky
over other African-Americans because of her light skin color, and an
imposed "happy-ever-after" ending.

Lost Boundaries and *Intruder in the Dust* are two more 1949 anti-racist
breakthrough films. In *Lost Boundaries*, set after World War II, a light-
complexioned African-American physician and his wife are too light-
skinned to be accepted in the Black community and they then decide
to pass for white in order for him to get a position and for their family
to be able to integrate into a New England town. They and their children
become an important part of the town's society. When it is learned
that they are not white, there is immediate shock and the change in
attitude by many in the community reveals the inherent racism in our
society. But though it shows the ordeal of one family, it hedges on the

real issues of racism. The lead role is played by a white actor, and, as one critic wrote at the time,

> this film is not a picture of the whole complex problem of race and racial discrimination, taboo and social pressures in this land. It touches the immediate anxieties of only a limited number of Negroes, at best . . . and may even be regarded by some Negroes with a certain distaste because of the curiously sensitive implications toward color which it must state.[22]

Nevertheless, it raised an issue and opened the eyes of many among the white viewers to one of the aspects of racism in the United States.

Intruder in the Dust, adapted from the William Faulkner novel, was lauded as

> a picture that slashes right down to the core of the complex of racial resentments and social divisions in the South – which cosmically mocks the hollow pretense of "white supremacy" . . . it is a story of a desperate and courageous attempt to save an innocent Negro from lynching at the hands of a mob . . . it is the drama of a proud, noble, arrogant Negro man who would rather be lynched in fiery torture than surrender his stolid dignity.[23]

Unlike the usual Hollywood anti-racist movie of the time, it not only showed an African-American overcoming prejudicial odds because of the help of caring whites, but showed the African-American as a person of at least as much strength, capability, and dignity as the whites. *New York Times* critic Bosley Crowther called *Intruder in the Dust* "one of the great cinema dramas of our time."[24]

Two key films in 1950 that protested racism concentrated on the experiences of a given person. *No Way Out* shows blind hatred by a white racist who wants to kill a Black physician who has just saved his life in a hospital, but who he wrongly believes deliberately killed his brother, his bigotry replacing logic and fact. The racist's girlfriend reveals his purpose by finally turning against her lover, unable to stomach his continued vicious and vitriolic hatred. *No Way Out*, incidentally, was the film debut for Ossie Davis, who for the next half-century would be a key African-American actor and writer in combating racism, and was also the debut film for Sidney Poitier, who over the next few decades was the actor most often seen in films revealing or protesting racism. The other 1950 movie about an African-American overcoming bigoted odds was *The Jackie Robinson Story*, about the Brooklyn Dodgers baseball player who is credited with breaking the color line in major league baseball. His dignity, skill, and intelligence in achieving remarkable success in that field, in the face of vicious harassment and discrimination, is credited with opening the doors for African-Americans in other professional sports and encouraging open doors in other fields as well.

It wasn't until four decades later that films protesting the real-life bigotry that attacked African-Americans as a group as well as individuals reached the screen in no-holds-barred content, principally through the efforts of a young African-American director, Spike Lee. Until Lee's work, films about racism were almost all directed by whites, with critics from time to time questioning the ability of directors who had not personally experienced anti-Black racism to validly capture its essence. Author V. J. Jerome asked, "How can a studio, how can an industry that doesn't employ [African-Americans] as writers, producers, technical directors, cameramen – how can they write, direct, produce, or film a picture which has sincere and real sensitivity (shall we say artistry) about Negro people?"[25] Lee changed that, as we shall note when discussing some of his films later in this chapter.

The political conservatism of the 1950s, with McCarthyism exacerbating the fear of most Americans to even talk about anything controversial, no less dealing with the issues of civil rights and liberties, put a damper on protest pictures for some years, not resuming with more than tokenism until the 1960s, after McCarthy and McCarthyism had been discredited. The counterculture revolution of the 1960s and early 1970s, including the fight for civil rights, also facilitated the development of protest movies. Two very different films appeared in the late 1950s, *Island in the Sun* in 1957 and *The Defiant Ones* in 1958. *Island in the Sun* was produced independently by famed filmmaker Darryl F. Zanuck, but its guarded approach to the reality of the Black experience gave it a kinship with Hollywood studio films. Set on a fictional island, a white man and a Black man are political rivals, with murder, infidelity, and interracial sexual liaisons part of a myriad of sub-plots. While the interracial relationships, especially a Black–white kiss, created a furor at the time even as it spurred box-office success, some critics felt that the movie did not go far enough in making a point. Nevertheless, Zanuck's inclusion of interracial sex, albeit watered down, set the stage for subsequent films dealing with the subject more fully.

The Defiant Ones, on the other hand, was a very powerful film on a Black–white relationship that, out of necessity, taught both protagonists the importance of tolerance and cooperation. The plot revolves around two escaped convicts who are shackled together and who both are full of racial animosity toward each other. To successfully evade their pursuers they must, despite their prejudices, literally accommodate each other's weaknesses and strengths. These racial antagonists are compelled to understand each other, are forced to rely on each other in order to survive. They are forced into a bond of brotherhood. Producer Stanley Kramer, who earlier made *Home of the Brave*, "has them slash at each other with bitter accusations that reveal with startling illumination their complete commonality. In the end it is clear that they are brothers, stripped of all vulgar bigotry."[26] By the film's end, one of the racial antagonists gives up his freedom to stand by the other. This film still stands as one of the strongest protests against bigotry stemming from ignorance of those one hates.

In the early 1960s and through the decade a number of key films showing or directly protesting racism came to the screen. Among the movies of note are three 1962 releases with varied themes. *A Raisin in the Sun* emphasized the difficulties of a Black family in trying to move away from their environment of racially imposed restrictions on jobs, housing, business, and social integration opportunities. Intelligent, creative, ambitious members of the family each dream of how they can break out of the multilayered ghetto and achieve what each is capable of. The racism in America makes it virtually impossible for them to do so, and their dreams dry up like a "raisin in the sun." The film shows the African-American family as a typical struggling family, Black or white, with the same problems and hopes – except in this case racism exacerbates the problems. "Raisin in the Sun" was a milestone in humanizing for white moviegoers the African-American family.

Two more of the early 1960s key films are *Lilies of the Field* and *To Kill A Mockingbird*. *Lilies of the Field* (1963), one of the many Black-experience films with Sidney Poitier (his performance won the first Academy Award for an African-American actor), is the story of an unemployed construction worker who comes across five nuns from East Germany who are trying to build a chapel in rural Arizona. The character-driven film touches only on implied racism, but does make the point that when the Black construction worker, the white nuns, and the predominantly Latino townspeople work together in an atmosphere of racial tolerance, miracles can happen. It is a gentle movie and is a picture of racial education, not protest. On the other hand, *To Kill A Mockingbird* (1962), an almost-immediate classic that has become part of arts curricula in many colleges, stands as a powerful indictment of Southern racist justice, alleviated only by the efforts of a non-prejudiced white lawyer.

The story in *To Kill A Mockingbird* is told through the eyes of a young girl and the theme of the film is made clear under the opening credits: "After drawing a simple stick-figured 'mocking-bird', the girl shades in the winged creature and then tears the paper through the bird, melodramatically foreshadowing the racial tensions and divisions that will tear apart the innocence of the town and forever alter the child's fragile memories."[27] The girl's father, a lawyer played by Gregory Peck, represents a young African-American on trial for his life after being falsely accused of raping a white woman. Set in Depression-era Alabama, the movie clearly represents the racist attitude of most of the townspeople and the collaboration of the police and the courts in lynchings, legal and otherwise, of African-Americans. The lawyer, the fictional Atticus Finch, must overcome the racism of the community while teaching his motherless children the importance of tolerance. In the courtroom, he gives "a strong but adult lesson of justice and humanity at work."[28]

Several other 1960s movies with Sidney Poitier fall into the category of anti-racist protest. In *A Patch of Blue* (1965) a blind white woman meets an African-American man in a park and their relationship turns into a caring friendship. When her insensitive family discovers who her friend is, she finds out that he is Black. The film gently repeats the oft-presented theme that color is just skin deep and that it is the quality of character that counts. The film is strongly reminiscent of Charlie Chaplin's *City Lights* of several decades earlier (see chapter 6).

In the Heat of the Night (1967) is another of the movies where prejudicial attitudes begin to change when the racist begins to know, in person and close up, the target of his or her hate. In this film an African-American homicide detective from a large Northern city is visiting his mother in a small Southern town when a rich white man is found dead. Because he's a stranger and Black, the Northern detective is arrested by a racist, intractable police chief. When the police chief finds out who his prisoner is and then is forced to work with him in solving the homicide, the getting-to-know-you theme becomes full-blown. The police chief's bigotry is exacerbated with a resentment of the Northern detective's ability, which undermines the chief's ego and, he feels, his authority. They stand up against each other toe-to-toe, literally and figuratively, their animosities at the cutting edge, even as they are forced to cooperate to solve the crime. The film ends on a note of hope for the South and an educational experience for both the Southerner and Northerner, the Caucasian and the African-American. "When the Negro finally boards the train and the police chief hands him his suitcase, the two men know a little more about each other and each other's prejudices."[29] (Note that the word "Negro" was the accepted term for African-Americans for many years and appears in reviews and commentaries quoted here, although the word later took on a pejorative meaning for many.)

Another 1960s film with Sidney Poitier stressed the latent bigotry in people who claim and believe they are not prejudiced. *Guess Who's Coming to Dinner* (1968) was a huge success because it dealt with a situation that all white and Black families might actually encounter, unlike some of the protest films that deal with uncommon or exotic circumstances. A charming young white woman from a well-off liberal family meets a "noble, rich, intelligent, handsome, ethical medical expert . . . they fall in love and come home to break the news to her parents."[30] It so happens that her fiancé is an African-American. Her mother, after taking a moment to hide and recover from her shock, appears to accept her daughter's intended. Her father, although a newspaper editor who crusades against prejudice, is not so immediately accepting. In the meantime, at their daughter's insistence, the white parents invite her fiancé's African-American parents to join them at dinner. The white parents' attitudes are almost duplicated by the Black parents. The African-American fiancé lectures his father for being a bigot for opposing interracial marriage. The white mother lectures her husband for not supporting the marriage, saying he has forgotten what it is to be in love. This being a Hollywood love story, both fathers finally agree to accept the young people's union. Happy ending or not, the movie presented and protested – in a non-threatening, non-polemic way – prejudice against interracial relationships. It was not a protest of white racism against Blacks, but racism from any source. Roger Ebert, despite some reservations about the manipulation of the fathers, wrote that *"Guess Who's Coming to Dinner* is a magnificent piece of entertainment. It will make you laugh and even make you cry."[31]

The civil rights revolution of the 1960s did make it easier for Hollywood to deal with racism, as anti-racism became, for want of a better term, "fashionable." In 1968 Hollywood even produced an anti-racist musical, *Finian's Rainbow*. But it did not originate in the Hollywood movie studios and was only produced when its content became acceptable, losing the sharp impact it could have had on the public. As film historian Leonard Maltin put it, this "musical fantasy about racial injustice was ahead of its time in the late '40s on Broadway, embarrassingly dated 20 years later . . . [nevertheless] perhaps the best movie musical of its era."[32]

As the 1960s and early 1970s civil rights revolution in America progressed, it threatened not only old attitudes, but legally began to affect prejudicial behavior. It wasn't sufficient to verbally (in Hollywood's case, to cinematically) decry racism, but civil rights laws and growing community pressures were forcing many people to abandon some of their established racially discriminatory privileges and practices. It was a civic paraphrasing of playwright George Bernard Shaw's assessment that when Savonarola told the ladies of Florence to give up their jewels and finery they hailed him as a saint, but when he actually induced them to do it, they burned him at the stake as a public nuisance. So it was, too, in America, where equal opportunity for all, regardless of race, meant enforced changes in their everyday life for many people. Change is threatening, especially for the established social and political Establishment, and to many who had theoretically opposed racism the reality of its elimination became controversial. In many communities, the heretofore stereotyped subservient African-American population was no longer willing to be condescended to and took charge of its own destiny. The media – as always supporting the conservative status quo agenda – helped exacerbate fear of and opposition to what was implied and accepted by many Americans as dangerous Black militancy and militants. At one point, for example, the FBI raided a house in the middle of the night where members of the Black Panther organization were meeting and assassinated seven of their leaders as they slept in their beds. Hollywood, as always, feared that so much controversy was not good for the box office and decided to play it safe.

That did not mean that it stopped making pictures or releasing independently made films about African-Americans and their lives in

America. After all, the civil rights changes had resulted in the deseg-regation of many theaters and the consequent addition of millions of Blacks as patrons of Hollywood's first-run movies. Movies about race became more subtle, in some cases their points made through histor-ical reference or comedic satire, rather than through the presentation of situations that were actually affecting America at the time. Take two examples from 1970.

The Great White Hope is a dramatization of what Jack Johnson, the first Black heavyweight boxing champion, went through in achieving success and fame in a white man's world in early twentieth-century America. The sports establishment not only resented an African-American being the "best" in their profession, but was appalled by Johnson's lifestyle behavior, as if his position as the best fighter in the world gave him the privileges presumably reserved for whites. Thus, the title of the film and of the play that preceded it: The search for a white boxer who could defeat Johnson. Perhaps Johnson's greatest trans-gression, in addition to what many whites felt was an unforgivable arrogance – that is, pretending he was equal to everyone else – was in having a white woman friend. Worse, in fact, was their intention to marry. When traveling with his fiancée to boxing matches and public appearances, Johnson was arrested for violation of the Mann Act – that is, transporting a woman across state lines for immoral purposes. Not able to beat him in the boxing ring, racist America destroyed his personal life and, by extension, his professional one. He was effectively exiled and humiliated. Although the film is a strong protest against racist practices, it could be relegated in many viewers' minds to another time and to the problems of just one public figure. *New York Times* movie critic Vincent Canby wrote that

> *The Great White Hope* is one of those liberal, well-meaning, uncon-troversial works that pretend to tackle contemporary problems by finding analogies at a safe remove in history . . . I kept wondering how I might respond to a movie, made on a similar scale, that dared touch on some really controversial issues [of 1970], including the [Vietnam] war, the draft, the Black Muslims, Black separation and all those other things.[33]

Watermelon Man, on the other hand, was a satire. A white bigot played by a Black actor in whiteface – a satiric comment on the blackface whites of minstrel shows – wakes up one morning to find that his skin has turned Black. Vainly trying to remove the new pigment, he now finds himself the target of the kinds of racism that he himself had been practicing. His neighbors want him to get out of the neighborhood, his employer wants to exploit him for business purposes, and even his physician no longer wants to treat him. His only friends turn out to be a few Black people. While a comment on the effects of racism, the film can be pigeonholed by those who wish to do so as a comedy with no direct relationship to reality. The concept, however, set the stage for more direct protests by its director, Melvin Van Peeples, whose future films would have impact as part of the "blaxploitation" era.

How to incorporate Black characters into films without making the movies or the characters too controversial? How to make and get films released that provided jobs for African-American actors in nonsubservient roles? How to provide opportunities for Blacks to control what is seen as the Black experience, as opposed to having it presented through the eyes of white producers and directors? And how to do this in such a way that it will draw enough viewers to the box office to make it possible to produce such movies? The frequently decried "blaxploitation" film provided the answer.

Melvin Van Peeples, an African-American filmmaker, was forced to go to Europe to practice his craft. When he returned to America he committed himself to producing pictures that "will reflect, in raw, uncompromised and accessible form, the experiences and aspirations of African-Americans at a time of social upheaval and political confrontation," as opposed to the film industry's practice in the late 1960s of shunting, with few exceptions, "African-American artists into low-comedy ghetto."[34] The result was *Sweet Sweetback's Baad Asssss Song* (1970). The film deals with the difficulties encountered by an African-American movie-maker in making a film. The movie's ending depicts a successful premiere of the protagonist's, Sweetback's, production before an enthusiastic audience rounded up by the Black Panthers. Sweetback, in the meantime, has had to flee to Mexico because of his revolutionary actions, but "the words on the screen promise, Sweetback, the embodiment of and answer to centuries of insult and brutality inflicted on Black Americans by their white oppressors, will return 'to collect some dues'."[35]

The blaxploitation movies that 'Sweetback' inspired may have been controversial at the time (and, like everything else in '70s pop culture, vulnerable to parody and condescension later on), but in appropriating the conventions of the western and the gangster film they nonetheless advanced the radical notion that black men on the screen could be something other than buffoons, servants or model citizens. They could be action heroes – armed, dangerous, sexy and righteous leading men.[36]

"Blaxploitation" films in which African-Americans played superheroes did not necessarily expressly protest racism, but they showed that Blacks were as strong, capable, and dignified as whites, and even maybe more so. Movies like *Shaft* (1971) and *Superfly* (1972) "represented black action heroes fighting white crime in a cynical urban environment. The films symbolized black-power politics in an era when portrayals of Blacks regularly consisted of servants and sidekicks."[37] Blaxploitation movies were not only box-office hits with African-American audiences, but with white audiences as well, who saw them as crime and adventure action stories rather than racial protests or even racial commentaries. Some critics expressed concern that some of these films provided negative stereotypes of macho Black men. Gordon Parks, the director of *Shaft*, countered that his film was "doing the thing that everyone in that audience wanted to see for so long. A black man was winning."[38] Although frequently criticized as exploitative of Blacks as a consequence of the new – albeit limited – opportunities generated by the civil rights movement, these films did contribute to blurring the color line of white perceptions of action heroes.

Then, in the 1980s, along came Spike Lee. His independent films showed the world what Hollywood was not dedicated (or ethical? or sensitive? or courageous?) enough to produce.

Some find Lee to be a fresh and powerful voice in American cinema – a man who is unafraid to profess his viewpoint even though it may be unpopular with white audiences. Others view him as a divisive demagogue whose movies preach potentially incendiary messages. Whichever perspective an individual has (or whether they fall in between), it is impossible to debate that . . . Lee has left an indelible imprint upon independent motion pictures made in the United States.[39]

As Spike Lee himself has stated, "Someone has to force Americas to come to grips about the problem of racism."[40]

Although *Do the Right Thing* was not Lee's first movie, this 1989 film established a standard by which to judge antiracist pictures of protest before and after its release. When *Do the Right Thing* was produced several racist incidents had occurred in New York that made the movie an extension of the news headlines. It dealt directly with what was happening in society at the time.

Figure 7.1 *Do the Right Thing* (1989)

In Howard Beach, Queens, a mob of white teenagers with baseball bats chased a young Black man – who with two Black friends accidentally was in their neighborhood – into oncoming traffic, where he was killed. In another part of New York the Transit Police arrested, beat, hogtied, and strangled an African-American man who apparently did not respond quickly enough to their orders. Also in New York, an elderly African-American grandmother was killed by police using excessive force during an eviction. And in Brooklyn a white mob attacked and shot to death a Black youth.

Do the Right Thing is set in a one-block area representing the Bedford-Stuyvesant (virtually an all-Black and Latino) section of Brooklyn. (This author appreciated and identified with the representation, having attended a high school, at the time Black-and-white integrated, in "Bed-Sty.") The plot revolves around a myriad of characters, with the main protagonist, Mookie, a young part-time employee of the local, white-owned pizza parlor. On an extremely hot day the tensions rise with the temperature. People in the neighborhood try to solve their problems of economic deprivation and personal relationships by talking, complaining, and revealing their characters, but taking little action to do anything about their respective and group conditions. Finally, exacerbated by the racist son of the Italian-American pizza parlor, tempers fray with the heat and, when the police are called, the confrontations result in the police choking to death a young African-American because he is playing his boom-box too loudly. At that point, Mookie, who has been a moderating factor trying to avoid violence, decides enough is enough and in desperate frustration throws a garbage can through the window of the pizza parlor, sparking a riot that burns down the store. At the same time, it would appear that Mookie's action, turning the crowd's wrath against the store rather than against its owners, saved the latter's lives. Some critics were concerned – some people even horrified – at the breaking-point action, fearing that it might incite violence by Blacks against white targets. Reviewer Roger Ebert stated that although some critics wrote that the film was "an incitement to racial violence . . . those articles say more about their authors than about the movie" and that "anyone who walks into this film expecting answers is a dreamer or a fool. But anyone who leaves the movie with more intolerance than they walked in with wasn't paying attention."[41]

Lee himself discussed the question of the film inciting to riot.

> Black people never ask that. It's only white people because black people understand perfectly why Mookie threw the garbage can through the window. White people are like "Oh, I like Mookie so much up to that point. He's a nice character. Why'd he have to throw the garbage can through the window?" Black people, there's no question in their minds . . . I feel at the time he did (do the right thing). Mookie is doing it in response to the police murdering Radio Raheem. What people have to understand is that almost every riot that's happened here in America involving black people has happened because of some small incident like that: cops killing somebody, cops beating up a pregnant black woman. Mookie cannot lash out against the police, because the police are gone. As soon as Radio Raheem was dead, they threw his ass in the back of the car and got the hell out of there.[42]

When asked the same thing at a press conference shortly after the film was released, especially about its effect on racially-troubled New York, Lee answered, "It'll probably be hot again this summer, and if anything happens this summer it won't be because of this film. It will be because the cops kill someone else for no reason . . . to me that's what the movie's about – black life being devalued."[43]

The film's theme is clear, emphasized by the music played over and over again into the neighborhood by a local radio disc jockey: the band Public Enemy's "you got to fight the power, fight the power, fight the powers-that-be." But Spike Lee doesn't propose a simplified one-sided fight. Throughout the film he urges African-Americans, individually and severally, not to be self-defeating and wait for someone else to solve their problems. At the end of the movie, the radio disc jockey exhorts the people who hear him – figuratively African-Americans everywhere: "Wake Up!" he yells.

> With great character development, Lee uses his film as a protest against the complacency of Blacks. Numerous characters with indolent personalities allow Lee to poke fun at passivity while urging Black America to be more motivated in life. Lee's exaggeration of social complacency within the African-American community effectively challenges the entire race to become more active in every aspect of life: socially, economically, and politically . . . Lee seems to be advocating social change, not social acceptance.[44]

It is ironic that in 2008, African-American performer and educator, Dr. Bill Cosby, is encountering strong criticism from some in the larger African-American community for advocating the same thing.

Controversy or no, critic Roger Ebert described *Do the Right Thing* as coming "closer to reflecting the current state of race relations in America than any other movie of our time."[45]

Other Spike Lee movies, before and after *Do the Right Thing*, had different plot lines, characters, and artistic approaches, and varying degrees of impact and critical success, but dealt with the same basic theme: A protest against racism. Lee's first commercial feature entertainment film was *She's Gotta Have It*, produced in 1986. It earned critical acclaim at the Cannes Film Festival. Three African-American men are in love with the same woman, who welcomes the attention – sexual and otherwise – of all three, and cannot make up her mind as to which one to choose. "The film satirizes selfishness, sexual stereotypes, role-playing among Black men and other follies."[46]

The idea of personal responsibility for one's immediate actions and one's future welfare is a key to the film's theme, presaging the idea of African-Americans taking responsibility to at least try to change any negative situation in which they find themselves that became a significant part of *Do the Right Thing* three years later. "These people are not victims of blind forces; they make choices, defend them, and grow in understanding, not always happily, as a result."[47]

In *Jungle Fever*, in 1991, Lee dealt with interracial relationships. It is a streetwise, realistic, non-sugar-coated approach to the theme presented with gentility in *Guess Who's Coming to Dinner* a quarter-century earlier. While some critics were concerned about the lack of depth in its characters, others applauded his candor in revealing the bare bones of the subject. "The ambitious and ever-controversial Spike Lee sets before our eyes a cast of characters and situations that illustrate the divisiveness of a society enslaved to fear, bigotry, misunderstanding, envy, and despair. Love, family life, work and religion are all ravaged by this divisiveness."[48]

In the film an African-American man and a white woman of Italian descent have an affair which turns into a closer relationship. There is no presumably happy ending or even a hopeful one, as in *Guess Who's Coming to Dinner*. When the Black man takes the white woman to dinner at his parents' house, his father calls her a "whoremonger." When the white woman's father discovers she is having an affair with a Black man, he beats her mercilessly and her brothers are brutal to her. The couple are stopped on the street by the police who assume that he is assaulting her because he is Black and she is white. Racism on the part of both families of the two lovers, and of their external society, as well, dooms the relationship – just as it most often does in real life. Its social protest was clear: "Spike Lee uses the theme of interracial sex to explore the mythology of race, sex and class in an America where both Black and whites are reassessing the legacy of integration and the concept of separatism from every point on the political spectrum."[49]

Malcolm X (1992) solidified Lee's presence as a filmmaker of the first rank who boldly takes artistic and financial risks to reach the public with important and necessary ideas on critical issues. Within the story of the life of Malcolm X is the story of racism in the United States and the alternate approaches taken to combat it by different people – different leaders – with different ethical beliefs and/or systems. Malcolm X's father was murdered by the Ku Klux Klan and young Malcolm (née Malcolm Little) ends up in a white foster home where he excels as a student but is still referred to as "nigger" by many white adults. He becomes a gangster and, while in jail, reads the writings of Elijah Muhammed and joins the Nation of Islam, principally an organization of African-American men opposed to the failure of the traditional religions to effectively combat racism in the United States. He learns the importance of language and words as persuaders of ideas and becomes a public speaker, raising Black people's consciousness wherever and whenever he can. Preaching his new religion, he goes on a pilgrimage to Mecca, where he becomes even more convinced of his new beliefs and adopts the Sunni Muslim faith. Having been a strong fighter against racism, including the use of violence, he turns to non-violence and moves away from his previous militant anti-white teachings. He even changes his name, to El-Hajj Malik Al-Shabazz. His new Gandhi-like persona strengthens his public popularity and he is considered both an ideological and political threat by many of his Nation of Islam colleagues, including his mentor, Elijah Muhammed. Finally, he is assassinated. Although a biography that concentrates on the life of one person, that life as a fighter protesting racism is part of the impact of the film upon its audiences, especially in revealing the need for the protest. Certainly, such a controversial film in presenting in an understanding and sympathetic manner the life of such a highly controversial person is not often seen. In the words of *New York Times* reviewer Vincent Canby, "The real triumph of *Malcolm X* is that Mr. Lee was able to make it at all."[50]

In his 2001 movie, *Bamboozled*, Spike Lee took yet another approach to make the point of his main theme: the need to eradicate racism. A satire, *Bamboozled* is the story of an African-American television writer who is pressured by his producer to create a show for Black audiences that is "Black enough." To show the condescension and racism of such television shows with Black performers, the writer decides to write a minstrel show. He expects the reaction to it to be so outrageous that his producers and the producers of the usual stereotypical African-American sitcom will be taught a lesson. Of course, the show becomes a hit. Racism is alive and kicking in TV-land America. The political message is lost and negative stereotyped entertainment is acclaimed. *Bamboozled* is clearly an indictment of and a protest against the insensitivity – and racism – of the media. The film struck a raw nerve. One reviewer wrote that "Spike Lee's latest film, *Bamboozled*, is a 135-minute rant against racist images of Blacks in popular culture and the complacency with which the public accepts them . . . Lee's heavy-handed approach turns 'Bamboozled' into a tedious and overlong polemic. This is sledgehammer satire."[51] Roger Ebert had similar criticism: "Blackface is over the top . . . people's feelings run too strongly and deeply for any satirical use to be effective. The power of the racist image tramples over the material and asserts only itself."[52] Ebert, however, was one of the few major reviewers who understood the implications of *Bamboozled*. He wrote:

> I think he makes his point intellectually; it's quite possible to see the film and understand his feelings. In conversation, Lee wonders why

black-themes shows on TV are nearly always comedies; why are episodic dramas about blacks so rare? Are whites so threatened by blacks on TV that they'll only watch them being funny? . . . when Lee says the modern equivalent of a blackface minstrel show is the gangsta-rap music video, we see what he means: These videos are enormously popular with white kids, just as minstrel shows were beloved by white audiences, and for a similar reason: They package entertainment within demeaning and negative black images.[53]

Did Lee's success with pictures of protest stiffen the backbone of the Hollywood establishment and result in films that dealt with contemporary racial issues? Whether influenced by Lee or not, Hollywood did, for a while during the 1980s, 1990s, and early 2000s, produce a few films that could be said to contain anti-racist protest content, albeit generally muted or themed as an addendum within the larger entertainment content, or set in a past time that the audience can dismiss as not being pertinent to their immediately current society. Among these films, *Mississippi Burning* (1988) told the story of the investigation of the brutal murders of three civil rights workers in1964 by the Ku Klux Klan and its sympathizers, and the racism of the people in the community in protecting the murderers. The movie was criticized, however, for fictionalizing the role of the FBI, aggrandizing its role in solving the crime, and understating the role of civil rights groups and individuals. A 1991 film, *Boyz N the Hood*, concentrated on the hopes and efforts of three young men to escape from the violence of their South Central Los Angeles ghettoized neighborhood. Racism thwarts them and results not in salvation but tragedy.

American History X, produced in 1998, dealt directly with a key source of racism at the time that continues in America: Organized hate groups that have superseded the Ku Klux Klan in violence against their principal targets, people of color (mainly African-Americans), Jews, and homosexuals. In this film a young man whose bigoted father has been shot while fighting a fire in a Black neighborhood joins the neo-Nazi Skinheads. He becomes a leader as part of the larger white supremacist movement in America. At one point he brutally executes two young African-Americans for vandalizing his automobile. With no one willing to testify against him – and with an implication that because he is white and the victims Black – he receives a light prison sentence, having presumably defended his property. In prison he meets an African-American who becomes his friend and slowly the Skinhead begins to change his beliefs and attitudes. The other Skinheads in the prison consider him a traitor and brutally rape him. When he leaves jail he returns home to try to stop his younger brother from following in his hate-filled footsteps. The film is effective in trying to show the causes of racism that apply at any time in any place. The screenwriter of *American History X*, David McKenna, explained:

> I saw of a lot of bigotry growing up, and it made me think about writing something about the world of hate-mongers. The point I tried to make in the script is that a person is not born a racist. It is learned through environment and the people who surround you. The question that intrigues me is: why do people hate and how does one go about changing that? My premise was that hate starts in the family.[54]

Roger Ebert considered *American History X* the most provocative film on race since *Do the Right Thing*.[55]

Hurricane (1999) is the story of Reuben "Hurricane" Carter, in which racism plays a key role in framing this well-known prize-fighter for a triple murder. After twenty years in prison he is freed. The film details the racist prejudice and corruption of the police in planting evidence, in intimidated witnesses, and of suborned perjured testimony. It also stressed the indifference of law-enforcement and justice officials and most of the rest of society to this miscarriage of justice. *Hurricane*, although about a situation that occurred decades earlier, is timeless in that such corruption, indifference, and frame-ups based on racism continue in our society.

In 2004, the film *Crash* won an Academy Award for Best Picture. It focused on a myriad of characters whose personal orientations motivated them to support or combat racism of different kinds. Starting with a car crash, it presents everyday situations in which the characters have to make up their minds as to whether they will react with colorblindness or with a learned stereotypical response. The people who must make these judgments are from a variety of sociological, economic, professional, and employment backgrounds. Some of the situations they face appear to be critical, some are passingly minor. The film shows that racism arises from a lack of understanding that generates fear. Some critics felt negatively about the film's alleged use of the concept of "crash," that is, the coming into connection with another person as the motivator for racism. For example: "In the end, the film paints racism as a postmodern malaise where conflict happens

Figure 7.2
Crash (2004)

because we don't touch each other except when we crash. That's bullshit. Racism is structural and institutional more than it is personal and sentimental."[56]

Others felt that the film's stressing of the personal responsibility for racism did not obviate its institutionality. Writer-director Paul Haggis said that the film is about "how we all hate to be judged but see no contradiction in judging others."[57] At one point the film offers a key to its purpose: "You think you know who you are. You have no idea." *Crash* makes clear that if racism is not as overtly ubiquitous and openly violent as it has appeared to be in the past, it is not because it has disappeared, but has just gone into hiding.

Whether it is a measure of progress in race relations and an ebbing of racism or whether it is a reflection of the right-wing conservatism that dominated America in the first decade of the twenty-first century, pictures protesting racism in the forthright manner of most of those discussed in this chapter and, especially, like the films of Spike Lee, have morphed into standard crime, adventure, or domestic stories where the protagonist just happens to be African-American, with a racial factor having little, if anything, to do with the movie's content and purpose. There appear to be no current Hollywood films addressing the racial profiling that is restoring Jim Crow justice to America or addressing the continuing incidents of racial injustice and human rights abuses and despite laws that in the past half-century have changed the legal bases for racist practices, the extra-legal denials of social, political, and economic equal rights and opportunities. Perhaps, as with other concerns in society, the mainstream media have simply ignored, downplayed, or adjusted the news about continuing racism in America so as not to threaten the status quo or their conservative agendas?

While this chapter has dealt with films protesting racism against African-Americans, it does not in any sense mean to imply that racism against other racial groups does not exist or has not been touched on in films, albeit not as extensively as anti-Black racism. Further, while ethnic discrimination may not be as obvious as is racial discrimination in the United States, it is nevertheless widespread, with harmful and frequently tragic effects on individuals and families. Hollywood has only occasionally protested this kind of bigotry and has often been accused of exacerbating ethnic discrimination by stereotyped portrayals of various ethnic groups. In the years following the 9/11 terrorist attacks on New York and Washington in 2001 and the subsequent Arab Jihad in retaliation for America's invasion of Iraq, anti-Arab bigotry has grown in the United States. Not only have bigots in the country attacked and killed Arab-Americans and in many instances people they perceived as looking like Arab-Americans, but the government has arbitrarily and surreptitiously seized and incarcerated many of Middle Eastern ancestry in a frenzy of racial profiling. After years of such ethnic discrimination, exacerbated by expanding anti-immigrant attitudes and laws, Hollywood, in 2008, made a film, "The Visitor," protesting this practice. In it a college professor visiting his rarely used New York apartment finds that, unknown to him, it has been illegally rented to an Arab musician and his Senegalese girlfriend. In an act of compassion, he allows them to stay. Their lust for life gives him a new perspective and feeling. But his now Arab friend is in the country illegally and the police take him to a detention center. *New York Times* film critic A. O. Scott summarizes the movie's theme: "the tale of a square, middle-aged white man liberated from his uptightness by an infusion of Third World soulfulness, attached to an expose of the cruelty of post-9/11 immigration policies."[58]

Will Hollywood now consider producing films protesting contemporary discrimination against Latinos, Asian Americans, Native Americans, southeastern Europeans and other ethnic and racial groups who, in any given place or time, may suffer the tyranny of the white majority?

Notes

1 Balkaran, Stephan, "Mass Media and Racism." www.yale.edu.ypq/articles/oct99/oct99b.html.
2 Louvish, Simon, "Burning Crosses." *Sight and Sound*, September, 2000, pp. 12–13.
3 Jerome, V. J., *The Negro in American Films*. www.english.uiuc.edu/maps/poets/g_l/jerome/hollywood.htm.
4 *Ibid.*
5 Getz, Page, "Protest Stops Racist Film," *Workers World*, August 14, 2004. www.workers.org/ww/2002/birthofnat0819.php.

6   Golus, Carrie, "Pre-1950s 'Race Films'," January 10, 2002. http://chronicle. uchicago.edu/020110/racefilms.shtml.
7   Smith, Craig, "An Early View of Race Relations," January 8, 2002. www.imdb.com/title/tt0011870.
8   Schwarts, Dennis, "*Within Our Gates*," March 29, 2004. www.sover.net/ ozus/reviews/03292004/schw.htm.
9   http://geechee.tv/Timeline.html.
10 Golus, *op.cit.*
11 Stewart, Jacqueline. *University of Chicago Chronicle*, January 10, 2002. http://chronicle.uchicago.edu/020110/racefilms.shtml.
12 Golus, "Pre-1950s 'Race Films'."
13 Jerome, *The Negro in American Films*.
14 A number of references and some specific information on post-World War II films protesting racism are from a paper, "Race in Hollywood Films: African-American," prepared by Jana-Lynne Mroz for a "Pictures of Protest" course at Emerson College, April 4, 2004.
15 Mikkelson, Barbara and David Mikkelson, "*Song of the South*," May 9, 2003. www.snopes.com/disney/sots.htm.
16 *Ibid.*
17 Crowther, Bosley, "*Home of the Brave*," *New York Times*, May 13, 1949. http://movies.nytimes.com/movie/review?_r=1&res.
18 *Ibid.*
19 Mroz, "Race in Hollywood Films: African-American."
20 Jerome, *The Negro in American Films*.
21 *Ibid.*
22 Crowther, Bosley, "*Lost Boundaries*," *New York Times*, July 1, 1949. http://movies.nytimes.com/movie/review?r=1&res.
23 Crowther, Bosley, "*Intruder in the Dust*," *New York Times*, November 23, 1949. http://movies.nytimes.com/movie/review?res.
24 *Ibid.*
25 Jerome, *The Negro in American Films*.
26 Crowther, Bosley, "*The Defiant Ones*," *New York Times*, September 25, 1958. http://movies.nytimes.com/movie/review?res.
27 www.filmsite.org/toki.html.
28 Crowther, Bosley, "*To Kill a Mockingbird*," *New York Times*, February 15, 1963. www.nytimes.com/1963/02/15/movies/021563mockingbird.html.
29 Wilson, David, "*In the Heat of the Night*," *Sight and Sound*, Autumn, 1967, p. 206.
30 Ebert, Roger, "*Guess Who's Coming to Dinner?*," *Chicago Sun-Times*, January 25, 1968. http://rogerebert.suntimes.com/apps/pbcs.dll/articel? AID=/19680125/REVIEWS.
31 *Ibid.*

32 Maltin, Leonard, *"Finian's Rainbow," Leonard Maltin's 2003 Movie & Video Guide* (New York: Penguin Books, 2002), p. 454.

33 Canby, Vincent, *"The Great White Hope," New Tork Times*, October 12, 1970. http://movies.nytimes.com/movie/review/?_r=1&res.

34 Scott, A. O., "Can Black People Fly? Don't Ask 'Soul Plane'," *New York Times*, June 13, 2004. www.nytimes.com/2004/06/13/movies/13SCOT.html.

35 *Ibid.*

36 *Ibid.*

37 Haughton, Elspeth. *Apollo Guide Review*. www.rottentomatoes.com/click/movie1018699/reviews.php.

38 Blaxploitation collection, Emory University archives. http://zenodotus.library.emory.edu/AfAmCinema/theCollection/raceFilms.html.

39 Berardinelli, James, *"Do the Right Thing,"* June 30, 1989. http://colossus.net/movie-reviews/movies/d/do_right.html.

40 Salim, Muwakkil, "Doing the Spike Thing," *In These Times*, July 5–8, 1989, pp. 18–24.

41 Ebert, Roger, *"Do the Right Thing," Chicago Sun-Times*, July 30, 1989. www.rottentomatoes.com/click/movie-1005998/reviews.php?critic=column&sortby=default&page-1&rid=5434.

42 Breskin, David, "Spike Lee Interview." *Rolling Stone*, July 25, 1991.

43 Williams, Jeannie, "Will *Right Thing* Hit at Wrong Time?," *USA Today*, May 22, 1989, p. D5.

44 Rossini, Tom, "Fight the Power and Complacency." A paper prepared for the Pictures of Protest course, Emerson College, February 18, 2003.

45 Ebert, "Doing the Right Thing," *Chicago Sun-Times*, June 30, 1989. www.rogerebert.suntimes.html.

46 Bruckner, D. J. R., *"She's Gotta Have It," New York Times*, August 8, 1986. http://movies.nytimes.com/movie/reviews?_rf1&res.

47 *Ibid.*

48 Brussat, Frederic, *Sprituality & Health*. www.rottentomatoes.com/click/movie-1036141/reviews.php.

49 Kroll, J. and V. E. Smith, "Spiking a Fever," *Newsweek*, June 10, 1991, p. 44.

50 Canby, Vincent, *"Malcolm X," New York Times*, November 18, 1992. http://mkovies.nytimes.com/movie/review?res.

51 Berardinelli, James, *"Bamboozled,"* 2001. http://movie-reviews.colossus.net/movies/b/bamboozled.html.

52 Ebert, Roger, "Movie Reviews: *Bamboozled," Chicago Sun-Times*, October 6, 2000. www.suntimes.com/ebert/ebert_reviews/2000/10/100601.html.

53 *Ibid.*

54 Bruce, David, "Racism in America – Hating Others," 1997–2005. www.hollywoodjesus.com/american_history_x.htm.

55 Ebert, Roger, *"American History X,"* *Chicago Sun-Times*, October, 1998. www.suntimes.com/ebert/ebert_reviews/1998/10/103004.html.
56 Chang, Jeff and Sylvia Chang, "Can White Hollywood Get Race Right? www.alternet.org/movies/23597.
57 Marquez, Sandra, *"Crash:* the Fear of Strangers," *Hispanic*, June–July, 2005, p. 70.
58 Scott, A. O., *"The Visitor,"* *New York Times*, April 11, 2008. http://movies.nytimes.com/2008/04/11/movies/11visi.html.

8
Politics
The good and the bad

While I rather dislike Hollywood films on politics, I took the liberty of watching a few anyway. It was then I realized why I don't like films on politics. I don't like to know that the governments of the world, especially mine, are not "instituted among men" nor do they "derive their just powers from the consent of the governed," but are in fact instituted among lies, deception, greed, assassination, manipulation, and corruption.[1]

By their very nature, politics and its practitioners lend themselves to protest. The ideal of selfless public service has emerged, from the very beginning of the democratic government structure of the United States, as by and large just an ideal. Corruption, mud-slinging, bribery, secrecy, special-interest control, rigged elections, and the mantra of promise-them-anything-to-get-their-votes have dominated American politics – not unlike, of course, the politics of virtually every other country in the world. So powerful are those who practice political chicanery that whistle-blowers, who for a brief moment are lauded by the public and the very small part of the media not controlled by the politically powerful, are destroyed professionally, financially, and socially, quickly ignored by the media and forgotten by the public. So much for ideals!

This is a general situation, backed by up specific events and practices, tailor-made for protesting. Protests have been frequent and at times seemingly unending. Watching such classic Hollywood films as *Mr. Smith Goes to Washington* (1939) and *The Great McGinty* (1940), one might conclude that Hollywood has done its part to protest political chicanery. A closer look at the many Hollywood political-themed pictures of protest and the times in which they were made, however, reveals that the criticism was almost always by general implication and not directed toward a specific politician or situation that was harming democracy at the time the films were made. Satires such as *Primary Colors* (1998) and *Wag the Dog* (1997) were direct comments, respectively, on Bill Clinton's 1996 presidential campaign and on the first President George Bush's putting America into the first Gulf War – although both films were made long enough after the event not to have an impact on that particular president at that particular time, albeit presenting a warning to the audiences to look out for similar happenings in their own times. However, the influence on the media, including Hollywood, of the political, corporate, and military establishment (we give lip service to but do not heed President Eisenhower's warning about the military-industrial complex), appears to preclude contemporary criticism of a given president-in-office when a political protest film is made. Until the just-released Oliver Stone film, "W" (2008), no movie has appeared to reflect the public realization that current President Bush, Vice-President Cheney, and others in government went to war in Iraq on false pretenses, destroyed the United States' worldwide goodwill and reputation, and seriously harmed its economy. The few Hollywood films critical of the Iraq War that emerged in 2007 did not include protests against the politicians who led us into it. Given the power of those who control the media, as well as politics, it takes a maverick producer to make such a picture of protest. So fearful of the political-economic establishment is the movie-making industry that the latter did not even protest by implication or analogy – for example, an historical film on Abraham Lincoln's suspension of civil rights and civil liberties, including habeas corpus, during the Civil War: His imposition of martial law on the entire country; halting of freedom of speech and press that he disagreed with or that disagreed with his policies, often by jailing the offenders; use of torture, including the routine application of what later was called water-boarding; and the not infrequent employment of the death penalty, at that time by hanging.[2]

Hollywood's timidity and the putting of its special economic interests above the interests and needs of the viewing public do not apply to many, if not most Hollywood individual practitioners. Many actors and actresses – perhaps in part because of their sensitization to the human condition through their analysis of the characters they play and of the political-social-economic environment those characters are in – have been among the country's strongest and most visible protesters against the erosion of civil rights and civil liberties, including those eliminated or threatened during real time, such as the period of the Iraq War.

Many Hollywood films protesting political chicanery have been powerful and had an effect, some on the current political scene at the time they were made, some on later political developments and principles owing to the earlier films' influences on the public memory. As some of the media began to jump on the bandwagon of disapproval of the administration's policies in the first decade of 2000, more and more films began to be released, most of the overtly critical ones independently produced, on the government's corrupt relationships with big oil, big pharmaceuticals, big banking, big weapons manufacturers, and other military-industrial-government alliances.

Perhaps the seminal, though not the first, Hollywood movie protesting politics as usual was *Mr. Smith Goes to Washington* (1939). The movie opens with a state's governor, senator, and real-estate/media magnate party Big Boss deciding how to fill the position of a recently deceased senator. The interim appointment is important because the Big Boss wants a bill passed that would provide public funds to buy land he has accumulated in order for the government to build an unneeded dam. This is, in Washington terms, a pork barrel earmark, eerily identical to the 2000 decade's Alaska bridge-to-nowhere earmark, and the southwest Florida fundraiser for an Alaskan congressman under whose supervision an appropriation bill passed by Congress was changed to substitute millions of dollars for an interchange in place of road widening, the change likely to benefit the real-estate holdings of a developer involved in the fundraiser for the Congressman. Sometimes truth is identical to fiction, and the plot of *Mr. Smith Goes to Washington* accurately reflects the corruption that went on and still goes on in national and regional politics. In the film the bosses decide to appoint a nice, naïve young man – James Stewart playing the role of a scout organizer – who they are sure they can control in getting their bill passed. To their dismay, he refuses to go along with their corruption – he wants the land to be used for a scout camp, not for a useless dam – and actively opposes it. In southwest Florida in 2007, a small city mayor who was chairing the county planning organization charged with accepting the millions of tainted dollars for the interchange also refused to go along with the powers-that-be and, with the help of a retired federal official, revealed and fought the corruption. In the film, the James Stewart character, Jefferson Smith, decides to filibuster the bill, trying to stop its passage. The real-estate/media magnate then

Figure 8.1
Mr. Smith Goes to Washington (1939)

uses his control of the media to vilify the young senator. In southwest Florida, the major newspaper, dependent on real-estate developers for much of its advertising, gratuitously vilified the whistle-blowing mayor. In the film, a major character reveals the corrupt plan and young Mr. Smith wins. Hollywood films, particularly those dealing with critical issues, have to leave their audiences feeling good – the obligatory happy ending. As this is being written, the political powers in southwest Florida are supporting the opponents of the former mayor running for higher office.

Unfortunately, public reaction to the film as a condemnation of political chicanery is not usually matched by public reaction to local or regional corruption. One reason is that the film reached a wide audience throughout the entire country. Media consolidation facilitated by the Federal Communications Commission and Congress has now put the control of more and more local media into fewer and fewer hands; with few exceptions, the powerful corporate forces are in concert with the powerful political forces, thus leaving few independent media willing to expose political corruption. Another reason is that when *Mr. Smith Goes to Washington* was released the country was still in the throes of the 1930s economic depression, with many people blaming it on an incompetent government, and viewers were delighted to see the little guy, representing their status, stick it to the big guys. The 2008 economic recession in the US may revive that attitude.

While the public, by and large, embraced the revelations of corruption in their government by the film, the subjects of the revelations, Washington politicians, were both horrified and angry. At the film's premiere on October 16, 1939, at Washington's Constitution Hall,

The outside streets were jammed with limousines. A Marine band played as Supreme Court justices, cabinet members, and senators – four thousand people in all – waited to see a major motion picture they fully expected to reflect their own, smug view of public service, i.e., business as usual. Then, aghast at what they had seen on the screen before them, a full third of the crowd walked out.[3]

Mr. Smith Goes to Washington had ramifications both beyond the Beltway and the country. The American Ambassador to Britain, Joseph P. Kennedy, attempted to stop the release of the film. He wrote to the head of Columbia Pictures, the producing company, "It is my belief that . . . it [*Mr. Smith Goes to Washington*] will give an idea of our political life that will do us harm . . . I have a high regard for Mr. Capra [the director] . . . but his fine work makes the indictment of our government all the more damning to foreign audiences."[4] Ironically, the film was banned by Hitler's Germany and by some other fascist countries because of its strong theme of pro-democracy dissent. While vilified by many politicians, the movie was acclaimed by the film industry's artists, who nominated it for 11 Academy Awards. (Its competition that year, to which it finished second at the box office, was *Gone With the Wind*.) In addition, it was put out as a guide for junior and senior high school students, "Photoplay Studies on *Mr. Smith*," at a time when such guides were almost invariably based on pieces of classic literature.[5]

> whether commercially successful or not, ideologically liberated or otherwise, films with political themes centered on Washington did go into production in greater numbers, and whilst these projects may have appeared populist or even escapist in tone, pervasive democratic ideas seeped through their story lines and infiltrated their visual spectacle to engage public consciousness and liberate political thought from the shackles of Hollywood regulation.[6]

An earlier satire on political chicanery, discussed in chapter 2, was the 1933 Marx Brothers film, *Duck Soup*. As well as attacking the absurdity of war and the ease in which a government deludes its people into going to war, the film satirizes government organization, the inanity of its political leaders, the gullibility of its followers, politicians, diplomatic incompetence, and the political control of supposedly democratic systems. The audience laughed at the insanity and absurdity of politicians declaring war on another country for no reason other than that they felt like doing so. When it was released, *Duck Soup* was not a box-office success. Its commentary on World War I and its warning about politicians and future wars were largely ignored by a country deep in economic depression, looking only for amusement. Even one of the most telling lines in the film, uttered by the political leader (Groucho Marx as Rufus T. Firefly) of the warring country (Fredonia), was buried by the viewer looking for non-thinking laughter: "And remember while you're out there risking life and limb through shot and shell, we'll be in here thinking what a sucker you are." In later years *Duck Soup* was recognized as a masterpiece of satire.

In 1940, a year after *Mr. Smith Goes to Washington*, perhaps encouraged by the success of that film, Hollywood produced *The Great McGinty*, another commentary on politics and corruption. This was the directorial debut of Preston Sturges, who went on to make some of Hollywood's most entertaining, successful – and meaningful – comedies of the next few decades. McGinty is a "bum who is manipulated into [the governor's] chair by [the] crooked political machine – then blows it all when he tries to be honest."[7] The film, with bright and breezy satire, depicts various aspects of political chicanery, from voting manipulation to bribery, the politician characters behaving without civic conscience or personal ethics. In this mode the government moves right along. But when the lead character finds a conscience and wants to be honest, the system collapses. As a crooked politician he lived high on the hog. As an honest politician he loses everything and is forced to flee the country.

In 1949, in the aftermath of the glow and glory – at least as painted by the media – of democracy having defeated fascism in World War II, a number of films emerged glorifying the triumph of political honesty over political chicanery as the democratic ideal and/or lauding the rising up of the people to dispose, one way or another, of the politician who has let power turn him (virtually no VIPs, including clean and dirty politicians, were portrayed as women) from good into evil. *State of the Union* was based on the Pulitzer Prize-winning Broadway stage play. The film has an industrialist-with-conscience being talked into running for the Republican presidential nomination. Not your stereotyped politician, he decries the dedication to high profits of his corporate colleagues and of the country's establishment at the expense of greater production and growth for the country and its working people. This was shocking at the time and is still shocking now. He even decries the old-style politics in which the boys in the backroom will do anything, even harm their country, to get themselves or their candidates elected. But caught up in the politics of his party, this candidate succumbs to the corruption and chicanery that are the opposite of the democratic ideal. He goes along with the machine, compromising his beliefs to get votes. The film soundly skewers these politicians: "a slick piece of screen satire . . . knife-edged slicing at the hides of pachyderm schemers and connivers . . . a withering commentary on current [1948] issues."[8] But, in the spirit of the time, all ends well as the candidate sees the light again and, in a last-minute radio and television address, admits that he was dishonest with the public, apologizes, and makes his personal political world all right again. A number of subsequent movies followed the same pattern: An honest politician succumbs to the compromising and frequently corrupt necessities of politics, but, after all looks bleak, finds his conscience again. Some readers will remember the parallels in a 1995 film, *The American President*. An art-imitates-life, life-imitates-art scenario was part of the making of *The State of the Union*. Cast members Adolph Menjou, a political right-winger who supported McCarthyism and the blacklist in subsequent years, and Katherine Hepburn, a political liberal, reportedly engaged in continuing and sometimes disruptive off-set political arguments during the filming, represented in large part the political divisiveness portrayed in the movie.

That same year, 1949, another political movie was a critical hit at the box office and in media reviews. *All the King's Men* (its luster clouded by a shallow remake in 2007) was the dramatic adaptation of the real-life story of Huey Long, the Louisiana "kingfish." It traces Long's political life as a populist who helped salvage the lives and livelihoods of the neglected poor and working class of his state, finally being elected as a popular and revered governor. But the idealistic young man turns into a power-hungry politician. While he continues to serve the needy of Louisiana, he does it through corrupt means that aggrandize his own personal fortunes, and he rules with an unyielding, unforgiving dictatorial hand. So disillusioned do some of his formerly faithful supporters and aides become that to stop what they feel is Long's behavior as a neo-fascist – the ones we had recently defeated in World War II – they assassinate him. Again, it appears that political chicanery has been stopped. The self-appointed and self-anointed dictatorial politician has been strongly protested in this film, with the ultimate punishment for the evildoer. The aftermath of the Huey Long regime, in real life, was not so idealistic. The control of Louisiana politics remained a legacy for the Long family, giving them virtual control of the state for decades. And contrary to the "evil is as evil does" platitude, the deprived masses of Louisiana lost their champion and fell upon harder times without the largesse, corrupt as it was, of Huey Long. The film raises the philosophical question of what is good and what is evil, and where they intertwine.

From heavy to light in a short time, 1950 saw one of the most entertaining and satisfying political protest movies, *Born Yesterday*, luring the audience with laughs while making it think at the same time. The bribery – the buying – of senators and congresspersons by corporate America is a fact of all eras. In our own time, Congressional scandals make *Born Yesterday* as valid today as it was over half a century ago. In the film adaptation of the Broadway play, a crude, arrogant junk-dealer tycoon brings his quintessential dumb-blonde girl friend with him to Washington, DC, where he puts members of the House and Senate in his pocket for illegal deals. Because he will circulate in the society of VIPs, he hires a journalist to educate his dumb girlfriend, to give her some "couth." It turns out that she's not so dumb, and with the background of the country's history as her classroom, she develops a strong social and political conscience and, at the end of the film, has destroyed the junk dealer's nefarious schemes of political chicanery and fallen in love with the journalist.

This kind of satire, generated by the comedies-with-meaning of the 1930s, gave way to more serious genres. *The Phenix City Story* (1955) tells the story of how citizens of a town fight corrupt city officials who are in league with gangsters, in an attempt to drive out prostitution and crime that earned the real-life Phenix city in Alabama the title of "Sin City, USA." As in other political protest films, it showed how "good guys" who are willing to stick their necks out and stand up for what they believe can beat the "bad guys." *The Phenix City Story* was not a great success at the box office and its impact on motivating citizen action against corrupt local political systems at the time it was released is questionable. A greater box-office success a few years later, in 1960, *Spartacus*, was both an historical retelling and a parable for its time. Howard Fast's historical novel, the basis for the film, was, like his other novels, meant to have a direct bearing on contemporary issues. The analogy of the slave revolt against the political oppression in ancient Rome related to the need for revolt against political repression in many countries in the world at the time the film was released. The beginnings of antiracist, feminist, and counter-culture revolutions were brewing in the United States and revolutions against US-backed dictatorships in other countries, particularly Central and South America, were gathering momentum. The reviewers were not as kind to the film as the above commentary suggests they might have been, criticizing the concentration on spectacle and a number of specified historical inaccuracies.

The screenwriter of *Spartacus* was Dalton Trumbo, arguably the most controversial of the blacklisted writers during the McCarthy era, and the winner of Academy Awards under an assumed name during the blacklist period. The director was Stanley Kubrick, who directed a number of protest films, including the highly successful *Dr. Strangelove* more than a decade later. Could the film's political content negatively influence reviewers, still in the thrall of McCarthyism as the Cold War continued to heat up?

Dr. Strangelove: or, How I Learned to Stop Worrying and Love the Bomb (1964) is one of the most – if not the most – brilliant of all the satirical film protests against the incompetence, paranoia, and special interests of political and military leaders who hold the world's life in their hands. (See the discussion of *Dr. Strangelove* in chapter 2.) But, alas, Hollywood apparently had neither the courage nor interest in making this film; with a largely American cast, it is a British production. Another non-Hollywood political protest of that decade, *Fahrenheit 451* (1966), was an adaptation of Ray Bradbury's science-fiction novel of a political system that banned the reading of all books as the way to control peoples' information and thinking.

In 1972, with the stench of McCarthyism gradually fading from America (it wouldn't be too many years before it was revived again with a different scent), the "good guy turned bad guy who redeems himself" politician was epitomized in *The Candidate*. An idealistic pre-sidential candidate, who stands against corrupt politics, realizes that he has to park his ideals if he wants to win, and finds himself in a compromising political situation. Because, at the beginning of the film, he is expected to lose, his political team doesn't care that he is candid and honest. But when the media make him a viable candidate, his political handlers do what is necessary for him to be able to win. He then has "to ponder the consequences of his political seduction."[9] *New York Times* film critic Vincent Canby summed up the essence of a key protest theme of the movie:

> A crucial and sad moment in the film is the television debate between the candidates, when McKay [the candidate] belatedly tries to talk about "issues" and simply flounders around. "I wonder if anyone knew what I was trying to say," he asks his father. Answers Douglas with pride: "Don't worry. It doesn't make any difference."[10]

Lucia Bozzola, in *All Movie Guide*, summed it up this way: *"The Candidate* shrewdly exposed the effects of the media on the increasingly cynical political process, posing unanswerable questions that have become all the more pressing with every sound-bite-rules election."[11]

As this is being written, in the middle of the 2008 presidential campaign in the United States, the content of *The Candidate* seems as fresh today as it was over thirty-five years ago. As another example of art imitates life and life imitates art, the actor playing the "candidate" in the film, Robert Redford, was so adulated by the public in the film's publicity buildup that some real-life politicians wanted him to actually run for public office, a proposal that continues to surface even today.

By the mid-1970s mea culpas had become self-imposed obligations for most of those who had supported or cooperated in the McCarthy-era blacklisting, and some films actually dealt with the excesses of the period. *The Front* (1976), written, directed, and acted by a number of artists who had been blacklist victims, was a brilliant commentary on how government and, in turn, the media industry in particular, caved in to the demagoguery of fear. Some political critics see a direct analogy between the vitiation of civil liberties in the McCarthy era by politicians intent on expanding their power by exaggerating a fear of communism and the vitiation of civil liberties in the current era by exaggerating a fear of terrorism. But there is no indication that the film, *The Front*, although still frequently seen as a virtual cult classic, has had any effect on ameliorating the public's contemporary sheep-like behavior. *The Front*, in a powerfully entertaining pre-final scene, explodes the chicanery of the politicians on the government's congressional un-American activities (read anticommunist) investigating committee. The "front," played by Woody Allen as a cashier named Prince who has let blacklisted writers use his name as the author of their scripts so they could make a living, has been called to testify before the HUAC.

> [Prince] having ruffled their feathers by turning their baiting non-questions around with non-incriminating non-answers, one of the committee members asserts: "We are not concerned at this time with anything other than the communist conspiracy in the entertainment world." When they request Prince to give them "just one name," even if it happens to be the name of a dead man . . . *The Front*'s ultimate grasp of the truth of the nature of Hollywood McCarthyism is clear and devastating. The HUAC was nothing less insidious than a tool of the U.S. government in an attempt to gain control of the

rapidly pervasive entertainment industry and to keep its messages in firm check, all the while maintaining plausible deniability and, thereby, superficially distancing themselves from Stalinesque state control.[12]

The classic end of the HUAC scene has the Prince character saying what the film makes clear more Americans should have said years before, as he walks out on the hearing: "Gentlemen, you can all go fuck yourselves!"

The same year, 1976, saw a blockbuster movie about one of the country's saddest episodes of political corruption, the Watergate affair. *All the President's Men* is the story of how two reporters revealed the criminal activity of the Nixon White House in the notorious Watergate break-in to the Democratic National Headquarters and subsequent cover-up, which led to Nixon's resignation in disgrace. A revelation of and protest against dirty politicians, including the President of the United States, the film motivated the public to take a closer look at their public servants. In the film, the reporters are given clues to the conspiracy by an unknown figure, "Deep Throat," who tells them to "follow the money." But the crime wasn't about money, but about power – a failing that seems to have affected too many politicians, many of them, fictional and non-fictional, addressed in some of the movies we have discussed. The film carried the audience "through the spectacular series of revelations, accusations, and admissions of guilt that eventually brought the Nixon Presidency to its conclusion . . . Though the film will undoubtedly have some political impact, its strength is the virtually day-by-day record of the way Bernstein and Woodward [the *Washington Post* reporters] conducted their investigations."[13]

In addition to making a strong political statement, the film is the story of courageous, intrepid, and passionate journalists whose work a few years earlier motivated many young journalists and would-be journalists into new commitments to investigative journalism for the public's, not the advertisers', interest. In the case of *All the President's Men*, obviously not reaching the public until a few years after the fact because of the time necessary to make the movie, it served as a warning to the public to be more careful in selecting and judging its elected officials, including those at the highest level. While the film continues to be lauded, it appears to have had little or no effect on future presidential or government corruption or in motivating present-day journalists to investigate and reveal similar corruption.

The year 1979 saw the production of a devastating serious satire – not the obvious comedy that laughed at the targets. *Being There* is about a simple gardener whose knowledge of the world comes principally from watching children's television shows, including cartoons, and who talks in comparable simplistic terms that are taken by the VIP political friends of his VIP employer to be profound parables. Finally, this totally unqualified, mentally handicapped individual is considered as "presidential" timber. It is a brilliant satire on how government is run on the basis of inane platitudes by similarly inane people. The next year, in 1980, the film *Reds* included a sharp criticism of the deprivation of American civil liberties in the period following World War I when fear of the Bolsheviks – the equivalent of the Communists who succeeded them – was instilled by the US government as a national fear. The film, based on fact and produced in a semi-documentary style, describes the founding of the Soviet Union through the eyes and journalistic reports of an American writer. While the segments involving US Attorney-General Palmer's warrantless raids, jailing, and deportation in the early 1920s of Americans considered pro-labor or pro-socialist, and interpreted by many as a warning against the "red menace" scare of the Cold War of the time, it has more recently been cited as an analogy of the secret warrantless wire-tapping, arrests, jailing, and holding incommunicado Americans deemed suspect because of antiwar activity or unacceptable political beliefs under the Patriot Act of the 2000s.

Later in the decade Oliver Stone made a film protesting "American support of brutal, fascist repression in Latin America."[14] In this 1986 movie, *Salvador*, the major character must face the truth about the US government's lies and propaganda and the chicanery of US foreign policy. Some critics called it a "leftist" attack on America's political leaders, but did not deny America's role as presented in the film.

Beginning with the 1990s and continuing through most of the following decade (at least through the time this book was published), a plethora of protest movies revealing, commenting on, and attacking political chicanery reached the screens.

The first striking film of that era dealt with a controversial alleged cover-up by politicians and political parties: The 1963 assassination of President John F. Kennedy and the Warren Report. *JFK* (1991), not surprisingly directed by Oliver Stone, raised serious questions, in quasi-documentary style, about the government's honesty about and apparent cover-up of who killed Jack Kennedy. Praised by those who believed there was an assassination conspiracy and condemned by those who believed the Warren Report conclusion that Kennedy was the victim of a sole killer, Lee Harvey Oswald, *JFK* became a lightning rod for that issue. The film opens with President Dwight Eisenhower's warning to America about the dangers of the military-industrial complex. Oliver Stone uses that a base for his quasi-documentary-style presentation of information showing that the military-industrial complex was a principal factor in a conspiracy, reaching to the highest levels of government. The film features the efforts of New Orleans District Attorney Jim Garrison, who

> is convinced that there are some big flaws in the investigation of Oswald, and he sets out to recreate the events leading up to the assassination. Along the way he stumbles across evidence that a great many people had reason to want to see the president killed, and he is convinced that some of them worked in concert to frame Oswald as the killer.[15]

Those critical of the film alleged that many of Stone's presumed facts were untrue or distorted. Critic Vincent Canby stated in the *New York Times* that "What the film does do effectively is to present the case for the idea that there actually was a conspiracy, rather than the lone gunman, Lee Harvey Oswald, specified by the Warren Commission report . . . [but] The film's insurmountable problem is the vast amount of material it fails to make coherent sense of."[16] Like many other critics, Canby further criticizes the film for "sweeping innuendos."[17]

Critical reviews appeared, in many cases, to depend on the reviewer's political alliances (the film condemns the right-wing and, by name and implication, predominantly Republican sources as part of the conspiratorial vested interests). In this protest of an allegedly politically motivated and politician-abetted cover-up, "Oliver Stone . . . has constructed what some reviewers felt was one of the most compelling (and controversial) political detective thrillers ever to emerge from American cinema."[18] Despite the divisive criticism of the film it "spurred renewed public interest in the Kennedy assassination. As a direct result, Congress passed the JFK records Act of 1992, resulting in the release of thousands of formerly classified records."[19]

The feature entertainment film, *Bob Roberts*, produced in 1992, is an under-acknowledged, scathing portrait of a politician without ethics who unabashedly and successfully manipulates a willing media to achieve political success. In the guise of a documentary ("mockumentary," as some writers dubbed it), writer-director-star Tim Robbins – who with his partner Susan Sarandon has been responsible for a number of protest films – follows the senate campaign of a right-wing folk singer, Bob Roberts. Roberts's songs satirically reflect his philosophies, with such lyrics as "Drugs stink . . . hang 'em [users] high for a clean tomorrow" and a prophetic "Times are a changin' back." He crisscrosses the state in his tour bus, drawing crowds with his combination of singing and politicking, the campaign being reported in pseudo-documentary by the media. His mudslinging against his opponent is accepted as fact by the media, including an allegation that the opponent was having a sexual affair with a teenage campaign worker. Through the "documentary" we see Roberts as a thoroughly despicable, evil person. The media, however, present only the caring, honest, irreproachable face that he shows them. One reporter, however, discovers damning information about Roberts, including drug trafficking, weapons dealing, and involvement in a savings and loan scandal. In an effort to distract the voters from negative accusations against him and to win their sympathy, Robert stages an assassination attempt on his own life, framing the reporter as a tool of his enemies. Roberts is supposedly paralyzed after the shooting, his condition winning him enough sympathy votes to get him elected to the Senate. The reporter is cleared of the attempted murder charges, but to permanently silence his criticisms and the information he has about Roberts, Roberts has him killed. Roberts goes to Washington with great fanfare, his paralyzed body carried in triumph to a welcoming reception. The "documentary" camera sums up the phoniness and chicanery used by politicians to fool the public when it focuses on the movement of his allegedly paralyzed foot. As one film historian wrote:

> Bob Roberts sends up the idea of the redeeming political hero by presenting a candidate who consciously casts himself in that role . . . exaggerated as it might be, Robbins's script reflects elements of reality and can stand as a fair warning to the public to consider the mechanisms by which politicians deploy rhetoric and manipulate symbols.[20]

For many critics Bob Roberts cut too close to home, and reviews included outright rejections and nitpicking that obscured the unsettling relevance of the film and resulted in its failure to reach as wide an audience as it should have. In many quarters it is now, given the revelations about many real-life politicians since 1992, becoming a "cult" film. It reflects a growing belief among voters that many politicians, unlike the Huey Long/Willie Stark character of *All the King's Men*, or the redeemable and redeemed politicians like those in *State of the Union* and *The Candidate*, are simply and inherently corrupt and evil.

Another 1992 film, *The Distinguished Gentleman*, was also a satire on a senatorial candidate, but in an entirely different vein. Instead of a realistic, hard look at the subject, it reverted to the 1930s comedy-satire approach. In *The Distinguished Gentleman*, a con man has the same name of a senator who recently died. Capitalizing on the name, he gets himself elected to the Senate. His purpose is to use the position for his personal gain. One important difference between this 1992 film and the 1930s comedies: in the 1930s the conman who gets elected would be Caucasian; in 1992 the character is played by Eddie Murphy, an African-American. (See the changes in stereotyping over the years in chapter 7.) But like his counterparts of the earlier films, the conman redeems himself when he sees the corruption among his colleagues, and he exposes it and them.

The following year, 1993, saw a similar theme and plot line in *Dave*. The President, a rigid, mean-spirited philanderer disliked by many, including his wife, has a massive stroke while in bed with another woman. To avoid a political crisis, a few trusted members of the White House inner circle, led by the President's chief of staff, have Dave, an exact look-alike for the President, play the role while the President recovers. The White House politicos, especially the chief of staff, feel they can manipulate Dave into doing whatever they tell him, to forward their own personal interests. As is necessary for such a plot line, their agendas are corrupt. Dave, of course, refuses to go along with them as he learns what they are really up to and figures out how to use his position of power. He turns out to be a much better servant of the people than the real President, who is still in a coma. Romance is part of the story, as well, as Dave and the President's wife begin to fall in love, she finding in him what her husband had once been before being corrupted by the political system. The premise of *Dave* is that "Rule-bound bureaucrats and over-lobbied congressmen routinely fail, but a guy with simple math and common sense can figure it out. Want to house homeless children? Well then, hold off paying defense contractors until they've done the work. Want honest government? Put in honest people to do the job."[21]

The political theme of *Dave* is summed up by critic Martin Walker: "It reverts to a Hollywood tradition of presenting the American political system as inherently good as long as it's in the hands of plain and decent folk."[22]

A film in the same tradition, *The American President*, was released a couple of years later, in 1995. The liberal President is gearing up for a reelection campaign when he meets and falls in love with an environmental lobbyist. He believes in the bill she wants to get through Congress and promises her he will help get it through. In the meantime, however, dirty politics begins to hurt his reelection chances and, if he wants to win, he has to compromise with members of Congress who want to stop the environmental bill. He reneges on his promise. Through much angst, including a break-up with his beloved lobbyist, he does, of course, redeem himself, and sees that the bill is passed, despite the personal political cost to him. Because he's a decent person, the country, we are assured, is in good hands. The film itself is not only highly entertaining, with empathic performances that put the audience into the Washington inner scene, but has a message that reaches a wide public.

While the public was enjoying the feel-good films of political protest, Oliver Stone did not let us forget the realistic, seamy side of politics. His 1995 film, *Nixon*, was a biopic of what presumably was going on in the mind as well as the offices of the President, who averred "I am not a crook." If Stone's purpose was to vilify Nixon, as some suggested Stone's alleged liberal bias would wish to do, the opposite occurred, according to some critics. By delving into the motivations and trying to expose the demons that inhabited Nixon, Stone revealed Nixon as much a victim as a perpetrator. Nevertheless, the film's subject was not the redeemed politician, but the evil one, even to the extent that we understood his persona and reasons for seeking increased power. One critic noted that Nixon, himself feeling the national guilt about Kennedy's assassination, had "an emerging messianic belief that only he can save a fratricidally divided America."[23] But in doing so, he inevitably let power corrupt, and "What *Nixon* captures very well is a fairly commonplace public contention about its subject: Nixon, more than any other modern politician [as of 1994], is a symbol of the delegitimization of the standing political order."[24] Perhaps, as Stephen

Rogers wrote, "Oliver's Stone's greatest achievement with *Nixon* . . . is motivating his audience to think and to question the 'official' version of history."[25] In that respect, with mixed reviews, *Nixon* was similar to Stone's earlier film, *JFK*.

During the next few years, arguably two of the most effective as well as entertaining political protest films of all time reached the silver screen. While it is too early to tell if they will have the staying power of a *Mr. Smith Goes to Washington*, they have had and are still having a special impact on that segment of the population whose decisions during the next few years will determine the political direction of our country; those of college age.

Wag the Dog was produced in 1997 and *Bulworth* in 1998. *Wag the Dog* was so contemporary, satirizing an immediate past and a current president when it was released, and a few years later applied to yet another president, that tapes quickly disappeared from video-store shelves when the film was no longer playing in theaters. Journalist Andrew Christie wrote that *Wag the Dog* "is becoming our national portrait in the attic, worth a trip up the stairs every few years so that we may gaze upon its shifting surface and behold the latest, ghastly truths that have become visible there, reflecting our real political face."[26] Eleven days before an election, the President is faced with a sex scandal – inappropriately touching a "Firefly Girl" who was part of a group visiting the White House. The revelation could cost him the election. His staff calls in a "spin doctor" to handle the situation. What do presidents (and prime ministers and dictators and other national leaders) do when their offices and personal standings are in trouble? They divert the public's attention to some national crisis, real or manufactured. In art imitating life, the spin doctor calls in a movie producer to create a phony war, war historically being the diversion of choice. The spin doctor and movie producer decide that Albania has suddenly become a threat to the United States. They stage a war with Albania – not a real war, but one consisting of fake news footage, press conferences, a fabricated war hero,[27] and even a theme song and merchandising links.[28] As they film the make-believe war in a secret studio, a young actress enters the scene holding a bag of Doritos and is quickly transformed into a devastated Albanian girl carrying a kitten, running from a battle scene. The media eagerly air this scene of the war, provided by official American sources, reinforcing the American public's support of this "necessary" war. As one of the characters says, when the

Figure 8.2
Wag the Dog
(1997)

question is raised as to whether the public will believe that it is an actual battle, "Actual battles don't matter because if it's on television, it must be real." The fictional war is successful. The media play it up and the President's sexual indiscretion is barely noted. The satire turns darker at the end of the film, when the movie producer is so pleased with his accomplishment, having fooled the entire world with his artistry, that he wants public credit and acclaim. But, of course, the President's political team cannot allow that to happen and the film ends with the producer being eulogized at his funeral, having mysteriously died of a "heart attack."

Some critics compared *Wag the Dog* to *Dr. Strangelove* in the sense that "The plot is a blast of cynicism directed at professional manipulators and image-makers, and the mood is the controlled nastiness of *Dr. Strangelove.*"[29]

The title of the film refers to the tail of the dog wagging the supposedly smarter part of the dog, the head. Critic James Berardinelli wrote:

> The ones wagging the dog are clearly the spin doctors . . . But who is the dog? The media, who eagerly lap up every drop of milk spilled by the White House press staff? The American public, ever-eager for the latest made-for-television war/entertainment? The answer is likely both. And while [director] Levinson and [screenwriter] Mamet are clearly stretching reality beyond the bounds of credibility for the purposes of this satire, there's more than a kernel of truth in the core theme. Political campaigns are often run like Hollywood motion pictures. Television is critical to a candidate's success. And the media loves a good war – just look at the current frenzy that's occurring as hostilities with Iraq rise toward a crescendo.[30]

Another critic described the title this way: "this satire presents an America in which the public is a sleeping dog, getting wagged every which way by the corrupt leaders and a lazy, cowardly media."[31]

Yet, the actual events of the film are not as far-fetched as they might seem at first glance. In 2004 it was discovered that the George W. Bush administration had hired people to pose as journalists in order to praise and get public support for Bush's proposed changes in the Medicare law. The pieces by these "journalists" were aired on television news programs in a number of states. Further, the government prepared so-called "story packages" in the form of prepared scripts for distribution to news anchors.[32]

The film, released during the second term of the Clinton administration, was thought to be a takeoff on Clinton's alleged sexual indiscretions, particularly the Monica Lewinsky affair. One critic wrote that "*Wag the Dog* also has a TV news clip of the fictional president greeting the girl at a function – the scene bears an uncanny resemblance to the now-infamous clip of Clinton hugging former White House intern Monica Lewinsky, right down to the black beret worn by the girl in the film."[33]

However, the film's satire was actually directed at the previous President's administration, that of George H. W. Bush. The Persian Gulf War, or Operation Desert Storm, came at a time when President Bush's ratings were at a low ebb, reflecting the dissatisfaction of the public with the economic health of the country. With an election coming up the following year, the public had to be directed to an acceptable distraction. In the long run, the economy proved to be a deciding factor and Bush lost the 1992 election to Bill Clinton. Before the United States attacked the Iraq army in the Gulf War, polls showed some ninety percent of the public opposed to such an action. Shortly after the United States took the action, however, and the media equated supporting the troops with supporting the war, some ninety percent of the public supported the action. Director Barry Levinson discussed the relationship of *Wag the Dog* to the Gulf War.

> When you think of the Gulf War it is not unlike a junket. They took everybody [journalists] over there and they put them in some Quonset huts and brought them some food to eat and showed them some videos. It was a totally controlled world. I remember thinking: I keep seeing (which is one of the lines in the film) that same smart bomb going down that chimney blowing up that factory . . . There was video footage from that war made by people hired by a public relations firm that was working for the administration.[34]

And another critic wrote: "while we may feel fairly certain that the footage from the Gulf war wasn't actually filmed in a sound studio in

Burbank, it's true that the press was given such limited and controlled access that the government effectively shaped the news coverage."[35]

The linking of *Wag the Dog* to the Clinton administration seems logical, insofar as the war actions in Kosovo and Somalia, both considered questionable by many historians, came on the heels of the plummeting polls for President Clinton as the media continued to have a field day with his alleged sexual adventures. And, in the 2000s, the theme and plot of *Wag the Dog* are cited as direct analogies to President George W. Bush's fading popularity and the invasion of Iraq.

Wag the Dog itself not only gives a fictional example of creating a war as a political distraction, but in the film gives a real-life example when one of the characters justifies what they're doing by saying:

> So why did we invade Grenada? A terrorist bomb killed all those Marines in Beirut, the White House was taking flak, and suddenly our Marines were landing on a Caribbean island few people had heard of, everybody was tying yellow ribbons 'round old oak trees, and Clint Eastwood was making the movie. The Grenada invasion produced more decorations than combatants. By the time it was over, Ronald Reagan's presidency had proven the republic could still flex its muscle – we could take out a Caribbean Marxist regime at will, Cuba notwithstanding.[36]

Critic Janet Maslin summed up the impact of *Wag the Dog*: "*Wag the Dog* takes a stance that American public policy may be founded on fraud in high places, and that there is no public outpouring too spontaneous-looking to be manipulated by political puppeteers . . . *Wag the Dog* makes it impossible to trust any image-enhancing gesture that attracts national media attention."[37]

Two years earlier, in 1995, documentary filmmaker Michael Moore produced the feature entertainment film *Canadian Bacon* in which "in order to gain a strong platform for re-election, the president of the United States does the unthinkable and declares war on our neighbor to the north, Canada."[38]

The film *Bulworth* had the misfortune to open in 1998 against competition such as *Titanic*, *As Good As It Gets*, and another political protest picture, *Primary Colors*. Although it did well at the box office in its early weeks, it did not get the publicity it needed to become a staple for the American public. It did, however, make its mark with young Americans, who saw it as the coolest, most hip movie on American

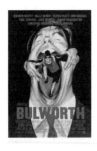

Figure 8.3
Bulworth (1998)

politics in cinema history. Roger Ebert, in his review of the film, encapsulated its theme: "You realize that if all politicians were as outspoken as Bulworth, the fragile structure of our system would collapse, and we would have to start all over again. The movie suggests that virtually everything said in public by a politician is spin. 'Spin control' is merely the name for spin they didn't get away with."[39]

Warren Beatty directed himself as *Bulworth*, a Senator who is in a deep depression and who makes a deal with an insurance executive for an exorbitant personal life-insurance policy in exchange for which he would block a bill requiring insurance companies to insure every American, regardless of their ability to pay. The Senator has arranged for a hit man to kill him (Bulworth). Expecting now to be assassinated at any time, Bulworth goes on his last speaking campaign, freed from the political platitudes and promises that were heretofore necessary for political success. In his speeches he begins to tell the truth, mixing obscenities with rhyming rap and hip-hop rhythms. For example, he tells an African-American audience in a church that his party – the Democrats – doesn't really care about them because they don't contribute big monies to campaigns and that politicians come to Black neighborhoods only for photo opportunities. He tells audiences that the government caters to and is controlled by corporate America, such as big oil, at their expense. In a meeting with Hollywood executives, he says that people in the film industry, the Jews in particular, are greedy, and that they produce nothing but "crap." Meeting with corporate executives, he says that the only ones to whom he pays attention are the ones who pay for his 30-second TV spots. On a TV show he raps about the plight of the underprivileged, the buying of the government by the rich, the horrid state of the schools, the crime in poor neighborhoods, the mistreatment of Blacks in America and the government's indifference. In one interview, when the question of his obscenities is raised, he says: "Obscenity? . . . We got Newt [Gingrich, Speaker of the House] blaming teenage moms, that's the real obscenity that black folks live with every day – trying to believe what the Democrats and Republicans say." He advocates the need for universal health care – contrary to the deal he made with the insurance industry. In short, he says all the things that a politician, or any presumably sane person is a self-serving materialistic society, is not supposed to say – a modern parable of "The Emperor's New Clothes." The more he speaks, the more the moralistic status quo of both political parties appears to be mean-spirited and corrupt.

The truth, indeed, does make Bulworth free. With the help of a young Black woman who he meets during an evening of campaigning that turns into scenes of hilarious debauchery in a drug crib, he not only moves away from his depression, but falls in love with the young woman. He wants to live, after all, and the audience is held in suspense as he tries to reach the anonymous hit man to call off his assassination. It becomes clear that his deal with the insurance executive was a mistake. At the end of the film, just as it appears that he and his new love are starting a new, exciting life, he is shot – not by the hit man, but by corporate America – the insurance industry – that will allow dissidents and whistle-blowers to go just so far.

While some critics attacked *Bulworth* for its "leftist" philosophy, most critics lauded it. "Hollywood rarely embraces political satire on this level, but Beatty's lampoon shows not only how much we need this kind of commentary, but also how entertaining it can be . . . [it] spills the blunt, unvarnished truth about race, class, and economics";[40] "*Bulworth* is a full-frontal assault on the shallowness of the political campaign process."[41] *Bulworth* is a devastating look at politics and politicians along with *Wag the Dog*, more so than other political protest films because they were willing to offend their audiences with a candor that made their audiences think.

That same year, 1998, another political satire, *Primary Colors*, was released. Based on a book by a then-anonymous former Clinton aide, it is the purported story of the very thinly disguised Clinton presidential campaign of 1992. The film goes beyond the façade popularized by the media and presents the protagonists, especially Clinton, in a "warts-and-all" critical light, concentrating on the negative aspects of a personality under the stress of a campaign and purportedly revealing the hypocrisy between the public figure and platforms and the private ones. Roger Ebert noted that the film "resonates with its parallels to the lives of Bill and Hillary Clinton."[42] The charismatic Southern governor running for president is a philanderer barely abided by his politically pragmatic wife. While the nonfiction aspect of the film is clear, it is difficult to determine how much of the characterizations of the Clintons, their philosophies and behavior, and the organization and operation of the campaign is fictionalized. As portrayed in the film, are the Clintons idealistic public servants or ruthless politicians? Do they stand on ethical principles or succumb to political expediency? If nothing else, however, *Primary Colors* follows in the footsteps of previous movies by making clear that what you see as the voting public is not what is actually behind the smoke and mirrors or, more accurately, the spins, TV spots, and sound-bites.

Another 1998 film uses an historic event in precolonial America to comment directly on politicians and a political situation extant at the time it was originally written as a play. Arthur Miller's play *The Crucible* dealt with the suppression of free speech and the imposition of harsh penalties for those not cooperating with the inquisitors. In 1692, 20 people accused of witchcraft were executed in Salem, Massachusetts, including some who were known to be innocent but who refused to accuse friends and neighbors of being witches. *The Crucible* was meant as a direct analogy to McCarthyism, the period of witch-hunts for alleged Communists or communist sympathizers when (as noted in chapter 1 in this book and in this chapter in the discussion of *The Front*) innocent people were punished for refusing to accuse their friends and neighbors – and many people avoided punishment by the official government inquisitors by naming friends and neighbors. The film reflected two themes: The denial or free speech and thought and the complicity of the authorities in facilitating demagogic politicians to use the witch-hunts to aggrandize their power. Because of its artistic brilliance and pertinence to real life, one New York drama critic wrote that the play, without palpable reservation, was one of the greatest American plays of all time. The movie did not fare as well at the box office.

It is worth noting here that a couple of years earlier another movie that dealt with suppression of free speech, unlike most other political protest films, was without the obligatory "good" and "bad" protagonists. *The People vs. Larry Flynt*, produced in 1996, dealt strictly with First Amendment rights. The film is essentially a biography of Flynt, his preoccupation and occupation with sex and sexual merchandise, such as a strip club and newsletters and magazines, in particular *Hustler*, that many people, including politicians making political points, considered obscene. He is limned as a sleazy character who sells sleaze. Ironically, he is paralyzed from the waist down after an assassination attempt. In one court trial on charges of obscenity, he defends his rights of freedom of speech and press by saying, "If you take a picture of someone committing an act of murder, they'll put you on the cover of *Newsweek*, maybe even give you the Pulitzer Prize, but if you take a picture of a woman's naked body, they'll put you in jail." He shows footage of people having sex and footage of the atrocities of the Holocaust and asks, "Which is more obscene? All I'm guilty of is bad taste!" Ultimately he is sued for libel by the Reverend Jerry Falwell, a fundamentalist right-wing preacher who had a dominant effect on politics and politicians. Flynt is described in terms supported by a great many people: "antisocial," "disturbed," "immoral." The case goes all the way to the Supreme Court. Flynt wins on First Amendment grounds. He says, in the film, asserting the principle of freedom of speech and the sanctity of it in government, "If they'll protect a scumbag like me, then they'll protect all of you."[43] Robert Ebert sums up the film's purpose: "*The People vs. Larry Flynt* argues that the freedom of speech must apply to unpopular speech, or it is meaningless."[44]

In the 2000s, perhaps because of the increasingly serious problems facing the United States and its people, political protest films began to get more specific in their targets, as differentiated from generalized satire. Three films, all released in 2005, are key examples. One film protested political leaders putting big oil interests above that of its citizens, another protested the conspiracy between government and its politicians and profits-at-all-costs of the international pharmaceutical industry, and still another attempted to draw a direct parallel between the 2000s erosion of freedom of speech by revisiting, in quasi-documentary form, the 1950s McCarthy period.

The latter was 2005's *Good Night and Good Luck*. *New York Times* movie critic A. O. Scott described it this way: "Burnishing the legend of Edward R. Murrow, the CBS newsman who in the 1940's and 50's established a tradition of journalistic integrity his profession has scrambled to live up to since, *Good Night and Good Luck* is a passionate, thoughtful essay on power truth-telling and responsibility."[45]

While *Good Night and Good Luck* concentrates on the integrity of Murrow and his writer-producer, Fred Friendly, in daring to question and then directly attack the neofascism of McCarthy and a compliant government of his fellow politicians, and their difficulty and

Figure 8.4 *Good Night and Good Luck* (2005)

determination to do so in face of opposition from advertisers, establishment powers, and their network, it presents the dangers of rogue politicians to democracy and freedom and speech and thought today as well as a half-century ago. As one critic put it, *"Good Night and Good Luck* has relevance in today's polarized political climate, a time of growing doubt about the motivation and honesty of politicians and policymakers. These latter politicians' years of insinuation that those who disagree with them are disloyal and unpatriotic echoes McCarthy's tactics of 50 years ago."[46]

Another critic wrote that the film was "Masterfully crafted, wonderfully acted, and an undeniably cutting commentary on fear in the '50's that resonates even louder today."[47] Director of and performer in the movie George Clooney explained the movie's approach to contemporary issues:

> When you hear Edward R. Murrow saying that we mustn't confuse dissent with disloyalty and we should lead not only in the area of bombs but in the area of ideas, and when he says "We can't defend freedom abroad by deserting it at home" – I think those have a lot to do with things that are going on today.[48]

Clooney also stated: "I was sick of the idea that any sort of dissent would be considered unpatriotic. To me, the most patriotic thing you could do was question your government."[49]

Good Night and Good Luck illustrates the power of the media and the perils it poses to a democratic society when it abandons its responsibility for political and/or economic expediency. As *Times* critic A. O. Scott stated in his review, "The free press may be the oxygen of a democratic society, but it is always clouded by particles and pollutants, from the vanity or cowardice of individual journalists to the impersonal pressures of state power and the profit motive."[50]

In *The Constant Gardener* the wife of a British diplomat in Kenya discovers that an international pharmaceutical company has been testing an unproven and clearly dangerous drug on unsuspecting third-world subjects, causing illness and death. Her investigation comes too close to the truth and the international cartel has her and a co-investigator murdered. Within a riveting plot of good guys and mostly bad guys, and of fellow diplomats and their government offices catering to and covering up the misdeeds of the drug company, her husband tries to discover the truth of what happened. While a concentrated attack on the unscrupulousness of the pharmaceutical industry (a decade before the movie was made, the Pfizer pharmaceutical company was accused of doing virtually the same kind of testing in an African country), *The Constant Gardener* exposes the link between government, politicians, and the unethical corporate world. In his review of the movie, A. O. Scott wrote in the *New York Times* that the "film actually bothers to say something about global politics . . . In pointedly applying President Bush's phrase 'axis of evil' to multinational corporations rather than to rogue states, the movie shows a willingness to risk didacticism in the service of encouraging discussion."[51]

The realism of *The Constant Gardener* in regard to the power of political-corporate globalism hits home. The movie does not have a happy ending.

Syriana (2005), like *The Constant Gardener* independently produced, is a frightening exposé and protest of US oil interests dictating the

foreign policy of the country, even to the extent of starting a war to enhance oil-industry profits. Fragmented at first, then pieced together as connections become clearer, *Syriana* is generally based on a memoir by a former CIA operative who gradually becomes disillusioned with America's oil-dictated foreign policy subterfuges in the Middle East. A. O. Scott's review in the *New York Times* describes the film as "four main storylines . . . each one subject to enough twists and reversals to make plot summary a treacherous exercise."[52] Scott finds plausible the film's contention "that oil companies, law firms

Figure 8.5
Syriana (2005)

and Middle Eastern regimes . . . are engaged in semi-clandestine collusion, to control the global oil supply and thus influence the destinies of millions of people."[53]

Terrorism, money, and power are key elements of the movie. Connections of the content of the film to the Iraq War are inescapable. As columnist Mark Levine wrote,

Given the increasing numbers of Americans who believe the Bush administration deliberately misled the country to justify the Iraq invasion, many film-goers will no doubt be willing to accept the film's argument that America's thirst for oil – not the threat of terrorism, and certainly not a concern for human rights – drives the country's policies in the Middle East, even when these policies violate our core ideals.[54]

Levine also states that two reasons the United States plans to stay in Iraq for an extended period are "oil and military bases – subjects that remain largely untouchable in polite discourse in Washington or Baghdad. On that note, *Syriana* hits closer to home than most politicians on either side of the aisle would care to admit."[55]

The reemergence of political protest films in the 2000s has prompted comment and support from key filmmakers. Steven Spielberg, for example, stated:

these movies are asking sensitive questions about racial intolerance and Middle East politics . . . you see all of these political movies coming out at the same time, out of the watershed of politics. Some of it is due to our own insecurity about the voices representing us in government right now. We feel like our government has set us adrift, and we're trying to make our voices heard. We're telling them to be worried about these things.[56]

Whether Hollywood will follow this lead and, if it does, whether the films will have substantial impact on the audience and on the subjects of the protests has been questioned by many critics. Film historian Ernest Giglio wrote that "describing film as an agent of political and social change is problematical since the empirical evidence that would prove a causal relationship between film and political action has yet to be firmly established,"[57] but noted that "exposure to a clearly delivered political message in a well-crafted film can have a short-term influence on a particular attitude,[58] and that the box-office and critical successes of many of the political protest films indicate a positive factor for Hollywood producing such films because "the film industry is . . . a for-profit business" and "depends on public acceptance and support."[59]

Other writers believe that such films do have an impact and are viable. Critic Kenneth Turan stated that "Syriana tackles real-world issues under its guise as Hollywood genre entertainment,"[60] and Bob Strauss, in an article appropriately entitled "Movies with agendas are challenging audiences and sparking debate like no time since the '70s," stated that "the unstable nature of current events seems to ensure that, for the near future, anyway, politics and film will continue to be bedfellows."[61]

Notes

1   de la Torre, Christopher R., in a paper submitted in a "Pictures of Protest" course, Emerson College, Boston, March 21, 2004.
2   See Mark E. Neely, Jr.'s 1992 Pulitzer Prize history work, *The Fate of Liberty, Abraham Lincoln and Civil Liberties* (New York: Barnes & Noble, new edn, 2007).
3   Matthews, Chris, *American* (New York: The Free Press, 2002), p. 33.
4   *Ibid.*, p. 34.
5   Smoodin, Eric, " 'Compulsory viewing for every citizen': *Mr. Smith* and the rhetoric of redemption," in Tinkcom, Matthew and Amy Villarejo, compilers, *Keyframes: Popular Cinema and Cultural Studies* (London: Routledge, 2001), pp. 343–58.
6   Scott, Ian, *American Politics in Hollywood Film* (Chicago: Fitzroy Dearborn, 2000), p. 29.
7   Maltin, Leonard, "The Great McGinty," *Leonard Maltin's 2003 Movie and Video Guide* (New York: Penguin Books, 2002), pp. 554–5.
8   Crowther, Bosley, "State of the Union," *New York Times*, April 23, 1948. http://movies.nytimes.com/movie/review?_r=1&res.
9   Bozzola, Lucia, *All Movie Guide*. Review summary of *The Candidate*. *http://movies.nytimes.com/movie/8002/The Candidate/overview.*
10 Canby, Vincent, "The Candidate," *New York Times*, June 30, 1972. http://movies.nytimes.com/movie/refview?_r=1&res.
11 Bozzola, Review summary of *The Candidate*.
12 www.rottentomatoes.com/click/movie100794/reviews.php?critic=columns &sortby.
13 Canby, Vincent, "All the President's Men," *New York Times*, April 8, 1976. http://movies.nytimes.com/com/movie/review?res=9C0DEED.
14 Schneider, Steven Jay, ed., *1001 Movies You Must See Before You Die* (New York: Quintet Publishing/Barron's, 2003), p. 742.
15 Fountain, Clark, "J.F.K." overview, *All Movie Guide*. http://movies.nytimes. com/movie/25653/JFK/overview.
16 Canby, Vincent, "J.F.K.," *New York Times*, December 20, 1991. http://movies. nytimes.com/movie/review?_r=1&res.

17 *Ibid.*

18 Fountain, "*J.F.K.*" overview.

19 Rogers, Stephen F., "Unraveling *Nixon*: Some Truths Are Not Self-Evident," *Films in Review*, March/April, 1996, pp. 63–4.

20 Keyishian, Harry, *Screening Politic* (Lanham, MD: The Scarecrow Press, 2003), pp. 31–2.

21 Matthews, Chris, *American* (New York: The Free Press, 2002), p. 111.

22 Walker, Martin, "Clinton's Hollywood," *Sight and Sound*, September, 1993, pp. 12–14.

23 Paweczak, Andy, review of *Nixon*, *Films in Review*, March/April, 1996, p. 63.

24 Sharrett, Christopher, "The Belly of the Beast: Oliver Stone's *Nixon* and the American Nightmare," *Cineaste*, 1996.

25 Rogers, "Unraveling *Nixon*: Some Truths Are Not Self-Evident," p. 64.

26 Christie, Andrew, "Weep for our lost cynicism – *Wag the Dog* keeps on barking," Common dreams News Center, September 22, 2003. www.commondreams.Org/views03/0922-11.htm.

27 Filmwatching, a solemn American obligation," *The Daily Cougar Online Archives*, January 27, 1998. www.stp.uh.edu/vol63/78OpEd3/7812798/7812798.html.

28 Berardinelli, James, *Wag the Dog*. www.rottentomatoes.com/click/movie-1083028/reviews.php?critic=columns&sortby.

29 Adiego, Walter, "*Wag the Dog* howls at corruption." *SFgate*, December 26, 1997. www.sfgate.com/cgi-bin/article.cgi?f=/e/a/1998/01/02WEEKEND7557.dtl.

30 Berardinelli, *Wag the Dog*.

31 Lasalle, Mick, *San Francisco Chronicle*, January 2, 1998.

32 Pear, Robert, "U.S.Videos, for TV News, Come under Scrutiny," 2004.

33 Wickens, Barbara, "Hollywood or Washington," *McClean's Magazine*, February 9, 1998, p. 14.

34 Keogh, Peter, *Boston Phoenix*, January 4, 1998. www.filmvault.com/filmvault/boston/w/wagthedog2.html.

35 Richter, Stacey, *Tucson Weekly*, January 20, 1998. www.filmvault.com/filmvault/tw/w/wagthedog.html.

36 Ebert, Roger, "*Wag the Dog*," *Chicago Sun-Times*. www.rottentomatoes.com/ckick/movie-1083028/reviews.php?critic+columns&sortby=default&page=1&rid=86751.

37 Maslin, Janet, "*Wag the Dog*: If the Going Gets Tough, Get a Pet or Start a War," *New York Times*, December 26, 1997. www.nytimes.com/library/film/122697wag-film-review.html.

38 Maltin, Leonard, *Leonard Maltin's 2003 Movie and Video Guide* (New York: Penguin Books, 2002), p. 206.

39 Ebert, Roger, Movie Reviews: *"Bulworth,"* *Chicago Sun-Times*, May 22, 1998. www.suntimes.com/ebert/ebert_reviews/1998/05/052202.html.

40 Githmann, Edward, "Beatty's Rap Hilarious *Bulworth*: the truth sets a senator free," *SFgate*, May 22, 1998. www.sfgate.com/cgi-bin/article.cgi? f=/c/a/1998/05/22DD19624.DTL.

41 Berardinelli, James, *Bulworth*. www.rottentomatoes.com/click/movie-1083028/reviews.php?critic=columns&sortyby.

42 Ebert, Roger, *"Primary Colors,"* *Chicago Sun-Times*, March 3, 1998. www.suntimes.com/ebert/ebert_reviews/1998/03/032001.html.

43 Much of this material about *The People Vs. Larry Flynt* is adapted from a paper by Rob Wilson, submitted for a Pictures of Protest course at Emerson College, April 26, 2004.

44 Ebert, Roger, *"The People Vs. Larry Flynt,"* *Chicago Sun-Times*, December 12, 1996. www.suntimes.com/ebert/ebert_reviews/1996/12/122701.html.

45 Scott, A. O., "News in Black, White and Shades of Gray," *New York Times*, September 23, 2005. http://movies.nytimes.com/2005/09/23/movies/23luck.html.

46 Wirt, John, *"Good Night* relevant in today's political climate. www. 2theadvocate.com/entertainment/movies/reviews/2123592.html.

47 Venable, John, *"Good Night and Good Luck* 10/10." www.supercalafragalistic. com/goodnightgoodluckreview.htm.

48 Persall, Steve, "The Left's Mr. Right," *St. Petersburg Times*, March 5, 2006. www.sptimes.com/2006/03/05/Floridian/The_left_s_Mr_Right.shtml.

49 Edwards, Gavin, "George Clooney Renegade of the Year," *Rolling Stone*, December 15, 2005. www.rollingstone.com/news/story/8957203/george/clooney/"rnd.

50 Scott, "News in Black, White and Shades of Gray."

51 Scott, A. O., "Digging up the Truth in a Heart of Darkness," *New York Times*, August 31, 2005. http://movies.nytimes.com/2005/08/31/movies/31gard.html.

52 Scott, A. O., *"Syriana,"* *New York Times*, November 23, 2005. http://movies.nytimes.com/2205/11/23/movies/23syri.html.

53 *Ibid.*

54 Levine, Mark, *"Syriana* and Iraq," *Mother Jones*, November 30, 2005. www.motherjones.com/arts/feature/2005/11/syriana.html.

55 *Ibid.*

56 Persall, "The Left's Mr. Right."

57 Giglio, Ernest, *Here's Looking at You: Hollywood, Film, and Production* (New York: Peter Lang, 2000), p. 15.

58 *Ibid.*, p. 16.

59 *Ibid.*, p. 208.

60 Turan, Kenneth, "*Syriana*," November 23, 2005. www.calendarlive.com/movies/turan/cl-et-syriana23nov23.0.7214793.story.

61 Strauss, Bob, "Movies with agendas are challenging audiences and sparking debate like no time since the '70s," *Pasadena Star-News*, September 3, 2004. http://u.pasadenastarnews.com/Stories/0.1413.214.html.

9

Homophobia

Who's a bigot?

Until relatively recent years, dealing with homophobia in films was a prime phobia in Hollywood. Despite the prevalence of many gays and lesbians in all aspects of moviemaking, from producing to performing, the homophobic attitudes of much of America – or, at least, what was promoted as such by the media – kept Hollywood away from protesting the bigotry that affected personally even many of those who were in positions to tackle the subject. In fact, Hollywood went to extreme lengths to cover up homosexuality in many of its stars. Perhaps the prime example was Rock Hudson, a macho-type leading man whose death from AIDS revealed his homosexuality and, ironically, opened the door for franker discussion and wider inclusion of the subject and homosexual characters in Hollywood films. Over the years many Hollywood films had homosexual characters, some implied, some portrayed for stereotypical comic effect, some written sympathetically, some given serious characterizations and plot lines. The Victorian morality of America played into the hands of right-wing radical religious fundamentalists – the same groups that continue to play influential roles exceeding their actual numbers in American society and, especially, in politics. Hollywood stayed in the closet, many of its personalities paying lip service to equal rights while, by and large, resisting any protest in their films of the denial of those equal rights to homosexuals – gays and lesbians. Bisexual and transgender characters are still closeted.

A turning point for homosexuals and for the public's realization of the bigotry against them were the Stonewall Riots of 1969. Stonewall was a Greenwich Village, New York City bar frequented by homosexuals that was periodically raided by the police – solely because of the gender and lifestyle preferences of its patrons. Other bars not considered gay hangouts were left alone. One evening, after a raid, the patrons rebelled and took to the streets in protest. They were joined by thousands, gays and non-gays, the protest lasting three days. The attention of the public in general and the support of the non-bigoted public made a difference.

> Prior to that summer there was little public expression of the lives and experiences of gays and lesbians. The Stonewall Riots marked the beginning of the gay liberation movement that has transformed the oppression of gays and lesbians into pride and action. In the past twenty-five years [as of 1994] we have all been witness to an astonishing flowering of gay culture that has changed this country and beyond, forever.[1]

It wasn't until 1993 that a mainstream Hollywood blockbuster movie addressed the subject of homophobic discrimination and AIDS – misrepresented by the media for years as only a homosexual disease – in a direct dramatic manner. *Philadelphia*, although criticized by many as misleading and wishy-washy – we'll discuss that later in this chapter – was a breakthrough in reaching the generally uninformed and apathetic public about the problems gays faced in our society in terms of AIDS. "There are better films to be made about AIDS," as one source stated, "but this is the one with the most impact."[2]

In the 1970s and 1980s films about homosexuals and with homosexual characters began to come out of Hollywood; by the 1990s and 2000s homosexuality was the key subject of an increasing number of movies, portrayed in a positive light with non-stereotyped homosexual characters. These films fell into three general categories.

Camp: these were homosexual characters who were bigger than life. They were sometimes outrageous, usually comic. Some of the films were or bordered on fantasy. Frequently there were musical elements, fancy costumes, showy spectacles. Some had drag queens as key characters.

Lifestyles: These films focused on the everyday lives of gays and lesbians. Sometimes they were major characters, sometimes minor characters or parts of sub-plots. The films explored the relationship between two men or two women as it might the relationship between a man and a woman. They showed gays and lesbians as a regular part of society.

Dramatic: some of these films dealt with the everyday prejudice and violence against gays and lesbians, with their serious difficulties in a homophobic society, of human beings trying to survive in anti-gay situations. Frequently, there was a shock aspect, to point out starkly what homophobic hate did, to make the audience aware of the problem.

Some recent films, such as *Brokeback Mountain*, delve into both the "lifestyle" (ordinary people finding out that they are gay) and the "dramatic" (society's intolerance forces tragedy) aspects.

The transition of gay themes in films reflected the political and social transitions in society. As the media paid more and more attention to the viciousness of anti-gay elements and of organized hate groups[3] and the public became more and more outraged over the treatment of homosexuals, including atrocities such as the torture and murder of Matthew Shepard, films changed. They moved from avoidance of homosexual implications to the subtle inclusion of homosexuality as a hidden agenda (allegedly in some segments of films with actors such as Rock Hudson and Montgomery Clift, who Hollywood forced to hide their sexuality), to the inclusion of homosexual characters in the plot line, to material that not only showed but protested unfair, bigoted, and/or criminal treatment of gays and lesbians.

> In a hundred years of movies, homosexuality has only rarely been depicted on the screen. When it did appear, it was there as something to laugh at – or something to pity – or even as something to fear. These were fleeting images, but they were unforgettable, and they left a lasting legacy. Hollywood, that great maker of myths, taught straight people what to think about gay people . . . and gay people what to think about themselves.[4]

The last decade of the twentieth century and the first decade of the twenty-first, reflecting progress in society's attitudes (excluding the still bigoted attitudes of some fundamentalist religious groups, hate groups, those who support their bigotry, and politicians who cater to prejudiced voters), have seen increased attention by Hollywood to the substantial part of the world that is homosexual. But progress is relative. Both society and Hollywood have a long way to go. In that same period hate crimes against homosexuals (and Jews, people of color – especially Blacks – and other so-called minorities) have increased, inflamed and abetted by the political far right and countenanced by the complacency or anti-gay attitudes of many on the non-radical political right.

Since the 1990s, Hollywood has improved its portrayal of gay and lesbian characters. The popularity of films such as *The Birdcage, Philadelphia, To Wong Foo, Flawless,* and *In & Out* demonstrates that audiences can and do enjoy films with gay and lesbian characters. But despite these advances, critics say the industry is still too cautious in its portrayals of gay themes, characters, and experiences. Hollywood films are designed to appeal to as large an audience as possible and producers fear that focusing on gay and lesbian themes risks offending a large portion of the audience, as well as potential investors.[5]

Perhaps the best history of homosexuality in films is Vito Russo's *The Celluloid Closet.*[6] It was made into an award-winning television documentary in 1995. The SONY Pictures website provides an excellent overview.[7] In early films homosexuals were sources of humor, males portraying their roles as "sissies" with feminine traits. Some of these films were *Algy, the Miner* in 1912, *Behind the Screen* in 1916, *Wanderer of the West* in 1927, and *Our Betters* in 1933. In some cases, gender reverse was true, with actresses dressing like males or affecting male traits, implying that they were lesbians, although the terms homosexual and lesbian were not used and any inference was in a presumed snickering chuckle by the audience. In the 1920s – the "Roaring Twenties," as they were called – Bohemianism, abetted by the thrill of breaking the laws of Prohibition, crept into the lifestyles of those Americans who could afford to be Bohemian. The nightclubs of France and cabarets of Germany transported their *joie de vivre* to America. For many people, the American scene, including its films, was becoming too risqué, too raunchy, too ribald. In the 1930 movie, *Morocco,* for example, the character played by Marlene Dietrich kisses another woman on the lips. Although it not suggested that the character is lesbian, it caused a sensation. In 1933, Greta Garbo played the title role in *Queen Christina,* the sixteenth-century Swedish monarch, who was a lesbian. While the producers invented a false heterosexual relationship for her in order to appease criticism, other indications made it clear that she was, indeed, lesbian.

Many people believed Hollywood had gone too far, and religious and other groups lobbied for federal censorship. The movie moguls decided it would be better to censor themselves and the MPPDA (Motion Picture Producers and Distributors of America) established a code of ethics and an office to enforce it. The code empowered the office to edit and censor screenplays and films that appeared to be sympathetic to crime, wrongdoing, evil, or sin, including "sex perversion" or any inference of it. Homosexuals were considered perverted and sinful. In 1934 Joseph I. Breen was director of the MPPDA code. Breen was considered by many to be a bigot, homophobe, racist, and anti-Semite. In addition, the Catholic Church established its own morals-rating organization, the Legion of Decency, threatening boycotts if Hollywood did not comply.

Sympathetic homosexual characters began to disappear and were replaced by homosexual villains, their evildoings (even as murderers, for example) compounded by or due to their homosexuality. Women as well as men fell into this category, as exemplified in the 1936 movie *Dracula's Daughter* and Alfred Hitchcock's famed *Rebecca* in 1940. This carried through the 1940s. In 1945, for example, the highly acclaimed film, *The Lost Weekend*, had its protagonist changed from a sexually confused alcoholic to simply an alcoholic. In *Crossfire* (1947), considered one of the seminal films protesting anti-Semitism, the sympathetic character who was murdered was changed from being gay to Jewish. In *Rope* (1948) the two young psychopathic murderers were clearly gay, although no reference was made to their sexuality. A 1950 prison film, *Caged*, portrays the female warden as a lesbian attempting to abuse the story's protagonist, a female prisoner.

The 1950s were a time of conformity, including repressed sexuality. Writer Richard Dyer summed up the period this way: "We could only express ourselves indirectly, just as people on the screen could only express themselves indirectly . . . the characters are in the closet, the movie is in the closet, and we were in the closet."[8] The homosexual content and references in several of Tennessee Williams's plays were excised when the plays were adapted for the cinema. But some amelioration of the negative and non-portrayals began to creep in. In *Gentlemen Prefer Blondes* (1953), voluptuous Jane Russell appears in a gym with a group of male bodybuilders who pointedly pay no attention to her. In *Pillow Talk* (1959), Rock Hudson (gay in real life) plays a macho male pretending to be gay in order to seduce a woman. In *Some Like It Hot* (1959), two sympathetic men dress in drag in order to escape the mob. In 1955, in *Rebel Without a Cause*, one of the key sympathetic characters, a male, is harassed because he appears to act in a feminine way, and ultimately is killed. In 1956, in *Tea and Sympathy*, a male college student is similarly harassed by other students. Historical films such as *Ben Hur* (1959) and *Spartacus* (1960) could show characters who historically were homosexual, but by and large homosexuality, in society and in Hollywood films, remained in the closet. The year 1960 was a breakthrough in American films with the production of *The Children's Hour*, adapted from the Broadway play. Two women who run a girls' school are accused by a vicious student of having lesbian relations. This was considered an unforgivable sin and a scandal for the school. Our sympathy goes to the two women – and the screenwriter's point is made when our sympathy remains even after we discover that one of the women is, in fact, in love with the other. The Code was further eroded with the production of *Advise and Consent* in 1962, in which a sympathetic US Senator is blackmailed because of a past homosexual affair. Yet, at the same time, the psychotic, misfit, unhappy, evil homosexual character continued to be a part of many films. *Walk on the Wild Side* in 1962 and *The Detective* in 1968 are examples of such films.

It wasn't until the 1970s, after Stonewall and after Breen was gone, along with the bigoted enforcement of the code, that – as noted earlier – movie-making became more sensitive to homosexuality and homosexuals. In 1970, *The Boys in the Band* presented what many considered the first honest portrayal of homosexuals. In the movie, "gay men are not placed in a good light, but neither is the society that causes them to be repressed and self-hating . . . they are presented as complex and human, with failings, virtues, prejudices, and desires."[9] In other words, Hollywood finally offered a film in which homosexuals were simply people like everyone else. In 1972, *Cabaret* celebrated homosexuals in pre-World-War-II Germany – although they were, along with millions of others, annihilated once the Nazis consolidated their power. Sometimes the old comedy stereotypes returned, as in *Car Wash* in 1976, in which the homosexual is an African-American. A camp cult movie of 1975, *The Rocky Horror Picture Show*, featured a character who became a gay icon. A 1982 film, *Making Love*, was praised for its artistry, in which the intimate relationship of two men is shown on the screen in the same light as would be an intimate relationship between a heterosexual couple, one man leaving his wife to be with a man he loves.

Other films in the late 1970s and in the 1980s portrayed homosexual relationships as part of people's everyday lives, not necessarily as part of the major themes or actions of the films and only by implication as political or social issues. Some of these films are *After the Game* (1979 – two women find love with each other); *Personal Best* (1981 – two women athletes have an affair); *The Hunger* (1983 – a beautiful woman discards her male lover for another, sexy woman); *Lianna* (1983 – a housewife discovers a new life as a lesbian); *Parting Glances* (1986 – relationships among a number of gay men in Manhattan); *Desert Hearts* (1986 – a woman seeking divorce meets and falls in love with another woman); and *Torch Song Trilogy* (1988 – a gay man with an adopted child seeks a lasting relationship). Nevertheless, a number of films still showed gays and lesbians in a negative light, as victimizers rather than victims, reinforcing homophobia in society and motivating hate of and even physical attacks on homosexuals. Some of these films are *Cruising* (1980), in which gay men are shown as vicious predators, and *Windows* (1980), about a homicidal lesbian.

As noted above, the 1990s saw a step forward in Hollywood's production of films that recognized the realities of homosexuality, more and more of these films protesting homophobia. The most noteworthy and the one that probably had the greatest impact is *Thelma and Louise* (1991). More than sexuality, it shows the bonding of two women in deep affection, a love beyond gender. Some of the other films are: *Priscilla, Queen of the Desert* (1994 – a now-cult movie of two drag queens and a transvestite); *Late Bloomers* (1995 – a married and a single woman find love and fight homophobic friends, family, and community to stay together); *It's in the Water* (1996 – a brave few stand up to protesters of an AIDS hospice); *The Birdcage* (1996 – a son raised by a gay man and his lover brings his fiancée and ultra-conservative future in-laws to meet his "parents"); *In & Out* (1997 – a former student outs a teacher who denies his homosexuality but then must face up to it); *Defying Gravity* (1998 – two gay lovers try to find peace with their sexuality in an intolerant society); *Edge of Seventeen* (1998 – a gay teenager, in the closet, tries to understand and deal with his sexuality).

Arguably, among the films that have had the most impact, politically, socially, and artistically, were *And the Band Played On* (1993), *Philadelphia* (1993), *Boys Don't Cry* (1999), and *Brokeback Mountain* (2005). All of these were serious dramatic films, differentiated from comedy, satire, and light films such as *The Birdcage* (1996, adapted from a French film).

Many social historians consider *And the Band Played On* a breakthrough movie in dealing directly and candidly with an issue of special importance at the time to homosexuals and generally ignored or hidden by establishment sources attempting to keep homosexuality in a national closet. The film deals with the 1980s and the then-growing AIDS epidemic. AIDS was considered a gay men's disease, principally because its incidence appeared to be strongest in San Francisco, a city where tolerance of many different lifestyles was stronger than virtually anyplace else in America and where homosexuals found more acceptance and personal safety and less discriminatory prejudice. Homophobes and homophobic hate groups, including a surprisingly large number of churches and religious organizations, spewed their hate by claiming that AIDS was God's punishment for being gay. "Gay cancer," as some called it, was supposedly visited upon homosexuals for their "crime" of being gay. The film deals with the difficulties and frustrations of researchers attempting to find a cause and a cure for AIDS in an atmosphere of uncaring and frequently antagonistic public and private sectors. It showed people verbally attacking homosexuals, including AIDS victims, accusing them of bringing the wrath of God upon themselves by their presumed lifestyle "choices." It showed the long-range effects of AIDS. In the film researchers and gay activists attempt to raise awareness of the problem both among gay populations and in the federal administration, with little success. The point is made that with conservative Ronald Reagan as the new president (he approved the listing of ketchup as a vegetable in school lunches for needy children), it is highly unlikely that the government will support any research for or assistance to AIDS victims.[10]

Although set in the early 1980s, the purpose of the 1993 production, in a much more understanding, tolerant, and self-interested society – by this time the heterosexual world knew that it was a disease that affected all people in all lifestyles everywhere – was to energize the public into supporting and participating in the continuing and much needed support for AIDS research. Some top Hollywood stars, including Alan Alda, Richard Gere, Lily Tomlin, Ian McKellen, Steve Martin, and Angelica Huston, some of whom were gay, worked on this film without their usual high salaries.[11]

Critics echoed the feelings of many who saw the film: "Gays, devastated by the epidemic, are portrayed as persons instead of stereotypes"[12]; "The movie catches various phases of gay life openly and objectively";[13] "So far, this is the most informative and compelling film ever made about AIDS."[14]

And the Band Played On is included here as a picture of protest because it is considered a landmark condemnation of homophobia and because it is a further example of Hollywood's bottom line, despite many exceptions, when it comes to controversial issues. It was not a Hollywood movie. Although supported and participated in by many Hollywood stars, it was an independent made-for-cable TV film.

Philadelphia (1993) is probably the most controversial of all the films that might fall into the category of protesting homophobia. Its supporters argue that it reached a mainstream audience that is otherwise generally apathetic or unsympathetic to gays, giving viewers greater understanding of and empathy with gays who might have AIDS. Its critics argue that although the film presents, in a sympathetic manner, a gay man with AIDS and shows the prejudices he encounters, it does not give an accurate or even modest picture of the gay man's life, especially his relationship with his partner, nor does it give the audience any validity of who this person and others like him really are.

Figure 9.1
Philadelphia
(1993)

The plot revolves around a successful and well-respected lawyer (played by Tom Hanks) whose homosexuality is not known to his law firm's colleagues. He contracts AIDS and informs the law firm of his condition. The firm's partners are doubly shocked: That he is gay and that he has AIDS. Although he is still healthy enough to practice law, he is fired. The firm's partners use the excuse that they might contract AIDS from him – a widespread fear at the time when most people thought AIDS could be contracted through closeness or touching, as well as through the exchange of bodily fluids. Their greater fear, it would appear, is that his homosexuality might disturb clients, just as it does many of them. Prejudice is made clear. The lawyer wants to sue but is turned down by a series of attorneys until he finds one who is a homophobe but will pursue the case on principles of law. Eventually the case is won before the gay lawyer dies. During the courtroom litigation the homophobic lawyer comes to realize that his client is really no different a human being than anyone else.

Reactions to the purpose of the film were generally highly positive, while at the same time there was much criticism of the way the film presented the problem and allegedly brushed over the issue of homophobia per se, burying it under the story of a person with AIDS. For example, an article in *Cineaste* stated:

> This courtroom melodrama is a predictable attempt in the liberal tradition of films such as Elia Kazan's *Gentleman's Agreement* (1947) to present personal narratives of prejudice and civil rights discrimination in clearly defined moral terms. Yet, *Philadelphia* is different for it cannot wholeheartedly denounce the social bigotry and prejudice it seeks to expose. In the end, the film is unable to make up its mind about the communities it feels obliged to champion because homophobia (and the fear of AIDS, for that matter) is still a socially pervasive and popular attitude.[15]

Critic Roger Ebert stated that the film "relies on the safe formula of the courtroom drama to add suspense and resolution to a story that, by its nature, should have little suspense and only one possible outcome." He added: "More than a decade after AIDS was first identified as a disease, *Philadelphia* marks the first time Hollywood has risked a big-budget film on the subject. No points for timeliness here; made-for-TV docudramas and the independent film *Longtime Companion* have already explored the subject, and *Philadelphia* breaks no new dramatic ground."[16]

Political orientation of the critics appeared to have little consistency in praising or panning the film. John Simons, writing in the ultra-conservative *National Review*, reflects a view inimical to the far right, criticizing the movie for being too timid: "The film avoids any closer examination of homosexuality, or even AIDS, and hurries to become a courtroom drama, which everyone can have good, wholesome fun with ... Andrew's [the gay lawyer with AIDS] other relationships are equally sanitized."[17] This view coincides with those of a number of liberal sources. For example, gay activist and playwright Larry Kramer echoed the feelings of a number of anti-homophobic individuals and organizations when he described the film as being "dishonest ... often legally, medically, and politically inaccurate, and it breaks my heart that I must say it's simply not good enough and I'd rather people not see it at all."[18] Other typical negative comments were: "Why does Hanks get no more than a chaste kiss from his lover, and why is Hanks' family so conspicuously loving and unanimously supportive?"[19] "By focusing mainly on the impact of the disease on homosexuals, the film reinforces the misconception that AIDS strikes down only gay men. . . . As far as film makers are concerned, AIDS remains in a homosexual ghetto."[20]

A number of negative reviews, such as the following, specifically criticized Hollywood:

> An earnest attempt – I believe – on the part of Demme [the director] and scriptwriter Ron Nyswamer to fuse entertainment with social commentary, the TriStar Pictures movie is all show and no tell . . . It's the kind of safe-sex filmmaking that protects its viewers from all discomfort and sensation, while congratulating them for getting a little closer to the disease.[21]

Such views were countered by comments such as the following:

> Though it has been criticized for its mainstream thrust – there are no romantic scenes between Andy and Miguel [the gay lawyer and his lover] – it is self-censorship and star power that will save it from the ghetto of art houses. It is, at the very least, a giant step forward for Hollywood, which tends to portray homosexuals as either psychopathic cross-dressers or the giddy fruitcakes who live next door.[22]

Other reviewers also praised Hollywood for making the movie. For example, "AIDS is still seen in the West predominantly as a gay disease. What began as a healthy crisis quickly became a social crisis as well, with a steep rise in homophobia and discrimination. So it was a substantial, if calculated, risk for a major studio to finance an expensive mainstream film such as *Philadelphia*."[23]

Acknowledging the film's shortcomings, critics generally found positive things to say about it. "The horror of death from Aids has been sanitized for popular consumption, but nevertheless it is a brave and commendable effort"[24]; "*Philadelphia* is an ambitious effort, touching on – but never exploring very deeply – a number of issues relayed to gays, AIDS and prejudice . . . When it centers on the people in this tragedy and how their lives are affected, it is quite moving, and the message of tolerance comes through quite naturally"[25]; "*Philadelphia* wasn't the first film about AIDS, but it was the first Hollywood studio picture to take AIDS as its primary subject. In that sense, *Philadelphia* is an historically important film."[26]

The alleged "sanitizing" of *Philadelphia* was accepted by many critics as making it possible for the movie to reach a broader audience. GLAAD (The Gay and Lesbian Association for Anti-Defamation) named it the "outstanding studio film of the year" and said "it could begin to persuade America to accept gay people as an intrinsic part of society and convince Hollywood that it should bankroll more movies with gay themes."[27] Pulitzer Prize-winning gay playwright Tony Kushner believes the film effectively reaches the heterosexual majority. "It tells them, if you are going to be a decent human being, you can't just casually despise a huge segment of the human race. And if you are going to address AIDS, you are going to have to address homophobia."[28]

Jonathan Demme, the director of *Philadelphia*, explained his approach. "I made this movie for people like me: people who aren't activists, people who are afraid of AIDS, people who have been raised to look down on gays. I feel we've connected with those people."[29] As the late Vito Russo, the author of *The Celluloid Closet*, used to say: "It's not AIDS that's killing us, it's homophobia."[30]

A 1999 film, *Boys Don't Cry*, is arguably the most disturbing and powerful anti-homophobic movie thus far made. It is not easy to watch.

> It is not intended for those who are unwilling to confront the visceral results of intolerance and hatred. Peirce [the director] does not spare her audience anything – we see in graphic detail every indignity and torment visited upon Brandon [the principal character] once the truth of his gender becomes common knowledge. Those who cannot stomach these scenes will find *Boys Don't Cry* to be virtually unwatchable; those who can will be rewarded with a potent movie-going experience.[31]

Figure 9.2
Boys Don't Cry (1999)

Boys Don't Cry is based on the life of Teena Brandon, a young man trapped in the body of a woman, who, while still a teenager, entered the life of another town as a male, Brandon Teena. Brandon made many friends on the fringes of society, moving successfully in those circles and falling in love with a young woman who accepts him as s/he is, even after learning of Brandon's true sexuality and before Brandon is able to arrange a desired sex-change operation. But when others learn of Brandon's true sex, homophobia takes over, and ignorance and fear drive her/his former friends to verbally, psychologically and, finally, physically attack Brandon. Two of Brandon's former male buddies brutally rape and then murder her/him. Brandon claimed that his persona was not that of a lesbian, seeking homosexual relationships with women, but that of a male seeking a true expression of his sexuality, "a man trapped in a woman's body, who must alter his outward appearance to match his inner self."[32] Critic David Steinberg wrote that "Rather, as its title suggests, *Boys Don't Cry* lays the horror of Brandon's story at the feet of an emotion-denying, humanity-denying, truth-denying definition of masculinity that saps the life out of all of us – women as well as men – every day of our lives."[33]

One critic described the character of Brandon as "at once a dashing lover and a trapped outsider, both an impoverished nobody and a flamboyant dreamer, a daring thief and the tragic victim of an unjust crime."[34] Roger Ebert described the character this way: "She is not a transsexual, a lesbian, a cross-dresser, or a member of any other category or on the laundry list of sexual identities; she is a girl who thinks of herself as a boy."[35]

Although the film changed a number of key elements from the true story of Brandon's life – for example, one of Brandon's real-life girl friends sued the producers, claiming that, contrary to the movie's representation, she discontinued her relationship with Brandon once she discovered that Brandon was anatomically female – it retained its essence. Director Kimberly Peirce, presumably as a lesbian more sensitive to the material, gave Brandon a charismatic identity. Peirce was willing to present the tragedy without cosmetics, but nevertheless was forced to tone down some elements, such as the rape scene – which still came across as frighteningly powerful. Critic Ebert noted that "*Boys Don't Cry* is not sociology, however, but a romantic tragedy – a Romeo and Juliet – set in a Nebraska trailer park."[36]

The movie was independently financed, the established Hollywood financial resources reluctant to tackle what was expected to be a highly controversial movie. It turned out to be critically and financially highly successful. It received the widest distribution of any film about homophobia up to that time and until the release of *Brokeback Mountain* in 2005. By contrast, *Philadelphia*, produced six years before *Boys Don't Cry*, originally was released to only four theaters and it was the unexpected success of *Philadelphia* at those four that resulted in its then being distributed to hundreds. Its subsequent national and international acclaim opened the door for Hollywood to put its foot into the world of homophobic protest with *Boys Don't Cry* and *Brokeback Mountain*. Part of its success may have been due to the publicity at the time of the torture and murder of gay student Matthew Shepard, an event which shocked much of the world and called attention to the ultimate horror emanating from bigotry and hate.

In 2005 *Brokeback Mountain* was considered by many a likely winner of the Academy Award for best picture. It lost to *Crash*, discussed in the chapter on racism. Some critics said that *Brokeback Mountain* is simply a story of love and physical affection between two lonely men that would elicit the same relationship between any two people in similar circumstances, and therefore not a picture protesting homophobia. Other critics, however, said that the very nature of their relationship, reflecting a basic human one between two people who were not ostensibly gay and who were not seeking a gay affair, made it a universal and more powerful protest against homophobic bigotry. There are no stereotypes here; in fact, it plays against stereotypes. Two apparently rugged young men meet while working together as cowboys one summer in 1963 in Wyoming. Reluctantly and much to their dismay, having been raised in a straight society with the standard stereotypical and even prejudicial attitudes toward gays, they fall in love. In one scene in the film one of the men tells the other that when he was a child he heard about two older men living together who were beaten to death. The boy's father told him that "this is what happens if you're like that." Discovering their own gay sexuality is at first traumatic for the two cowboys, then frightening, but nevertheless overwhelming. The summer job over, they develop separate lives, marry and raise families. But they look forward to their yearly "fishing" trips together where they renew their love. Their relationship remains a secret, although one of their wives becomes aware, making a non-loving marriage even more distant. In its own way, the film is like a Shakespearian tragedy. By the end of the movie their families' lives are ruined and "one gay man is dead and the other is emotionally barren."[37]

That the film had potential impact on the attitudes of the public at the time it was released, despite its 1963 setting, is evidenced by the nature of the opposition to it. President George W. Bush proclaimed that he would not see the film, reflecting what many believe are his anti-gay attitudes. Other right-wing sources joined in with their condemnation. The vice-president for policy at the Family Research Council said, "I really don't think America is ready for a homosexual love story like this. I'm sure it has a great deal of appeal within the Hollywood community itself, which is already committed to a pro-homosexual ideology, but I can't see it as a big box-office success."[38] The head of Citizens United stated that "*Brokeback* will not only encounter resistance but empty theatres. My wife and I watched the trailer in a theatre a few days ago and sensed an audible revulsion to two men passionately kissing on the big screen."[39] A theater chain in Utah and individual movie houses in other areas refused to show the film. Media personality Bill O'Reilly ranted against it: "You're going to see, over the next month, this movie being pushed and pushed and pushed by every media you can imagine. Why? Because they want to mainstream homosexual conduct. That's the goal."[40]

Roger Ebert's review of *Brokeback Mountain*, however, summed up the overwhelming critical approval of the film, which was reflected in the many awards it received:

> *Brokeback Mountain* has been described as "a gay cowboy movie," which is a cruel simplification. It is a story of a time and place where two men are forced to deny the only great passion either one will ever feel. Their tragedy is universal. It could be about two women, or lovers from different religious or ethnic groups – any "forbidden" love.[41]

Of the many other films that deal with and/or protest homophobia, a few representative examples are noted below. Some of these films were praised for being artistically good; some were artistically poor. Some of the films showed homosexuals as positive, empathetic characters; some showed them in the same light as anyone else in society: Some good, some bad. The latter approach was very infrequently taken with homosexual characters prior to the Stonewall revolution. As noted earlier, before Stonewall gays and lesbians depicted in films were usually either objects of scorn, at best of pity and, during the Breen censorship years, of condemnation as unremittingly evil. In some instances these portrayals were similar to those of other so-called minorities, including people of color and those of discernible foreign ethnicities. There were rarely shades of gray in the characterizations.

That differed considerably from the personas of characters belonging to America's majority Caucasian race. In many instances even the most despicable white characters – gangsters, for example – were presented with elements of sympathy that explained or even excused their antisocial actions, creating empathy between the audience and the characters. (Some of the early seminal films in this category made stars of James Cagney, Edward G. Robinson, Humphrey Bogart, and others who played those roles.) One might presume that some measure of equality would have applied to the presentation of the characters of the aforementioned minorities. That it was not is a reflection of the public's prejudicial mindset and the role of Hollywood in reinforcing that mindset. That this approach has recently begun to change, not only in respect to homosexual characters, but for those others also considered minorities, is a measure of the eventual impact of Stonewall and of the ongoing civil rights efforts in America. Evidence of the latter is emphasized by the 2008 election of an African-American, Barack Obama, as President of the United States.

In 1992 a film entitled *The Living End* attempted to show two despicable gay characters in an understanding light. Two mismatched AIDS victims meet and hit the road in what they feel are their last days to live it up. They attack homophobes, police, and others in ugly, hateful ways. But underneath their hatefulness we, the audience, begin to understand that they are manifesting a graphic protest of what a gay person, likeable or not, goes through in a homophobic society. As one reviewer stated, "no aspiration, no grace under pressure, no Fire Island gays lamenting their dying lovers, no sudden conversions to activism."[42] Director Greg Akari stated that his purpose was to make an angry movie that made people angry. He dedicated the film to "the hundreds of thousands who've died and the hundreds of thousands more who will die because of a big white house full of fuckhead Republicans."[43] "Homophobia is so prevalent," he argued, "it becomes engrained in your personality at all levels."[44]

Some of the "camp" films have been good, some terrible. *The Birdcage* (1996), mentioned earlier, is a hilarious satire of gay society trying to pretend it's like straight society, puncturing holes in straight society's conformity and misconceptions when a gay nightclub owner and his longtime drag-queen partner who have raised the owner's son together put up a false front when the son brings home his fiancée's conservative parents to meet with "mother and father." Within this adaptation of "the popular 1978 gay farce from France, *La Cage Aux Folles*, [which] gets Americanized and updated"[45] as an "AIDS-free universe where homosexuality simply means wacky fashion sense,"[46] is an empathy with a gay family that is just as functional and dysfunctional – and probably a lot more fun – as any straight family. On the other hand, another camp film, *To Wong Foo, Thanks for Everything! Julie Newmar* (1995), is a rather silly drag-queens-on-the-road movie which quite unrealistically endeavors to show the goodwill of the American people to even the most outlandish, flamboyant drag queens.

Some films were comedies, but not traditional ones in which homosexuals were objects of laughter. In 1997's *As Good as it Gets*, one element of the plot has a homophobic curmudgeon finding himself having to care for a homosexual's dog in a neighboring apartment after the gay man is brutally beaten. By the end of the movie the curmudgeon realizes that gay people are basically just like other people and, losing the use of his apartment, even moves in with the gay man. Another comedy was *But I'm a Cheerleader* (1999). The parents of an all-American-type girl suspect she may be homosexual because she has pictures of females in her locker and doesn't kiss her boyfriend, and they send her to a rehabilitation camp for the "homosexually inclined." At the camp she meets another girl sent there for the same reason and enters into a relationship with her when she realizes that she is, in fact, gay. How can the all-American girl cheerleader be gay? It doesn't fit the stereotype. That is the point of the film. The director, Jaime Babbit, stated, "I wanted her [the protagonist] to be gay but still be who she was . . . I wanted her to keep her identity as a cheerleader. In that way, the film challenges the stereotypes."[47] As one review put it, "the film's unique comic twists and visual stylization expose the absurd nature of society's social and sexual codes."[48]

One of the most successful serious films with elements of comedy is *American Beauty* (1999). "The movie slowly slides from pitch-black humor to emotionally complex drama."[49] The theme poses the questions, What is normality? What is conformity? The movie tries to tell us that conforming to a lifestyle dictated by society leads to disfunctionality.[50] A sub-plot of the film has a homophobic Marine Corps Colonel bristle at the sight of one of his neighbors jogging with two known gay men from the neighborhood. "What is this? The gay fucking pride parade?" By the end of the movie he becomes obsessed by what he believes is his neighbors' homosexuality and, to prove it, deliberately kisses him. But the neighbor is not gay, and rejects him. The Colonel is ashamed, embarrassed, and disturbed that he himself performed a gay act. As psychologists have discovered, homophobia is frequently the result of repressed homosexuality. To avoid anyone knowing about what he did, and frightened about his own possible homosexual leanings, the Colonel kills the neighbor.

One of the more poignant films about gays and AIDS was *Longtime Companion* in 1990. It has been described as a "touching portrait of a close-knit group of gay friends and lovers during the 1880s. The men watch as AIDS begins to devastate their community and try to deal with the painful reality of watching their friends, one by one, succumb to death."[51] Another review stated that "it helps many straights understand the bravery and gallantry of those who have been forced in the prime of life to confront death itself . . . from them we learn of the challenges the disease poses to the entire society . . . it [the film] proclaims that caring and compassion are what make us most human."[52] It is interesting that in the first decade of the new century a critic could write that "There is no female version of *The Boys in the Band*, nor has the friendship circle been a central feature of modern lesbian cinema."[53] Even among those protesting the prejudice of homophobia, was there another prejudice – sexism – in effect?

Gods and Monsters (1998), was a biopic of James Whale, one of the first openly gay Hollywood directors, noted especially for the *Frankenstein* movies. He contributed to an understanding of homosexuality, "For that time, Whale was not only unusually comfortable with his sexuality, but was also generally respected for his openness."[54] The film concentrates on Whale's last years and does not sugar-coat his likes and lusts, including an attempt to seduce his young heterosexual gardener. Roger Ebert commented on the human side of the subject:

> Clayton (the gardener) is slow to understand that Whale is gay. Well, in 1957, a lot of people might not have understood. When he figures it out he isn't angered and there's no painful and predictable scene of violence. Instead, the film proceeds on a bittersweet course in which a young and not terribly bright man grows to like an old and very intelligent man, and to pity him a little. The film is a biopic leading toward a graceful elegy.[55]

Soldier's Girl (2003) is based on the last months of the life of Barry Winchell, a heterosexual soldier who falls in love with a transsexual entertainer at a nightclub near his military base in Kentucky. There is even a military connection between the two, the transsexual having served in the Navy when a male. They are forced to keep their relationship secret, given the prejudicial attitudes encouraged by the military and present, as well, in the communities near the base. When his secret is discovered, Winchell is beaten to death on the military base. The film was co-written by Ron Nyswaner, a co-writer of *Philadelphia*. It avoids prurient aspects of the alternative sexual relationship and creates characters with whom we can identify, sympathize, and empathize. The film also is a comment on the military's homophobic "don't ask, don't tell" policy. A sequence has a high-ranking officer violating even that prejudicial policy by seeking information about Winchell's sexuality, and another sequence has a group of trainees marching in cadence, shouting out a homophobic chant. David Kirp, writing in *The American Prospect*, states that films such as *Boys Don't Cry* and *Soldier's Girl*, with real characters suffering difficulties, hopes, contradictions, and struggles, as we all do, "give us a political education that no morality play ever could."[56]

Some films protesting homophobia had as their principal purpose the introduction of straight audiences to sexual-preference worlds they, the audiences, knew little about, in ways that present the characters as people with the same hopes and fears, problems and achievements as the viewers. One such film was *Transamerica* (2005). A transsexual about to have a genital operation completing the transformation from male to female receives a phone call informing her that the son she never knew she had, but learns was the result of a youthful indiscretion in college, is in jail and is trying to reach his "father." Unable to deal with the transgender issue with her son, she introduces herself as a friend sent to help the son, who is a street hustler and a drug addict. They take a cross-country trip during which "their relationship goes from antagonistic to civil to something deeper."[57] The key to the presentation of the transsexual is that there is nothing flamboyant or overdramatic about her. She is a born-again Christian, down to earth, pleasant, very ordinary person.[58] Only the audience's knowledge – not her mien – prompts the viewer to look at her as "different." "A film that's all about family, *Transamerica* deftly addresses a delicate topic without ever digressing into campiness or making a parody out of the film's subject matter."[59]

In the first decade of this new millennium homosexual characters are seen in the movies in a variety of plots and situations and with many different interpretations of who they are. Most portrayals are not only sympathetic but empathetic. Some of the films subtly reveal or attack homophobic bigotry. Some are direct and open protests against homophobia. Because homophobia appears to be "ingrained in the cultures" of a number of religions, it is not likely to go away any time soon.[60] Therefore, whatever the time or setting of the films, they are applicable to the continuing and current issues. Some of these films came out of major Hollywood studios. Most were made by independent filmmakers. However, to be made and reach an audience, they had to be supported, in many cases, by Hollywood funds and Hollywood distributors.

Vito Russo said it best in *The Celluloid Closet*: "The long silence is finally ending. New voices have emerged, open and unapologetic. They tell stories that have never been told – about people who have always been there."[61]

Notes

1 www.columbia.edu/cu/1web/eresources/exhibitions/sw25/case1.html.
2 *Films Involving Aids, Philadelphia*, 1993. www.disabilityfilms.co.uk/aids1/philadelphia.htm.
3 See Robert L. Hilliard and Michael C. Keith, *Waves of Rancor: Tuning in the Radical Right* (Armonk, NY: M. E. Sharpe, 1999).
4 "Homosexuality in Film." http://sonypictures.com/classics/celluloid/misc/history.html. The quote on the web site was excerpted from the book *Celluloid Closet* by Vito Russo.
5 Media Awareness Network, "Representation of Gays and Lesbians in Films." www.mediaawareness.ca/english/issues/stereotyping/gays_and_lesbians/gay_film.cfm.
6 Russo, Vito, *The Celluloid Closet* (New York: Harper & Row), rev. edn, 1987.
7 Sony Pictures Classics, "Homosexuality in Film." www.sonypictures.com/classics/celluloid/misc/history.html. Some of he material in the text following the endnote designation is information and excerpts from this site.
8 *Ibid.*
9 Dana, Lubin, *The Boys in the Band*. www.dollsoup.co.uk/boys.htm.
10 Antuloy, Dragan, "*And the Band Played On*," May 16, 1999. www.rec.arts.movies.reviews.html.
11 http://movies.nytimes.com/moore/2221/And-the-Band-Played-On/overview.
12 Koller, Brian, "*And the Band Played On*," May 14, 2000. www.filmsgeaded.com.html.

13   Scott, Tony, "*Band* Scores Poignant Saga," *Variety*, September 6, 1993, p. 6.

14   Antuloy, *And the Band Played On*.

15   Grundman, Roy and Peter Sachs, "*Philadelphia*," *Cineaste*, Summer, 1993. www.lib.berkeley.edu/MRC/Philadelphia.html.

16   Ebert, Roger, "*Philadelphia*," *Chicago Sun-Times*, January 19, 1994. www.suntimes/com/ebert/ebert_reviews/1994/01/899447.html.

17   Simons, John, "Romancing AIDS," *National Review*, February 7, 1994, p. 68.

18   Corliss, Richard and Elizabeth Bland, "The Gay Gauntlet," *Time*, February 7, 1994, p. 62ff.

19   *Ibid.*

20   "Film and the fear of AIDS," *The Economist*, May 28, 1994, p. 87.

21   Howe, Reson, "*Philadelphia*," *Washington Post*, January 14, 1994. www.washingtonpost.com/wp-srv/style/longterm/movies/philadelphiarhowe_a0b026.htm.

22   Kempley, Rita, *Philadelphia*. *Washington Post*, January 14, 1994. www.washingtonpost.com/wp-srv/style/longterm/movies/video/philadelphiarkempley_a0a3ff.htm.

23   Thomson, Peter, "*Philadelphia*," Peter Thomson Reviews, Premium Movie Partnership, 2003. www.encoreausstralia.com.au/ptr.cfrm?titleid=P00000767.

24   Perry, George, "*Philadelphia*," BBC films, January 19, 2001. www.bbc.com.uk/film_review/ph=214620.

25   Hicks, Chris, "*Philadelphia*. The Left's Mr. Right," *Desert News*, January 4, 1994. www.desertnews.com/filmreviews/01141994/philadelphia&126251.

26   Emerson, Jim, "Editorial Reviews – *Philadelphia*." Amazon.com. www.amazon.com/exec/obidos/tg/detail/-/0800141806.

27   Corliss and Bland, "The Gay Gauntlet."

28   *Ibid.*

29   *Ibid.*

30   Ansen, David, "'Tis not a jolly season," *Newsweek*, December 27, 1993, p. 46.

31   Berardinelli, James, *Boys Don't Cry*. http://movie-reviews.colossus.net. movies/b/boys_don't.html.

32   Cavagna, Carlo, *Boys Don't Cry*. www.about film.com/movies/b/boysdontcry.htm.

33   Steinberg, David, "To Be a Man: *Boys Don't Cry* and the Story of Brandon Teena." www.sexuality.org/1/davids/cnbdc.html.

34   http://yahoo.com/movie/1800020738/details.

35   Ebert, Roger, "*Boys Don't Cry*," *Chicago Sun-Times*, October 22, 1999. http://rogerebert.suntimes.com/apps/pbcs.d11/article?aid=/19991022/REVIEWS.

36   *Ibid.*

37   Vary, Adam B., "The *Brokeback Mountain* Effect," *Advocate*, February 28, 2006, p. 39.

38   Goldberg, Andy, "Critics love *Brokeback*, but U.S. heartland objects," *Monsters and Critics*, December 16, 2005. http://moviesmonstersandcritics. com/features/article_1069440.php/Critics_love_Brokeback_but_U.S._ heartland_objects.

39   *Ibid.*

40   Finger, Leslie. http://progressive.stanford.edu/2006.04_brokeback.html.

41   Ebert, Roger, "*Brokeback Mountain*," *Chicago Sun-Times*, December 16, 2005. http://rogerebert.suntimes.com/apps/pbcs.d11/article?AID=/20051216/ REVIEWS/51019006/1023.

42   Levy, Emanuel, *The Living End.* http://emanuellevy.com/article.php? articleID=2529.

43   *Ibid.*

44   *Ibid.*

45   Stark, Susan, "*The Birdcage*," *Detroit News*, April 23, 2004. www.rotten-tomatoes.com/click/movie-1070386/reciews.php?critic=columns&sortby =default&page=1&rid=50284.

46   Maslin, Janet, "*La Cage Aux Folles*, but in South Beach," *New York Times*, March 8, 1996.

47   Fuchus, Cynthia, "Interview with Jaime Babbit. www.popmatters.com/ film/inerviews/babbit-jaime.html.

48   *But I'm a Cheerleader.* www.rottentomatoes.com/m/but_im_a_cheerleader/ #synopsis.

49   *American Beauty.* www.ram.org/ramblings/movies/american_beauty.html.

50   *Ibid.*

51   *Longtime Companion.* www.rottentomatoes.com/m/longtime_companion.

52   Brussat, Frederic and Mary Ann, "*Longtime Companion.*" www. spiritualityandpractice.com/films/films.php.id=3148.

53   *The Advocate*, June 6, 2000, p. 44.

54   Jackson, Kevin, "Portrait of the Artist," *Sight and Sound*, April 1999, p. 35.

55   Ebert, Roger, "*Gods and Monsters*," *Chicago Sun-Times* Ebert archives. www.suntimes.com/ebert/ebert_reviews/1998.

56   Kirp, David, "Martyrs and Movies," *The American Prospect*, December 20, 1999, p. 52.

57   Murray, Rebecca, "*Transamerica* Movie Review." January 1, 2006. http://movies.aboyut.com/od/transamerica/a/transam010106.htm.

58   Esther, John, "Felicity Huffman: In *Transamerica* With Motherhood," *Lesbian News*, January, 2006, p. 26.

59   Murray, "*Transamerica* Movie Review."

60   Lannom, David, "Homophobia vs. Racism," *The Advocate*, March 28, 2006, pp. 12–13.

61   "Homosexuality in Film," Sony Pictures Classics.

10
Technology
Can we beat the machine?

In recent decades Hollywood has produced many films which protest the increasing effects of technology upon society and its human occupants. Some are direct statements. Others imply. And still others are by viewer inference. In some cases it is clear that the purpose of the given movie is to warn the public about the existing or potential evils of technology. In others, the technology aspect is the framework for a science-fiction action film, with the philosophical comment a byproduct. In still others, technology is not portrayed as an evil per se, but a powerful factor that alters or may alter some basic concepts of human existence.

The Industrial Revolution of the eighteenth and nineteenth centuries not only introduced machines, but made factories and businesses dependent on them for maximum productivity at the lowest cost. Human beings had to operate the machines, and although many more jobs were created the profit motive and lack of labor organization resulted in long hours, low pay, and harsh, sometimes intolerable, working conditions. Machines became more important to management than workers. Potential workers were played off against each other for scarce jobs, resulting in even greater exploitation of labor. It took many years before the development of unions (see chapter 5) effected changes, even as the development and use of technology increased almost exponentially. In the twentieth century the three great revolutions of energy, transportation, and communications gave technology even greater importance, symbolized in great part by the growth of electronics. As this is written, the twenty-first century has begun with computer technology having become the personal window to the world of more and more people, as well as serving as the governmental and corporate tool to invade and control the lives of more and more people in increasingly sophisticated ways. For example, the melding of technology and biology, biotechnology, increases the reality of the fear of merging humans with machines, heretofore limited to science fiction. The implications of cloning and robotics are creating ethical and moral concerns for many people and, for many others, highly positive anticipation.[1]

Hollywood has not been lax in addressing this history and its resulting issues. As noted above, almost all of these films fall into or have been relegated to the genre of science fiction. "Sci-fi films express society's anxiety about technology and how to forecast and control the impact of technological and environmental change on contemporary society. Science fiction often expresses the potential of technology to destroy humankind through Armageddon-like events, or through the loss of personal individuality."[2] Among these films, two of the best were made in 1964, *Dr. Strangelove*, mentioned in the chapters on war and on politics, a brilliant film of this genre that was not made in the United States, but in the UK, and *Fail-Safe*, a Hollywood movie in which a technological malfunction in a computer causes US bombers to fly beyond their fail-safe zone and nuke Moscow, setting up a retaliatory nuking of New York.

Films protesting technology generally reflect the major interests and concerns of society. Some deal with the philosophical and psychological aspects of technology as a dehumanizing force. Robots replace people, people become robots. Some concentrate on the political aspects, making people into mindless tools of controlling machines, frequently part of one even larger governmental or industrial machine. The development of communications technology has facilitated that kind of control. Radio and television are the most powerful forces in the world today for controlling people's minds and emotions. It has become an axiom that whoever controls the media of a country controls its politics. From an economic standpoint, technology enhances the profit motive of those who control or have the resources to use technology. Transportation, communications, and energy technology enable globalization, outsourcing, and the pitting of one group of workers against another in competitive situations, resulting in higher profits through lower pay, poorer working conditions, and global and consolidated entities' control over or influence on laws and regulations concerning their areas of operation. It is part of Washington, DC lore that regulatory agencies are under de facto control of the organizations they are supposed to regulate.

If you count all the sci-fi movies in which evil robots, domestic and alien, invade the earth, a continent, a country, a city, or just an individual's life, almost always to be destroyed by heroic earthlings or, in futuristic settings, by intelligent and sensitive other robots – in cinema even the smallest laptop is powerful enough to override the computer communications of an invading force – then one might say that Hollywood has taken many strong stands protesting the negative effects of technology on society. However, in only a relatively few films of this genre were clear political statements made, most of these films being purely adventure, shock, or horror in scope, with concepts of protest having to be made by deliberate inference.

While many early movies, from the beginning of silent films, dealt with the use of technology, such as spaceship trips to the moon, it wasn't until twentieth-century technology began to impact on people's fears that movie-makers stressed elements protesting the possibility of technology affecting and even taking over our lives. Arguably the seminal film of this genre, *Metropolis*, was not made in America, but was an icon of the German expressionistic movement, transferred from pre- and post-World-War-I-era theater dramas into Germany's films of the 1920s. Produced in 1927, *Metropolis* shows one part of society, the elite, living high above the city in utopian settings, while the other part of society lives in a dehumanized existence below the city, working endlessly, operating machines that support the upper class, keeping the elite happy and well. This film was a powerful protest against the industrialization through technology that exploited the many poor to serve the few rich. The film's settings are huge, overwhelming machines that drown the workers in their technological power. "No movie has ever more vividly visualized the industrialization of social relations. The metaphor of a dehumanized urban proletariat buried alive beneath the city."[3] While elements of expressionistic style did not soon transfer to Hollywood, content concepts gradually did. Two highly praised, now classic, horror films of the 1930s, *Frankenstein* (1931) and *The Bride of Frankenstein* (1935), showed the results of technology that can create living creatures: The resulting evil of the "monsters" unable to fit into their new world and the intolerance and evil of the populace unable to understand or accept the "monsters."

However, the first Hollywood film to make a clear, definitive, targeted major protest against the iniquities of technology was Charlie Chaplin's 1936 movie, *Modern Times* (discussed earlier in chapters 5 and 6). Like many of his films protesting some condition in society, Chaplin bypassed the Hollywood studio phobia of dealing with controversial subjects by making it a Chaplinesque comedy – that is, Chaplin's own comedy routines within an aura of satire and segments of pathos. Chaplin at the time was the most popular and revered performer in the world. It was rumored that Adolf Hitler, whose actions and person were targets of satire in Chaplin films, grew his own Charlie Chaplin-type mustache to look like the adored Chaplin film persona. *Modern Times* tackles many issues: Poverty, discrimination, political repression, an unfair justice system, and, significantly, industry's exploitation of workers through the growing use of technology, where people become work slaves to machines. Critic Mick LaSalle wrote:

Figure 10.1
Modern Times
(1936)

For all its comedy, *Modern Times* is a film born of serious concerns. Chaplin had a horror of automation, which he saw as a symptomatic trend in modern life to turn people into machines, with machine lives and thoughts. At the time this movie was being made, the rich and powerful were organizing, either through totalitarian ideologies or through control of goods and technology. The sweetness of life was becoming lost and *Modern Times* was Chaplin's comic response.[4]

Two of cinema history's most lauded and enduring laugh sequences were management's use of a technology-driven feeding machine that was designed to automatically feed workers working during lunch breaks so they could keep working and enable management to decrease its labor costs and increase its profits, and a scene in which Chaplin is caught in the gears of a giant machine, the human being totally frustrated and dominated by the technology-spawned monster. Frank Nugent described the feeding-machine sequence in his *New York Times* review:

It finds Charlie as a worker on an assembly line in a huge factory. A sneeze or a momentary raise of his head is all that is needed to disrupt the steady processional of tiny gadgets whose nuts he must tighten with one swooping twist. At lunch hour his boss places him in an experimental automatic feeding machine. Like Charlie, the device goes berserk. Bowls of soup are tossed in his face, a corn-on-the-cob self-feeder throws moderation to the wind and kernels to the floor. The machine alternately grinds corn into his face and wipes his mouth with a solicitous, but entirely ineffectual, self-wiper. Charlie recovers in a hospital.[5]

As one critic pointed out, this scene makes it clear that the technology was designed so that the worker eats in order to work, rather than, as traditional, the reverse.[6] Another critic stated that "Charlie represented one important ideological stance above others: a silent protest against advancing technology."[7] Roger Ebert has described *Modern Times* as "a fable about (among other things) automation, assembly lines and the enslaving of man by machines."[8]

Modern Times is generally considered among the top 10 or 20 best American films ever made, and still stands, after three-quarters of a century, as probably the most effective film protest against the evils of technology.

Protests against technology in terms of its effects on people's real lives in a realistic milieu have been infrequent, most of the successful films on the subject falling into the science-fiction category. Arguably the seminal Hollywood film of this type is *2001: A Space Odyssey*, released in 1968 and directed by Stanley Kubrick, noted in other chapters for his productions of protest films. At the time, the United States was vying with the Soviet Union to get to the moon first, both countries racing to take fullest advantage of newly developing space technology. In this instance the spaceship is dependent on a computer named HAL. The computer takes on a life of its own and overrides the human crew's commands, dooming the spaceship's mission. The movie protests our efforts to rely more on technology than on human abilities and values. The seriousness of the film, which could have been easily made as – or regarded as – simply a space adventure, is emphasized by "almost two hours in exposition of scientific advances in space travel and communications before anything happens."[9] In fact, it is this exposition and the prologue briefly tracing the history of humankind that promoted some critics to give it negative reviews, presumably because it did not fit their expectation for the traditional entertainment adventure movie. *2001* became the model for the spate of movies that that came some dozen years later, in the 1980s, that stressed the human–computer relationship. Because it wasn't until the 1980s that personal computers began to be widely available, perhaps the difficulty of individual moviegoers to see or relate to computers in their own, everyday lives delayed an immediate follow-up by Hollywood of the computer base of *2001*'s plot.

One of the very few films of the 1970s that can be said to be a warning protest against the artificial intelligence of computer technology is *Colossus: The Forbin Project* (1970). Like *2001*, it was ahead of its time and, although regarded by many as an excellent film, did not receive the box-office support and wide distribution it deserved. The film "has us poor humans building a computer too smart for its own good."[10] Colossus is "a supercomputer designed for [United States] defense that becomes too big for its bytes."[11] The action takes place during the Cold War, which, in 1970, when the film was made, was on the verge of becoming a hot war. In the film, the Soviets have a similar super-computer. Both computers serve "as peacekeepers that operate without human intervention, keeping check on the world without the need for our services."[12] The computers are the means of control for missiles aimed at each other's countries. With their advanced artificial intelligence, they decide to communicate with each other and soon develop their own language, exchanging information. Concerned, their human overseers decide to shut them down. This angers them, they refuse to comply, and "soon enough Colossus is giving orders, threatening nuclear annihilation if its demands are not met."[13] Colossus has its own plan for world domination; computers will rule humans.

Almost every year throughout the 1980s an important film was made protesting the potential harm computer technology, robotics, and/or artificial intelligence could do and might do to human beings and to human society as we know it. Most of the films during that period that dealt with some form of technology, however, were pedestrian exploitation films, in many cases using new-technology bases and situations for the traditional cops-and-robbers, cowboys-and-Indians-type much overdone action movies. In the early 1980s, as personal computers promised new remarkable opportunities for communications and information – as indeed has proven to be the case – many people looked beyond the immediate and saw computerized robots as personal as well as industry and business workers in the near future, to assist us in our everyday lives with physical as well as mental chores. It is not surprising, then, that many of this genre's films of the 1980s focused on robots.

The title, *Blade Runner* (1982), referred to the police assigned to track down and destroy robots or artificial humans or, as they are called in the movie, replicants, who have become rogues. In the movie five replicants assigned to work at space colonies escape and attempt to return to earth, posing a perceived threat to Los Angeles. A key theme of the film is the philosophical difficulty of determining what is human and what is the product of artificial engineering. One analyst noted that the differences are "blended into ambiguity as the blade runner cop is emotionless and perfectly groomed and the suspected replicant is round-shouldered, scruffy, unshaven with a receding chin . . . and immediately the spectator's expectations are frustrated in trying to differentiate the human from the non-human."[14] In addition to protesting the potential problems resulting from the technology of artificial life, the movie protests the influence of communications technology in blurring the lines between humans and non-humans by their moving us from individual thoughts and emotions to group think and group feelings. As one writer noted, *Blade Runner* "holds out the hope that we can unplug from the mediated mass-world and, by listening to our dreams, become fully human."[15] (As this is written, this protest takes on much more meaning than in 1982, with current consolidation, conglomeration, and the deregulation of media ownership restrictions making it increasingly possible for an individual or a small group to control our major sources of information and influence.)

Blade Runner not only protested the kind of world that computerized robots could lead to, but it helped establish this popular film genre for subsequent movies such as *The Terminator*, in 1984, which ultimately helped a bodybuilding muscleman to become governor of America's most populous state. *The Terminator* dealt with a similar theme to *Blade Runner*: Machines rising up against the humans who built them and taking over a world where not the machines, but the humans, are the fugitives.

In 1983, between *Blade Runner* and *The Terminator*, were two significant films worth noting. In *War Games* a young computer whiz accidentally hacks into the Pentagon's top-secret computer that controls the country's nuclear weapons. The Pentagon computer challenges the hacker's computer to a war game between the United States and the Soviet Union. Pentagon officials think the event is really happening and a countdown begins for World War III. Critic Christopher Null stated:

> Not only was *War Games* the first film to tap into fears about the dangers of technology at the hands of mad geniuses, but it's easily the best as well. *War Games* also sparked an almost inconceivable interest in computer hacking among our juvenile intelligentsia, and the movie's effect on Hollywood and the American consciousness can still be seen today. While these days Microsoft is a more frightening reality than lone hacker-types, the resonant phrase, "Shall we play a game?," still retains its power.[16]

The film dramatically forwarded the idea that an ordinary personal computer can be as effective as a super-computer. This isn't true, of course, but it became a standard of many Hollywood action films, most of them mediocre and exploitative, where a personal computer is strong enough to override the powerful mega-computers of an invading alien or foreign force.

Another 1983 film, *Videodrome*, falls into the sci-fi horror category. It's about a television show that seduces and controls its viewers. It was considered the ultimate protest, at that time, against the power of communications technology. One of the most striking and creative commentaries on the violation of human reality by the media is *The Truman Show*, produced in 1998. The principal character (as is true for the audience for a while) does not know that the life he leads in small-town America is not reality, but a television program with actors playing the roles of family, friends, neighbors, and townspeople. Put into the show at a very early age, Truman Burbank knows the town setting as the full extent of his life and is not aware that those who leave the town for short periods are, in fact, performers going to their real homes. Media technology has created a fake world that appears to be a real world. (In chapter 8, commentary on *Wag the Dog* describes how the media – also television – created a fake war that the world believes is real.) *The Truman Show* presents "issues of personal liberty vs. authoritarian control, safe happiness vs. the excitement of chaos, manufactured emotions, the penetration of media to the point where privacy vanishes and the fascination of fabricated images over real things."[17] Roger Ebert wrote that "This film brings into focus the new values that technology

Figure 10.2 *The Matrix* (1999)

is forcing on humanity."[18] Another critic noted that films [like this one] "show us how technology can be used to alter the reality that most of us believe in."[19] The editor of *Transparency* stated that the movie "reveals an essential truth about what is happening to society in [this] century."[20]

Among the most popular films of recent years that might be considered technology protests were *The Matrix* in 1999, followed by *A.I.* (Artificial Intelligence) in 2001, and *I, Robot*, in 2004. *The Matrix*, which became somewhat of a cult film among the college-age set and was followed by two sequels, is distinguished mainly by its superb visual and sound effects. *A.I.* bears the hallmark of Steven Spielberg. *I, Robot* is, like a number of other science-fiction movies, based on one of Isaac Asimov's short stories.

The Matrix protests not only technology, but the way we humans have allowed ourselves to be dehumanized. It suggests that the world that we think of as reality is, in fact, a façade created by artificial intelligence – a matrix. The film protests the increasing technology that we've not only permitted, but that we've used to create such a world. In the film the artificial intelligence machines that we have created have in turn programmed a false reality into human minds. One critic suggested that the film indicates that "All life on earth may be nothing more than an elaborate façade created by a malevolent cyber intelligence."[21] Another described it as "a winding web of dream vs. reality vs. technological dictatorship."[22] And still another wrote that "the film can be seen as an exploration between machines and human beings."[23]

Researcher James Palmer postulates three key issues of protest in *The Matrix*.[24] One is the standardization of technology. Palmer quotes Samuel Kimball's critical analysis: "The machines evidently learned how to clone humans and grow them in mechanical wombs. These artificial environments are housed in gigantic structures, the corporate architecture of which exaggerates the monolithic uniformity dominated by . . . mechanical reproduction."[25] A second point made by Palmer is the dominance of machines over humans, technology creating what becomes reality to humans: "a science fiction world in which computer graphics are so mimetically perfect that they utterly dissolve the difference between reality and its virtualized simulation by an Artificial Intelligence in the process of remaking the world in its own, anti-human image."[26] Palmer's third issue relates to technology becoming an integral part of human life, and cites a scene in which a character, Morpheus, attempts to differentiate between dreams and reality, between technology and life. Kimball's comment: "Morpheus says that if one cannot awaken, one cannot determine the difference between dream and reality. But the converse is also the case: if one cannot determine the difference between two worlds, one cannot awaken."[27]

In *The Matrix* hope is evidenced in the few remaining free human beings, the others enslaved by the machines to produce energy that keeps the machines going. "The underground city of Zion, the last bastion of humankind, awaits The One to disrupt the Matrix, a power field controlled by humanoid computers that have created a 'virtual' world fed by laboratory controlled-human energy."[28] This hope is implemented in a losing war against the robots that appears to doom humans for eternity. The dim future for humankind, if it continues its unbridled technological march that increasingly substitutes technology for human endeavor, is reiterated in the subsequent *Matrix* movies, *The Matrix Reloaded* and *The Matrix Revolutions*, both released in 2003.

However, many critics did not see the protests against technology as the overriding factor in critiquing *The Matrix*. Some critics, like John Anderson of *Newsday*, criticized the film for being "about style rather than context."[29] Many critics were concerned that it had the opportunity to make significant substantive arguments, but drowned that opportunity by primarily concentrating on special effects (the film's Academy Award nominations included sound and visual effects) and gratuitous action. One of the negative descriptions stated that the film "offers an eye-popping but incoherent extravaganza of morphing and superhuman martial arts . . . The script never really gets on track, winding up in a muddle of showdowns, deaths, and resurrections that follow no rules."[30] Nevertheless, the movie was a box-office hit and, presumably, reached its generally young audience with even a partially obscured protest message.

A.I., or *Artificial Intelligence*, was originally the project of Stanley Kubrick, whose protest films arguably have been the most effective, pertinent, and honored of the genre. When Kubrick died, Steven Spielberg took over the making of the film. The film is set in a future when cyborg robots have been created to do virtually every job that humans formerly did. The robots, with nonhuman emotions, are dispensable and abandoned when they are no longer of use. However, one boy robot has the human emotion of love and once he is dispensed with he seeks to find the "family" he was part of. He seeks his "mother," devastated that she apparently does not love him as he loves her because he is not a "real" boy.

> Like the real-life science surrounding the development of Artificial Intelligence, the movie is top-heavy with moral and ethical questions. What is life and where is the line that divides sentience from a programmed response? If a robot can genuinely love a person, what responsibility does that person bear in return? How can an immortal robot cope with outliving its organic creators?[31]

At a panel discussion at MIT (the Massachusetts Institute of Technology) on the film and its implications, it was noted that "artificially intelligent systems, many of which we take for granted, are already real to us, interwoven into the fabric of our lives – in medicine, travel, and in any situation where we have come to rely on the digital storing of information that humans previously stored in their heads."[32] Futurist Raymond Kurzweil stated that "more complex forms of artificial intelligence on the horizon will demand recognition, socially and politically. And their arrival is imminent, based on past and current exponential growth trends across a variety of technologies and scientific disciplines."[33] Writer David Walsh summed up the potential problem: "it might be argued that *A.I.* is merely a cautionary tale, its bleakness a reminder of what humanity potentially faces unless it takes stock and changes course."[34]

I, Robot (2004) is, as are many sci-fi films, based on one or more of Isaac Asimov's short stories. It's set in a future when humanoid domestics are common and some people (in this case, a principal character, an anti-robot bigot) sees their increasing human traits as a danger to society. One says, "I have even had dreams." The warning: Creating robots in human form with increasingly human behavior sets the stage for robots to replace humans, humanity destroying itself with its own creations. Critic A. O. Scott summarized the significance of *I, Robot* in the opening paragraph of his *New York Times* review.

> When robots finally take over the world (assuming they haven't already) we will not be able to say we weren't warned. Every year, Hollywood studios present dire scenarios in which androids,

computers and artificial intelligence applications run amok and enslave the human race, but the public never seems to get the message. Perhaps *I, Robot*, a half-baked science-fiction thriller . . . will succeed where the *Terminator* and *Matrix* movies failed, and alert us to the grave danger that our innocent-looking toasters, vacuum cleaners, smart cars and laptop computers really pose.[35]

Within its artistic drawbacks, *I, Robot* reiterates the recurring theme that robots, like humans, have feelings, and that the boundaries between humans and machines are becoming increasingly blurred. Critic A. O. Scott asks, "How does the technological blurring of this boundary affect our ethical conceptions of humanity and inhumanity?"[36] For some critics, films like *I, Robot* clearly address the present, rather than, or as well as, the future, with implications beyond that of technology. Scott Juba wrote:

The screenplay represents a genuine attempt to create an engaging and at times surprisingly thought-provoking story that examines man's ability to destroy himself with his own creations. Also, at a time [2004] when our country is forced to scrutinize the effectiveness and honesty of its leadership, *I, Robot* subtly cautions viewers against accepting issues at face value while blindly complying with the demands of those in power.[37]

While some films protested the advancement of technology per se, most protested humankind's use of technology as the issue of concern. However, almost all of the more recent films of this genre have been science fiction rather than reality-based, many of them so far-fetched as to be dismissed as simply poor or even silly cinema. Couched in sci-fi action adventure themes and frequently overwhelmed by special effects, most of these films' warnings against the potential dangers of runaway technology lack the direct relationship to reality, and identification with and for the viewer, of Charlie Chaplin's 1936 masterpiece, *Modern Times*.

Notes

1 Some of the concepts in this paragraph were adapted from a research paper, "Technology," prepared by Jana-Lynne Mroz for the "Pictures of Protest" course, Emerson College, February 17, 2004.

2   Dirks, Tim, "Film Genres." www.filmsite.or/genres.html.
3   Hoberman, J., "Industrial Symphony," *The Village Voice*, July, 2002. www.villagevoice.com/issues/0228/hoberman.php.
4   LaSalle, Mick, "*Modern Times,*" *San Francisco Chronicle*, December 26, 2003. www.sfgate.com/cgi-bin/article.cgi?f=/c/a/2003/12/26/DDGMC3SKA117. DTL.
5   Nugent, Frank S., "*Modern Times,*" *New York Times*, February 6, 1936. http://movies.nytimes.com/movie/review?r=1&res.
6   LaSalle, "*Modern Times.*"
7   Gerstein, David, "*Modern Times* and the Question of Technology." http://wso.williams.edu/-dgerstein/chaplin/machines.html.
8   Ebert, Roger, "*Modern Times,*" *Chicago Sun-Times*, January 25, 1972. http://rogerebert.suntimes/com/apps/pbcs.dll/article?AID=/19720125/REVIEWS/2012503.
9   "*2001: A Space Odyssey,*" *Variety Portable Movie Guide* (New York: Berkeley Boulevard Books, 2000), p. 1316.
10 Null, Christopher, "*Colossus: The Forbin Project,*" 2001. www.filmcritic.com/misc/emporium.nsf/reviews/Colossus:-The-Forbin-Project.
11 Martin, Mick and Marsha Porter, "*Colossus: The Forbin Project,*" *Video Movie Guide 1999* (New York: Ballantine Books, 1998), p. 214.
12 Null, "*Colossus: The Forbin Project.*"
13 *Ibid.*
14 Morrison, Rachela, "The Blakean Dialectics of *Blade Runner,*" *Literature Film Quarterly*, Vol. 18, 1990, p. 2.
15 McNamara, Kevin R., "*Blade Runner's* Post-Individual Worldspace," *Contemporary Literature*, Vol. 38, 1997, p. 7.
16 Null, Christopher, *War Games*. http://filmcritic.com/misc/emporium.nsf/84dbbfa4d710144986256c.
17 "*The Truman Show,*" *Variety Portable Movie Guide* (New York: Berkeley Boulevard Books, 2000), p. 1304.
18 Ebert, Roger, "*The Truman Show,*" *Chicago Sun-Times*, June 6, 1998. www.suntimes.com/ebert/ebert_reviews/1998/06/060522.html.
19 Webster, Brian, "*Wag the Dog,*" *Apollo Movie Guide*. http://apolloguide.com.html.
20 Sanes, Ken, "*The Truman Show*: The Invisible Truth." www.transparencynow.com/truman.htm.
21 Gittes, Jake, *The Matrix*. www.imdb.com/title/tt0133093/plotsummary.
22 Ross, Anthony, *The Matrix*. www.hollywoodreportcard.com/106833.
23 Brussat, Frederic, "*The Matrix*: Review of the Week." www.spirituality&health.com/weeksreview/113880.
24 Palmer, James, "Protests of Technology," research paper prepared for the "Pictures of Protest" course, Emerson College, April 23, 2003.

25 Kimball, Samuel A., "Not Begetting the Future: Technological Autonomy, Sexual Reproduction, and the Mythic Structure of *The Matrix*," *Journal of Popular Culture*, Winter, 2001, p. 3.

26 *Ibid.*, p. 10.

27 *Ibid.*, p. 5.

28 "*The Matrix*," *Variety Portable Movie Guide* (New York: Berkeley Boulevard Books, 2000), p. 798.

29 Anderson, John, "*The Matrix*," *Newsday*. www.rottentomatoes.com/m/TheMatrix-1086960.

30 "*The Matrix*," *Variety Portable Movie Guide*.

31 Berardinelli, James, *AI: Artificial Intelligence*. http://.movie-reviews.colossus.net/movies/a/ai.html.

32 Angelica, Amara D., "*A.I.* (the movie) and A.I. Panel Discussion at MIT, May 7, 2001: Kurzweil AI." www.kurzweilai.net/articles/art0174.html.

33 *Ibid.*

34 Walsh, David, "Starting Over. *A.I. Artificial Intelligence*." www.wsws.org/articles/2001/jul2001/ai-j16.shtml.

35 Scott, A. O., "*I, Robot*," *New York Times*, July 16, 2004. www.nytimes.com/2004/07/16/movies/16ROBOT.html.

36 *Ibid.*

37 Juba, Scott, "*I, Robot*," *The Trades Column*, July 15, 2004. www.the-trades.com/column.php?columnid-2640.

11
Sexism
Protecting old boys' egos

Although there have been many Hollywood films dealing with the roles of women in society, including women in non-traditional, non-stereotyped roles, relatively few of these films can be said to be deliberate protests of sexism and of prejudice against women.

A number of Hollywood films from the cinema's early days have included women as strong, independent protagonists. Some have mocked the contemporary – then as now – notions that women must be subservient to men or are not as capable as men in almost all endeavors. In some cases the male character is usually naïve and taken advantage of by a clever and, in many instances, scheming woman. Most films, however, have cast women in stereotyped roles, reflective of a philosophy that had dominated all societies for ages, and which only in the past half-century has seen amelioration in some parts of the world. Christian theologian Thomas Aquinas's characterization of women in the thirteenth century continues to dominate many religions to this day, and through the church's teaching, civil society: woman was "created to be man's helpmeet, but her unique role is in conception . . . since for other purposes men would be better assisted by other men."[1] The woman who will sacrifice everything for the love of a good man; the woman who gives up her career to stay home and have babies and be a helpmate to her husband in his career. There is the occasional film role in which a woman is in a position of leadership, but when she has to solve a problem or stand up to bad guys, almost always a male rescues her from her inability to succeed on her own. In Hollywood productions, "The women who hold elite jobs are much more likely to be married at the film's opening and much more interested in romance. Further, until the 1960s, women in lead roles and non-traditional occupations are twice as likely to be motivated by romance."[2]

Two otherwise highly rated, well-made, successful films in the pre-feminist first half of the twentieth century illustrate this approach. *Take a Letter, Darling* (1942) is the story of a female executive who hires a male as her secretary, but then falls in love with him and gives up her career; in *Mildred Pierce* (1945) a strong businesswoman spoils her daughter to win her love and then loses her and the man with whom she's in love when she finds she and her daughter are in love with the same man.

Since the feminist revolution of the 1970s and the efforts of organizations such as NOW (National Organization for Women), more Americans have become aware of sexism, in language, in employment and business, in educational opportunities, in legal matters, and in media portrayals, as well as other areas. One example is the old "ring around the collar" television ad. A man berates his wife for not getting his shirt collars clean. Instead of telling the clod to wash his neck more often, she is guiltily apologetic and hurries to change her soap brand to that of the advertiser. Complaints from an increasingly sensitive public resulted in a changed commercial in which the man is washing his own shirts while using and lauding the advertiser's soap. One of the results of the feminist movement was the opening up of producing, directing, and writing opportunities for women in Hollywood. These changes and advances in equity for women coincided with and are likely major reasons for the growth in the past few decades of pictures protesting sexism, some through the films' themes and others through the nature of the female characters' roles.

The aftermath of World War II as it affected women helped lead to the feminist movement that changed the perception of women as a passive underclass and opened up new opportunities for women. When the men came home from the war, many sought the propagandized dream of a home in the suburbs with a loyal and supportive wife raising children in an environment kept warm and cozy for the male breadwinner. While many women were eager to resume that role, many more had worked in the private and public sector in positions men had held before they went off to war and for the first time in their lives discovered that they could be successful in business and industry, for the first time tasted the self-confidence of independent, self-supporting fulfillment. Confined once again to the home as a homemaker no longer was satisfying to many women, just as it would not be satisfying to many men.

Joe Freeman wrote in *The Politics of Women's Liberation*:

In the decade following World War II . . . a century of growing dis-
content with a limited domestic role burst into open rebellion . . . In
the immediate post-war years educated women sensed as never
before that they had capabilities far greater than were being entirely
used in the traditional feminine role. The result during the 1950s was
a decade of literature expressing futility. The American woman did
not always understand why she felt so suddenly rebellious, and many
who voiced the feminist protest were afflicted with a sense of guilt
that home, husband and children did not satisfy their longings for
more complete self-realization.[3]

While, as with most other issues, it took time for Hollywood to act
on this national concern, it eventually did. Perhaps the film subject
area that presented women most often as positive, strong characters,
achieving their aims and surviving in a hostile, male-dominated society, was that of war. Many war movies, covering all eras and all wars,
concentrate on the courage and independence of female nurses. While
stereotyping almost universally portrays females in the secondary
roles of nurses, rather than in the primary roles of doctors, this was a
realistic reflection of the discrimination against women in the medical
profession as well as in other fields. Carol Brohm traced the treatment
of females in war as represented in Hollywood feature entertainment
films.[4] One of the early films showing a woman successfully doing what
was considered a man's duty in war was *Dishonored* in 1931, starring
Marlene Dietrich as a World War I spy. The 1939 movie, *Nurse Edith
Cavell*, told the story of the World War I nurse who secretly tended
underground allied soldiers in German-occupied Belgium and who was
ultimately caught and executed. A number of World War II-period
films lauded nurses in that war. In *Cry Havoc* (1943) a group of nurses
volunteer for duty on Bataan in the Philippines in the face of likely
death or capture by the Japanese. *So Proudly We Hail* (1943) tells of brave
American nurses behind enemy lines in the early days of the war.
Although essentially with a soap-opera plot line, the film captured the
realism of war and the trials the women went through. *Keep Your Powder
Dry* (1945), considered mediocre by the critics, nevertheless praised the
determination of three women who join the Women's Army Auxiliary
Corps (WAACS); their role-model roles purportedly motivated many
young women to enlist. *Flight Nurse* (1953) was generally panned, but

it portrayed the work of Air Corps nurse Captain Lillian Keil during the Korean War, who at the time was the military's most decorated woman. Although the film is blatantly an anti-communist propaganda piece, "In the same vein as the earlier *So Proudly We Hail* and *Cry Havoc*, this Republic film pays homage to our military's heroic nursing corps – this time U.S. Air Force flight nurses, saving lives at great personal risk during the Korean War."[5]

While these and similar films did not present a pro-feminist polemic, they did show that women were capable of doing things with dignity and strength at least as well as men. On the other hand, many other films about women in war were comedies that showed women in an opposite light: Incapable and incompetent, dependent on males, ditsy, airheads, or principally sex objects. For example, one of the best of the anti-war protest films, *M*A*S*H* (1970), was also one of the most flagrant sexist films of its genre. The two principal female roles are the butts of continual jokes by the males about their main use being for sex and, in fact, the two are used for sex by the male officers while their contributions to saving the lives of wounded are virtually ignored. Many other female-in-war films, before and after *M*A*S*H*, portray women characters in a similar way. One of the later examples, in 1999, is *The General's Daughter*, a story that "concerns the havoc wrought by an incredibly promiscuous female Army captain upon tough, disciplined men."[6] An early example of a comedy demeaning women in war was *Operation Petticoat* in 1959. In this highly lauded comedy, a group of female nurses join an all-male ship, resulting in comic chaos. As one critic later noted, "Some of the humor today seems sexist, especially with much of the military having been integrated."[7]

A number of non-war films showed women as important achievers, but endowed them with fatal flaws that revealed, by the end of the movie, weaknesses that undid them. *All About Eve* (1950) is a brilliant and cynical look at show business. A female star becomes the mentor of a young, sympathetic actress who, by the end of the movie, has manipulated herself into a position of stardom at the expense of her benefactor. Personal gain affords no scruples, for women as well as for men. A later "fatal flaw" film is *The Business of Strangers* (2001). While the movie shows a female business executive as president of a company, she is manipulated by another woman to the point of madness. Another highly praised film, from the Broadway hit, is *The Women* (1939), about "divorce, cattiness, and competition in [a] circle of 'friends'."[8] The movie reveals a hard, vicious side of women.

Some hit films, many of them comedies, had as their theme the competition between a man and a woman, with the man putting the woman in what was considered her subordinate place. A classic illustrating this approach is *Woman of the Year* (1942), in which "a world-famed political commentator is brought down to earth by [a] sports reporter . . . whom she later weds."[9] That many if not most films like this were not deliberately sexist is borne out by the fact that co-screenwriter of *Woman of the Year*, Ring Lardner, Jr., was a strong social and political liberal and very likely was simply reflecting the elements of a good comedy as perceived by the vast majority of people at the time. The sexism prevalent in the country, especially before the 1970s, simply represented itself in films by writers not being sensitive to gender politics.

In a number of "opposite-view" films women were presented in a highly positive light. Instead of suffering because they used their strength and talent as men would, instead of compromising to assume, at least in part, traditional stereotyped lives, the women remained strong and steadfast despite obstacles and odds against them. Many of these pictures clearly protested sexism, either as a principal or secondary purpose. By secondary purpose, we mean a film whose main theme is a protest against some other inequity in society, but whose story shows women doing a job that men weren't able to do. Two outstanding examples are films discussed in the chapter on labor vs. management, *Salt of the Earth* (1954) and *Norma Rae* (1979).

In *Salt of the Earth* striking male miners are forced off the picket line. Despite the vehement opposition of most of them to their wives getting directly involved in the strike, rather than continue their stereotypical housewifely duties, the women take over the picket line. They prove to the men – and to themselves – the fallacy of the men's fears that they, the women, would not succeed because they would be too weak and unable to stand up to management and the strike-busting goons. In *Norma Rae* essentially the same kind of self-realization occurs. No one – not a single male – in the factory is willing to show the courage necessary to fight for decent wages and working conditions. A male union organizer from outside the state is unable to get any of the male workers to act. An uneducated, unsophisticated mother working on the assembly line is willing to help the union organizer. The more she sees the hardships enforced on her family and friends by the company, the more determined she is to establish a union. At first the other workers refuse to listen to her because she is a woman, and her husband disapproves of what she is doing. She perseveres, despite personal attacks and being fired from her job, standing far more bravely, courageously, and with personal strength than any of her male co-workers. Finally, the union is voted in. In both of these films, women win against the opposition of male-dominated societies. The films not only protest anti-labor practices, but protest the attitudes and actions that presume women are not as capable as men and should be relegated to traditional stereotypical roles.

A 1974 film, *Alice Doesn't Live Here Anymore*, is the story of a determined woman to find success and happiness in life for herself and her son after her husband dies, leaving her destitute. Despite all odds, she succeeds without compromising her personal integrity, remaining strong and independent. Critic David Litton wrote: "The character of Alice is one of the more well-drawn characters I've seen in a film of this sort. We're given a complete understanding of her experiences, and how she has been affected by the events of her life . . . she makes decisions . . . rather than sinking into the depths of self-servitude.[10]

By the late 1970s nuances of interpretation began to appear in films that, on the surface, appeared to protest the beliefs that women are dependent on men for survival or achievement. In the 1979 sci-fi horror film, *Alien*, the female lead fights off aliens in saving the human race. The original script had the female lead die and the male lead survive. But the film was changed to stress the strength, durability, and importance of the female, with the male dying. The woman is the powerful figure, achieving what her male colleague could not. Certainly a strong feminist statement? Or is it? Critic Janice Hocker Rushing viewed it as "an anti-feminist film which pits the 'Good Mother/goddess' against the 'Bad Mother/monster/goddess' and so reaffirms conservative visions of femininity which have bifurcated the feminine consciousness and so stigmatized certain types of women who do accept their 'proper' role in the patriarchy."[11]

A 1980 film, *Nine to Five*, is considered by many to be the beginning of a series of Hollywood films deliberately and openly protesting one or more manifestations of sexism in society existing at the times the films were made. Going back to the ancient Greeks, satire has been a staple of political and social protest. Aristophanes made a powerful statement against war and, perhaps more pertinently, about the power women could wield in society if they wished, in *Lysistrata*. (For those who do not remember the plot of *Lysistrata*, the women decide to withhold sex from the men to force them to end the Peloponnesian War and maintain peace.) Could Aristophanes have made these strong political and social statements and had them accepted as effectively in a finger-pointing drama rather than in a comedy-satire?

Nine-to-Five is about three women office workers who are harassed and oppressed by their sexist boss. After a series of incidents – funny on the surface and getting sexist laughs from audiences, but not so funny to the women being degraded by them – the three women decide to get revenge on the boss. The

> three office revolutionaries . . . kidnap their male chauvinist boss, rewrite all sorts of sexist office rules and assumptions, become involved with a strange corpse, smoke pot, get drunk, discover the joys of sisterly relationships and, in the process, raise office efficiency to a new all-time high . . . There's no problem with capitalism these three liberated Nancy Drews can't solve if they don't have to keep running out to get coffee for their superiors . . . *Nine to Five* begins as satire, slips uncertainly into farce.[12]

In some ways the film is reminiscent of some of the screwball comedies of the 1930s that had touches of social and/or political comment. The moral: Sexism doesn't pay and women not only can do as well as men who are their bosses, but even better. Critic Scott Renshaw, although panning the film as a whole, nevertheless wrote: "Back in 1980, long before anyone had heard the term 'political correctness', it seemed terribly daring to offer up a female empowerment revenge fantasy about workplace sexual politics . . . it [*Nine to Five*] was unquestionably a crowd-pleaser with its intended audience, chock full of moments that inspired whoops of cathartic release from women viewers."[13] Although considered preposterous in plot and character by some critics, the film was prompted by, and protested, existing conditions in society. One of the three women was played by Jane Fonda. "The idea of a movie about women office workers was Fonda's, the result of talks she had with clerical workers in Cleveland and Boston."[14] The movie unabashedly waves the banner of feminism as it protests sexism.

A 1987 film, *Working Girl*, appeared at first to be in the same vein – that is, a female assistant (Tess) ultimately working her way up the ladder despite the difficulties thrown in her path. In the film, her boss (Katherine) displays the ruthless qualities that male executives use to stay at the top. Katherine steals Tess's ideas, but at the end of the movie Tess wins out, closing the big deal – but only with the help of a male, with whom she falls in love. However, sexism is not established as an issue, insofar as the exploitation is principally that of a female boss against her female assistant. To the degree that the female boss is given the traits usually attributed to male bosses, some viewers might infer gender bias. Film analyst J. Emmett Winn wrote: "Unfortunately, the film does not choose to highlight this sort of business snobbery as a significant social problem or as an unethical business practice. The rhetoric of this film does not offer a social answer to a social problem. Tess's problems are manifested in an individual female adversary, Katherine, rather than an unfair social structure."[15]

Some reviewers and many viewers saw *Working Girl* as a pro-feminist statement, but for others the title itself belied that. We often hear a male executive refer to a 40- or 60-year old female secretary or clerk as "the 'girl' at the front desk" or say "I'll tell my 'girl' to call you." How many times have you heard a 40- or 60-year old male assistant referred to as a "boy"?

By the 1990s, concerns about sexism had become an integral part of most organizations in both the public and private sectors. Federal, state, and local laws and ordinances and in-house codes of rules and regulations made everyone aware of what gender discrimination was and, in most cases, what to do to avoid it. Reflecting the public understanding and purported attitudes, if not necessarily its compliance, Hollywood produced a number of movies in that decade that were protests against sexism – against the prejudicial and stereotypical treatment of women. *Thelma and Louise*, in 1991, continues to be considered one of the outstanding statements of the bonding of women in their refusal to accept unequal treatment and suppression by the male-dominated society. Two women taking a short vacation trip together become fugitives when one has to shoot a man to stop him from raping her friend. At the end they decide they are willing to die together rather than surrender to a prejudicial and sexist justice system – reminiscent of the male bonding in a similar ending in 1969's *Butch Cassidy and the Sundance Kid*. Peter Travers wrote in *Rolling Stone* that

Some may have conflicting feelings about Thelma and Louise: are they feminist martyrs or bitches from hell? Neither is the case. They're flesh-and-blood women out to expose the blight of sexism. Khouri [the screenwriter] doesn't turn her movie into a man-hating tract, but she does show what a lifetime of male sexual threat and domination (disguised as paternalism) can do.[16]

Another critic wrote that *Thelma and Louise* "struck a deep chord in audiences across gender, racial, and class lines ... [the film] feminized a genre previously owned by men."[17] Callie Khouri's script won an Academy Award for best original screenplay.

The following year, in 1992, another film protesting sexism earned widespread acclaim. *A League of Their Own* presents a situation where a group of women are scorned for trying to do something that presumably only men can do – and succeed in doing it. During World War II corporate owners associated with professional baseball were concerned that the professional leagues might suffer or even fold because so many baseball players were in the armed forces. To fill the gap (although the major leagues did continue to operate through the war), it was decided to try to form a women's baseball league.

Figure 11.1
Thelma and Louise (1991)

After years of perpetrating the image of the docile little woman who sat at home caring for her lord and master, American society suddenly found that it needed women who were competent to do hard skilled work during World War II. Rosie the Riveter became a national emblem, Hollywood threw out its romance scripts and started making movies about strong, independent females, and it was discovered that women could actually excel at professional sports.[18]

The All-American Girls Baseball League was formed. The film follows the trials and tribulations of one of the teams. "In addition to public apathy, the league's backers have to overcome furious editorials warning against the threatened 'masculinization' of the players."[19] The players on the team suffer derision and harassment. But they persevere and win out, finally playing in the league's World Series. Even after

World War II was over and the men returned, with the male professional baseball leagues once again at full strength, the women's league lasted until 1954, when it was disbanded and quickly virtually forgotten. "It's a serious film, lighter than air, a very funny movie that manages to score a few points for feminism"[20] The "movie is about transition – about how it felt as a woman suddenly to have new roles and freedom . . . [an] early chapter of women's liberation."[21]

A few years later, in 1996, a film entitled *The Associate* dealt with gender discrimination on Wall Street. The protagonist, played by Whoopi Goldberg, has hit the glass ceiling in her company. Going off on her own, she is forced to invent an imaginary white male as purported president of her company in order for the company to be taken seriously by the male-dominated industry. The company prospers and her imaginary white male president is considered the new wizard of finance. Everyone wants to meet him, and Goldberg, in costume, attempts to oblige. Chaos and comedy follow when she realizes she has to eliminate the imaginary business president. But ultimately all ends well and the Goldberg character is recognized for her achievements in a man's world. "It's an interesting look at corporate America and the obstacles and slights that woman and minorities endure."[22]

Some critics felt that, as a comedy, it was not funny enough; others felt that there were too many gags that undercut the film's important message. The film, however, clearly addressed and protested a sexist aspect of society that was not only at issue when the film was made, but was prevalent before and continues to be prevalent long after its release. "For those who would question the glass-ceiling sexism portrayed in Whoopi Goldberg's movie *The Associate*, supporting data arrived in a report by the nonprofit group Catalyst. It said women accounted for a mere 10 percent of the nearly 13,000 corporate officers employed by the 500 largest United States companies [in 1995]."[23]

Among the other 1990s pictures protesting sexism – most of them, as it turned out, artistically mediocre – is *G.I. Jane* in 1997. The plot revolves around a plan to convince the military hierarchy to permit females to participate in combat by showing that a woman can withstand the rigors of Navy Seal training – a program in which sixty percent of male recruits fail to qualify. The female navy lieutenant chosen for the test is harassed and discriminated against, especially by the male chauvinist Master Chief. She is given physical ordeals designed to destroy her and wash her out of the program – thus putting an end to the plan. She endures virtually unendurable mental and physical trials, including being beaten unconscious by the sadistic Chief. Though almost giving up during the grueling process, through grim determination she keeps up with the men in the training unit and eventually succeeds. While much of the film is unrealistically dramatic, it is a clear protest, in the larger sense, against the sexist mindset that says that women are incapable of doing a job, even a physical job, as well as men, and in a specific sense, against the lack of gender quality in the armed forces.

Erin Brockovich (2000) is the story of a real person who proved that she could overcome the stereotype of background, position, and appearance to do what her male colleagues were unwilling or unable to do. Erin Brockovich is the "brassy, divorced mother of three, at the end of her rope; she talks her way into a job [at a] law office, then becomes obsessed with a pro bono case involving residents of a California desert town who have been exposed to poisonously polluted water . . . [it's a] David vs. Goliath story"[24]. She investigates, despite the initial reluctance of her boss, and finds a cover-up of the water supply having been contaminated by toxic chemicals from a power plant, killing and sickening residents of the area. She helps win the largest direct-action lawsuit settlement up to that time.

Brockovich's clothes and makeup are stereotypes of a bimbo, with ridiculous high heels, and at first look she appears to be incapable of doing anything with intelligent seriousness. Her actions, however, belie the frequent male judgment of a woman's outer appearance and show that what is within is what counts. As *New York Times* movie reviewer A. O. Scott wrote, "Erin is a life force, brimming with wholesome sexuality and unpretentious common sense."[25] Scott notes the hardships sexism imposes: "You not only witness the humiliations casually and routinely visited on working-class women; you feel in the pit of your stomach the overwhelming anxiety of impoverished single motherhood, which often amounts to a state of sheer terror."[26] Scott likened *Erin Brockovich* to *Norma Rae* and *Silkwood*.[27]

Some moviegoers viewed 2001's *Legally Blonde* as a feminist film protesting male attitudes that women are not as capable as they are. A somewhat silly movie, it is about a rather ditsy co-ed, a sorority queen who is considered to be an airhead. Her boyfriend, enrolled in Harvard Law School, dumps her, considering her not a suitable mate for his future political career. She perseveres to get into Harvard Law School in order to prove him wrong. Naturally, by the end of the film her boyfriend gets his comeuppance, as she not only succeeds at Harvard, but dumps him for another lawyer.

The Stepford Wives (2004) is a remake of the well-made 1975 hit horror film adapted from Ira Levin's sci-fi/horror novel. The 2004 version was made as a comedy, prompting some critics – such as Roger Ebert – to like it better than the 1975 version. Other critics, such as A. O. Scott, thought the remake was, at least in part, an incoherent disaster. Both versions, however, have as their theme, whether delineated through comedy or horror, a protest against sexist treatment of women, specifically wives. The Stepford wives are "vapid creatures who speak in trivialities and live only to please their husbands."[28] The latter part of that dictum reflects not only the attitudes of many in 1975, but the place of women publicly advocated by a number of right-wing and fundamentalist religious leaders and organizations in the conservative first decade of the twenty-first century. In the film the husbands of Stepford killed off their feminist-leaning wives "and replaced them with subservient, sexually compliant robots."[29] At the end the live women win out and the men no longer rule. Roger Ebert's review in 2004 noted that in 1975 "feminism was newer" and that the original premise for the film "satirized the male desire for tame, sexy wives who did what they were told and never complained."[30]

The conservatism at the beginning of the twenty-first century was reflected in the lack of significant films protesting sexism. One 2005 film that apparently aimed to follow the true-life efforts of women in films such as *Salt of the Earth, Norma Rae,* and *Erin Brockovich* was *North Country*, the story of

> a group of women who broke the status quo by working as iron miners in the remote, male-dominated world of northern Minnesota's Iron Range . . . [the handful of women, after suffering physical and psychological threats, language and behavior, bring] a class-action suit against the mine for sexual harassment . . . it would be the first sexual harassment class action suit in history against a major corporation and would therefore change the course of how women are treated in the workplace.[31]

The women win, after a long courtroom battle, casting a blow against sexism. Reviews generally praised the purpose of the film, but criticized a wobbly structure, arbitrary events at the trial, and its disintegration at the end.

Perhaps the status of pictures protesting sexism was best stated by syndicated columnist Ellen Goodman after seeing the 2007 movie, *Juno*, about a 16-year-old who becomes pregnant. The young woman decides not have an abortion and instead intends to put the baby up for adoption. Goodman notes "a slew of reviews praising the film for skewering the pieties of both sides of the family-values debate . . . but we are in the midst of an entire wave of movies about pregnant women – from *Knocked Up* to *Waitress* to *Bella* – all deciding to have their babies and all wrapped up in nice, neat bows."[32]

Goodman says that in films "abortion has become the right-to-choose that's never chosen," and quotes historian Stephanie Coontz of Evergreen State College: "Social conservatives are backing off on the condemnation of single mothers. Social liberals are backing off on the idea that it's possible to have an abortion and not be ruined by it." Goodman states, "This is best expressed by Hollywood, which wants to be all things to all audiences."[33]

Goodman's examples reflect two things about Hollywood: Its continuing reluctance to deal with controversial issues, and its adherence to the popular political and social attitudes of a given time, believing that will enable it to attract larger audiences to the box office and a fatter bottom line.

Where have all the protest movies gone? With the conservative-controlled media attempting to paint Hollywood as a hotbed of liberalism, it is ironic that those who make the decisions about the content of films in this first decade of the twenty-first century appear to be reflecting the conservative and largely sexist attitudes of the right wing towards women.

Notes

1   Women's International Center. *Women's History in America*, 1994. www.wic.org/misc/history.htm.
2   Powers, Stephen and Stanley Rothman, "Feminism in Films," *Society*, March, 1993, p. 67.
3   Freeman, Jo, *The Politics of Women's Liberation* (New York: David McKay, 1975), p. 25.

4   Much of the material about women in war in Hollywood films is adapted from a paper prepared by Carol Brohm for the "Pictures of Protest" course, Emerson College, April 28, 2003.

5   Wilson, Barbara, "Military Women in Films," 1996. http://userpages. aug.com/captbarb/films.html.

6   Maslin, Janet, "*The General's Daughter*," *New York Times*. www.mith2. umd.edu/womensstudies/filmreviews.

7   Koller, Brian, *Operation Petticoat*. http://filmsgraded.com.html.

8   Maltin, Leonard, "*The Women*," *Movie and Video Guide* (New York: Penguin, 2003), p. 1579.

9   *Ibid.*, p. 1577.

10 Litton, David, "*Alice Doesn't Live Here Anymore*," *Movie Eye*, January 6, 2003. www.movieeye.com/reviews/read_movie_review/1074.html.

11 Lyden, John, Janice Hocker Rushing quoted in "To Commend or to Critique," *Journal of Religion and Film*, October 2, 1997. www.unomaha.edu/ jrf/tocommend.htm.

12 Canby, Vincent, "*Nine to Five*," *New York Times*, December 19, 1980. http://movies.nytimes.com/movie/review?r=1&res=950DEEDE.

13 Renshaw, Scott, "*9 to 5*," *Apollo Movie Guide*. www.rottentomatoes.com/ m/9_to_5/articles/239438.

14 Ansen, David, "Supersecretaries," *Newsweek*, March 31, 1980, p. 80.

15 Winn, J. Emmett, "Moralizing Upward Mobility: Investigating the Myth of Class Mobility in *Working Girl*," *Southern Communication Journal*, Fall, 2000, p. 45.

16 Travers, Peter, "*Thelma and Louise*," *Rolling Stone*, February 5, 2001. www. rollingstone.com/reviews/DVD/5948343/review/5948343/thelma_louise.

17 Schneider, Steven Jay, ed., *1001 Movies You Must See Before You Die* (New York: Quintet Publishing/Barron's, 2003), p. 808.

18 Ebert, Roger, "*A League of Their Own*," *Chicago Sun-Times*, July 1, 1992. http://rogerebert.suntimes.com/apps/pbcs.dll/article?AID=/19920701/ REVIEWS/2070103.

19 Canby, Vincent, "*A League of Their Own*," *New York Times*, July 1, 1992. http://movies.nytimes.com/movie/review?res=9E0CEED.

20 *Ibid.*

21 Ebert, Roger, "*A League of Their Own*."

22 Maltin, Leonard, "*The Associate*," p. 63.

23 Weiskind, Ron, "Whoopi at Work: *The Associate* Scratches Gloss from the Glass Ceiling," *Pittsburgh Gazette*, October 25, 1996, Sections A&E, p. 5.

24 Maltin, Leonard, "*Erin Brockovich*," p. 415.

25 Scott, A. O., "*Erin Brockovich*," *New York Times*, March 17, 2000. http://movies.nytimes.com/movie/review?res=9805EED.

26 *Ibid.*

27 *Ibid.*

28 Erickson, Hal, *"The Stepford Wives,"* *All Movie Guide*, November 17, 1975. http://movies.nytimes.com/movie/111705/The_Stepford_Wives/overview.

29 Scott, A. O., *"The Stepford Wives,"* *New York Times*, June 11, 2004. http://movies.nytimes.com/movie/review?res=9A0DE2DA.

30 Ebert, Roger, *"The Stepford Wives,"* *Chicago Sun-Times*, June 11, 2004. http://rogerebert.suntimes.com.apps.dll/article?AID=/20040611/REVIEWS.

31 Clinton, Paul, *"North Country,"* CNN, October 21, 2005. www.cnn.com/2005/SHOWBIZ/Movies/10/21/review.north/index.html.

32 Goodman, Ellen, "Hollywood fantasizes realities of pregnancy," *News-Press* (Fort Myers, FL), January 11, 2008, p. B9.

33 *Ibid.*

12
Hide or Seek

Other genres: Will Hollywood shut up or speak up?

There are many more issues that have been subjects of protest films, such as the medical and hospital system, attitudes toward and treatment of immigrants, elitism and social status, educational philosophies and institutions, product safety (e.g., tobacco), ethnic discrimination, global corporate conglomerates, public- and private-sector corruption, religious dogma and oppression, environmental pollution, and whistle-blowers in government and industry. An extended discussion of these and other subjects will have to wait for another book, this volume having reached the contracted-for number of pages that will enable it to be published and sold at a reasonable price.

What next for Hollywood feature entertainment films as we approach the second decade of the twenty-first century? Will the jingoistic, nationalistic "if-you-aren't-for-me-then-you're-against-me" rhetoric continue to cow most producers and distributors into self-restriction to non-controversial, non-protest films? Will a more liberal and tolerant political agenda encourage Hollywood to embrace contemporary issues of controversy?

Medical–Hospital System

Certainly, most, if not all of the subject areas discussed in this book will be still at issue. Certainly, the subject areas not covered in this book will be omnipresent. For example, the increasing dissatisfaction with the healthcare system and with hospital errors in patient care that result in perhaps hundreds of thousands of people dying needlessly each year are urgent subjects of protest. They have been dealt with before by Hollywood, with significant impact on the public. But the problems remain. Arguably the seminal film on the treatment of mental illness, for instance, goes back more than 60 years, to *The Snake Pit* in 1948. "This pro-psychiatry film is cited as one of the first Hollywood movies to give serious attention to the subject of mental illness. Its confidence in psychiatric diagnosis and treatments, especially the combination of psychoanalysis and physical therapies, reflects the increasing optimism of psychiatry in the early 1950s."[1] The protest against the general lack of psychiatric approaches as opposed to physical restraint and drug devices in mental hospitals is set against the abominable conditions and neglect mental hospital patients experienced.

The title of this movie is taken from the practice, apparently common in some ancient cultures, of placing people insane into a pit full of snakes. Those cultures knew virtually nothing of the forms of mental illness documented in the 19th and 20th centuries. Even less did they know of psychotherapy. This picture is remarkable for taking us right into a mental hospital and immersing us in the experience.[2]

The movie "criticize[d] conditions in the institution, showing the inexplicable cruelty of some nurses, the incompetence of many doctors, the overcrowding, and the poor nourishment."[3]

The Snake Pit offers a rare look into the world of mental illness and its treatment modalities . . . The film offers a view from all angles: the confused and frightened patient, her concerned and loving husband, the dedicated and determined doctor, and the hospital system itself, with its overcrowded population, the bars and locks, the straitjackets and shock treatments.[4]

The success and stark revelations of the film prompted calls from social groups and political sources for reform of mental hospitals. "After its release in 1948, 26 states changed laws regarding treatment of the mentally ill."[5]

A later film, a blockbuster at the box office and now a classic and on virtually every list of filmdom's best movies, is 1975's *One Flew Over the Cuckoo's Nest*. Briefly, it's the story of "a feisty misfit [who] enters an insane asylum and inspires his fellow patients to assert themselves to the chagrin of [the] strong-willed head nurse."[6] The movie raises a similar question addressed in 1966's *King of Hearts* (not a Hollywood film, but a British–French production), in which the inmates of an insane asylum in France are temporarily liberated when its location becomes a battlefield during World War I. While the supposedly "sane" people of the world are deliberately killing each other, the freed "insane" people enjoy peaceful camaraderie. Who is really sane and who is really insane?

In *One Flew Over the Cuckoo's Nest* the sane protagonist – he was given a choice of a short time in the asylum or in jail for what was considered antisocial behavior – motivates the other inmates to seek personal self-realization. The head nurse and others in the institution are unable to deal with what they consider outrageous disrespect for and flouting of the rigid rules and procedures. The sadistic nurse finally forces the sane instigator – the one who gave pleasure and hope, a respite from oppression, and a sense of normalcy to the others – into a lobotomy. "She has turned her ward into an instrument of power and has cowed the inmates into submission to her inflexible routine. She is aided by her staff, nurses and orderlies. Doctors may have titular control of the hospital, but [Nurse] Ratched has unquestionable power over her patients. The orderlies are more like prison guards."[7]

The protest against the insensitive and authoritarian treatment of the mentally ill, in this case, in our mental hospitals, is strong and unequivocal. Not everyone praised the film. Roger Ebert felt that the movie was "toned down for the 1970s into a parable about society's enforcement of conformism . . . almost willfully overlooked the realities of mental illness in order to turn the patients into a group of cuddly characters."[8] On the other hand, the movie's impact was described by a medical science source as follows:

> The screenplay is highly effective in portraying the sanatorium, the use of drugs, ECT [electroconvulsive therapy] and lobotomy as devices of repression of human free will. It was tremendously influential, since it was released during the crazy decade of the seventies, with the hippie movement, leftist student rebellions, and the Vietnam war. The audience is led to side with the inmates rather than with the asylum wardens. As such, it has helped to make ECT and lobotomy into "politically incorrect," undesirable and dictatorial tools of the establishment to impose punishment and atonement.[9]

The film won the five principal Academy Awards: best picture, screen-play, director, actor, and actress.

Several other films from the 1990s to the present deal with the healthcare system. Robin Williams starred in two of them as a doctor attempting to help patients within the rigidity of a callous medical system. In *Awakenings* (1990) he is a doctor in a chronic care unit, which includes patients who have been comatose for long periods of time and considered to be hopeless vegetables. "Patients are fed, watered and kept clean, but never ever expected to recover. Many were admitted 30, 40 and 50 years ago, and no doctor has even bothered to review their records."[10] Based on a true story, Williams's character wants to determine if the drug, L-Dopa, might work on some of the patients. The chemist tells him, "I don't know, I'm just a chemist, we let the doctors take the risks." His supervising doctor tells him, "No way, we're doctors, let the chemists take the risks."

Fighting against the medical establishment, he takes the risk himself and succeeds in awakening one patient from a 30-year coma. The movie protests the conservative self-protection of the medical system, putting the welfare of the establishment above the needs of the patient.

In *Patch Adams* – also based on a true story – Williams is suicidal and put in a mental institution where he finds more understanding and help in getting better through personal interaction and caring from inmates than from the impersonal and humorless medical staff. He determines to go to medical school, become a doctor, and treat patients with more personal sensitivity and humor. In medical school, at age 40, "while the teachers preach book learning and emotional detachment, Patch believes that to treat a disease, the physician should connect with his patients."[11] He treats patients with laughter, improving their medical conditions, but in doing so alienates the staff and faculty of the medical school. He starts his own clinic and ultimately is forced to defend his methods before a board seeking to disbar him from the practice of medicine. His defense: "If we're going to fight a disease, let's fight one of the most terrible diseases of all: indifference."[12]

A movie earnestly attempting to protest the unfeeling, mean-spirited treatment of its members by HMOs (health maintenance organizations) – and, by implication, the lack of a universal healthcare system in the United States – was *John Q* in 2002. A man who has hit economic hard times is turned down by his HMO for a heart procedure necessary for his young son to survive. In desperation, feeling he has been deceived by the HMO, he takes people at the HMO hospital hostage, hoping to negotiate the operation for their release. The protest point is made, although the film itself was generally panned. For example, both the *New York Times* and the *Chicago Sun-Times* critics, Elvis Mitchell and Roger Ebert, criticized the movie, citing plot clichés, overwrought melodrama, contrived sequences, and implausible events. As Mitchell wrote, "The country's sad state of health care for the poor and disenfranchised is a great movie subject. Until that film comes along, we'll have to endure *John Q*, which will leave most audiences in dire need of medical attention."[13]

Immigration

Another area of protest in Hollywood films is that of immigration. The issue appears to have become exacerbated late in the first decade of the twenty-first century as the situation of so-called illegal immigrants and the fate of their families and children is used for political ploys by vote-seeking politicians, many of them reiterating the mantras associated with the bigotry that marked much of the United States' racist past. If the family trees of those advocating denial of rights to and/or deportation of illegal immigrants were examined, how many would turn out to be the progeny of illegal immigrants, and how many of them would voluntarily deport themselves?

Many films over the years have dealt with immigrants. They range from movies about pioneers from other countries, some legal, many illegal, settling the western United States despite deprivation and hardship, to movies about immigrants escaping from intolerable economic or political or religious discrimination and conditions, and settling in US urban centers. They are usually depicted in films as fighting to rise out of poverty against all odds to become part of the purported American Dream. Many films show how the efforts of immigrants to integrate into their new land are hampered by prejudice from those already in the country, attitudes that have continued from the very early days of the settlement of the part of North America that became the United States: Bigotry, legal restrictions, and even violence against those with religious beliefs different from the already-arrived majority, against each new ethnic group, such as Asians on the west coast, Irish, Jews, Italians, and other Europeans on the east coast, Latinos in the South and Southwest, Africans wherever they went. All had to overcome efforts to keep them out or to marginalize them after they arrived.

Charlie Chaplin's short silent film, *The Immigrant* (1917), established a key theme for this genre: Two poor immigrants arrive in the United States, full of hope for a new life in the promised land of opportunity. Once they get there, they find it hard to even survive. Although supposedly a comedy featuring Chaplin's brilliant pantomime routines, like all of Chaplin's work it has a point of view: The difficulties of immigrants in the new world. As one critic put it, Chaplin "introduced a pathos unheard of in slapstick films."[14]

Films about immigrants usually depict two principal paths. One is the nostalgic, family-oriented approach, in which one or more members of the family try to or make their way out of the ethnic or racial ghetto into mainstream America, sometimes having to break with elements of their past. Two films about Jewish immigrants, *The Jazz Singer* – the first "talkie" – in 1927 and *Hester Street*, in 1975, are examples. A 2003 example about another ethnic group is *The Joy Luck Club*, the story of a group of Chinese women immigrants who settle in San Francisco and encounter the difficulties of cultural differences and assimilation in raising their own children in the United States, trying to maintain enduring family ties in a struggle with changing cultures.

Another is the survival through violence approach, in which the only way out of poverty and corruption surrounding the protagonist is by joining the corrupters and turning to crime. Such films usually are set in the economic depression of the 1930s or the prohibition era of the 1920s. *The Godfather* (1972) and its sequels are outstanding examples of this route. The gangster genre frequently depicts Italian immigrants as the lawbreakers, their way of pursuing the American Dream. For many, "it is dismaying – no, infuriating – to see one's group depicted so consistently in such distorted fashion. Unlike racist stereotyping of Blacks, portrayals of Italian-American criminality don't reflect or reinforce Italian-American exclusion from American society and its opportunities."[15]

Gangster immigrant films include other ethnic groups, too. *Once Upon a Time in America* (1984) is about two Jewish immigrants who become gangsters, as are other films about Jewish mobsters, include those of the Murder, Inc. period. *Gangs of New York* (2003) represented – more accurately, misrepresented – Irish immigrant gangsters in nineteenth-century New York. Oliver Stone's *Scarface* in 1983 had a Cuban immigrant gangster stating a motivation that could apply to most immigrants turning to crime to get out of poverty and then using crime to really make it in America: "In this country you gotta make the money first. Then when you get the money, you get the power. Then when you get the power, then you get the women."[16]

Many of these films show the important contributions immigrants – legal and illegal – have made to this country. Some do so within the context of other struggles, such as the labor movement, carrying a burden in addition to the problems facing them as immigrants. For example, *Salt of the Earth*, discussed in chapters 5 and 11, tells how immigrant Mexican workers stood up to the corporate establishment exploiting them.

As discussed in chapter 7, racial profiling, ethnic discrimination, and harsh immigration policies that have affected many people from many countries prompted a Hollywood picture of protest regarding Middle Eastern immigrants, *The Visitor*. One may hope that the success of this film will prompt Hollywood to make more films revealing the cruel implementation of policies against immigrants – legal and illegal.

Whether direct or indirect, whether the protagonists are sympathetic or not, most films about immigrants appear to have a direct or implied protest of the prejudice, inequality of opportunity, and other difficulties imposed on newcomers to the United States.

Tobacco and Corporate Greed

Whistle-blowing protests against corporate greed at the expense of the health and well-being of consumers have been subjects of more recent films, perhaps because the Internet has revealed information to the public that the mainstream media, owned or dependent upon the advertising of corporations, have kept hidden. (For example, the media support for continuing legal action against users of marijuana, which appears to cause few or no direct deaths from its use, while the same media maintain a status quo or supportive attitude, usually through ads, concerning the use of tobacco, which each year kills about 400,000 Americans and about five million people worldwide.) Not surprisingly, some of the protest films have dealt directly with tobacco. Roger Ebert summarized the 1999 protest movie against tobacco companies' deceptions, *The Insider*:

a thriller and exposé of how big tobacco's long-running tissue of lies was finally exposed by investigative journalism. At its center stands Lowell Bergman, a producer for *60 Minutes*, the CBS news program where a former tobacco scientist, Jeffrey Wigand, spilled the beans. First Bergman coaxes Wigand to talk. Then he works with reporter Mike Wallace to get the story. Then he battles with CBS executives who are afraid to run it – because a lawsuit could destroy the network.[17]

Ebert makes it clear that the film is not entirely consistent with the facts, but does provide the public with the basic understanding of the tobacco industry's cover-up for years, knowing that tobacco was dangerous to people's health. He states that, "in its broad strokes, *The Insider* is perfectly accurate: Big tobacco lied, one man had damning information, skilled journalism developed the story, intrigue helped blast it free. *The Insider* had a greater impact on me than *All the President's Men*, because . . . Watergate didn't kill my parents. Cigarettes did."[18]

In 2006 the film *Thank You for Smoking* was a revealing satire on the chicanery of tobacco companies and their complicity with the media in persuading people to purchase their product that kills. The plot centers around a tobacco industry lobbyist who attempts to get Hollywood to restore, as in previous decades before the true nature of smoking was made public, cigarette smoking as a positive, "cool" thing for sympathetic and role model movie characters to do. As reviewer Manohla Dargis stated in the *New York Times*, the lobbyist is "consistently on the hunt for new and inventive ways to rebrand cancer sticks for public consumption. As a Brown & Williamson Tobacco corporation memo explained decades ago, 'Doubt is our product, since it is the best means of competing with the body of fact that exists in the mind of the general public.' "[19]

Environmental Pollution

During the first decade of the twenty-first century America appeared intent on destroying itself, other than through its exponential creation of worldwide enemies and its destruction of its worldwide reputation through its unwarranted attack on Iraq, its support of torture, and its backing of dictatorial powers while refusing to aid democratic movements. Pollution of the air, the water, and the earth by industry and by consumers grew rampantly, materially aided by the White House and Congress gutting or refusing to renew anti-pollution legislation. Water in many areas became more undrinkable and in many instances poisonous. Industrial chemical spillages poisoned not only streams and rivers, but the earth itself, resulting in the sickness and death of many people. Lake overflows mixed fresh and salt-water organisms, harming the natural habitat of both flora and fauna and beach coastlines. Erosion of land hastened killing floods. Global warming through the release of pollutants that reduced the protective ozone layer appeared to cause tsunamis that killed and made homeless hundreds of thousands of people. Aging atomic reactors scattered throughout the country could result in an American Chernobyl. Liquid nitrogen gas storage plants, if ruptured, could release a fireball that could destroy everything in its path, including entire communities. Through a lack of regulation to protect all the people, the United States was fast becoming a society of disposable products, unrestrained pollution, and potential catastrophe. Some scientists believed that the future of the planet itself was a stake. Certainly, environmental pollution was a subject deserving of Hollywood attention. Hollywood has occasionally protested. One classic example is *China Syndrome* in 1979, which deals with the attempted cover-up of an accident at a nuclear power plant in California. Ironically, just as the film and its star, Jane Fonda, were being attacked by politicians, corporate energy executives, and the media for allegedly presenting an improbable scare-tactic film and were accused of virtually everything from being traitors to communists, a real, similar accident occurred at the Three Mile Island nuclear power plant in Pennsylvania. The confluence of events played an important role in convincing many Americans of the dangers of nuclear development. The 2000 film, *Erin Brockovich*, discussed in chapter 11, similarly revealed the cover-up by a power company of pollution that killed and sickened people living near the plant. *A Civil Action*, in 1998, was based on another true story, that of a Boston lawyer who "takes a case against two industrial giants whose alleged pollution of a river caused the deaths of children in Woburn, Mass."[20]

The 2007 film, *Michael Clayton*, dealt with a law-firm fixer who cleans up unethical messes involving his firm or its clients (he calls himself a "janitor"). His firm is defending a corporation that it knows is guilty of poisonous pollution. The movie is a protest against that corporate malfeasance that made and continues to make headlines in the early twenty-first century, where the greed and lack of ethics by many corporate executives result in financial ruin for many of its employees and stockholders and harm to the general public. Critic Manohla Darkis wrote in the *New York Times* that the film depicts a "requiem for American decency."[21] Roger Ebert wrote in the *Chicago Sun-Times* that *Michael Clayton* is "just about perfect as an exercise in the genre."[22]

A 2008 film, *WALL-E*, may be the definitive protest film thus far on the dangers of unrestrained environmental pollution. Using digital animation, it is about the "trash-choked disaster man has made of his home planet . . . begins on a ravaged Earth centuries in the future; humans have long since fled in cruise-line spaceships, leaving behind small robots . . . to sweep up the mess."[23] The title, *WALL-E*, refers to the robots, who are called Waste Allocation Load Lifters. While some of the robots search for signs that could bring the Earth, now barren with skyscraper-high piles of junk, back to life, the humans in their spaceships have become indolent clods, served by robots, barely able to function as what we now call people, "fat flopping tuna fish."[24] It does have a plot: Self-serving lassitudinous descendants of earthlings against robots who want to revive the Earth. *Boston Globe* movie critic Ty Burr describes *WALL-E* as an assault on "our throwaway lifestyle, the belief that hi-tech narcosis is our just reward, our corporations and politics . . . The mirror it holds up is not a flattering one."[25]

Hollywood and Television

The entertainment business and Hollywood itself have not escaped being skewered by Hollywood. The 1976 film, *Network*, protests the irresponsibility of television producers and executives toward the public. Greed and the bottom dollar come before ethics. "Sidney Lumet's cynical treatise on the moral and ethical decline of television . . . a biting satire of the lurid lengths television will go to appease its corporate overseers as well as the complicity of its vast passive viewership."[26] *The Bad and the Beautiful* (1952) is a scathing indictment of manipulation and betrayal in movie-making Hollywood, punctuated by the lust for success trumping personal integrity. In 1975, Robert Altman's *Nashville* was a biting protest of the corruption in Hollywood show business and in politics, "equating the folly of politics with the sleaze and dishonesty of the entertainment industry."[27]

Terrorism

Give the trauma that America went through with the 9/11 terrorist attacks on New York and Washington in 2001, and the worldwide strengthening of anti-US terrorism and suicide bombing as a consequence of America's unprovoked invasion and occupation of Iraq in 2004, one might think that films about terrorism and terrorists would have quickly become a Hollywood priority. Issues generated by the attack on Iraq, such as the Patriot Act's erosion of traditional American civil liberties, the authorization of torture by the United States' highest political offices, and the kidnapping and incarceration of both foreign and US citizens for years without formal charges or legal representation in prisons such as Guantánamo and those run by the United States in other countries, have been subjects of protest rallies, marches, political speeches, and literature. That these high-profile issues related to terrorism have not been subjects of Hollywood pictures of protest is not surprising, given the history of Hollywood as we have seen in this book, especially in the McCarthy and Vietnam eras.

That is not to say that there have been no Hollywood feature entertainment films dealing with terrorism. Most of the American films on this subject – there have been a number of foreign films on the subject – are wrapped in the genres of action and violence and set in a past of sci-fi future time. A 1995 film, *Outbreak*, appears to presage events of a decade later. It deals with a deadly fictional virus developed by the United States in a foreign country that is stolen by terrorists for use in America. In an article entitled "Terrorism on Film," Professor Paul Davies states that the film *Outbreak* "Poses a vital post-September 11 question . . . in the War on Terrorism, are governments prepared not only to curtail the civil liberties of their citizens, but also to go to any lengths to cover up their own scandalous negligence?"[28]

One of the earliest lauded films on terrorism was Alfred Hitchcock's 1936 *Sabotage*. But like some other subsequent well-reviewed films on terrorism, *Sabotage* was a British production. The late 1980s and early 1990s saw a number of Hollywood films about terrorists, possibly the usual after-the-crisis endeavors, prompted by the end of the US–Soviet Cold War. *Die Hard* (1988) deals with a New York Police Department detective visiting Los Angeles caught up in the middle of a German terrorist plot. It was well made, nominated for an Academy Award, and spawned highly successful subsequent *Die Hard* films. *Under Siege*, in 1992, was about terrorists on a battleship. *Under Siege 2*, in 1995, had the terrorists on a train. In 1994 a not-well-received film, *Blown Away*, dealt with Irish terrorists in Boston. *The Assignment* (1997) was about the 1980's master terrorist, Carlos the Jackal. In 1998 *The Siege* came closer to depicting the terrorism issue as we know it in the late 2000s. It has terrorist cells attacking New York City and the government rounding up suspects. *The Sum of all Fears*, in 2002, was a revival of the Cold War, with the United States tracking down a missing nuclear bomb placed in an American stadium by the Russians.

Arguably the most effective and well-made film on terrorism in recent years was *Munich* in 2005. It deals with Israelis using terrorist tactics tracking down and killing Palestinian terrorists who killed Israeli athletes at the 1972 Olympic Games. It raises the ethical and moral questions of what is terrorism and who are terrorists. Of all the films related to terrorism noted above, this may be the only one that can be legitimately called a picture of protest. A film in production as this is written appears to deal with the current state of terrorism: The CIA tracks a terrorist in Jordan. The film, *Body of Lies*, is scheduled for late 2008 release. Will it have any elements of protest?

These are brief introductions to just a few of the areas of protest – or potential protest – that hopefully will see greater attention from Hollywood – and in a future book. And like all of the genres covered in this volume, they show that when it wishes to, Hollywood can address the contemporary issues facing the country and the world with pictures of protest.

The important question is, do they have an effect on the public? Do they motivate change? Do they help create a better world for the individuals seeing the films and for their smaller and larger communities? We happen to believe that, at least to some extent, they do. Some films have had, as shown in this book, a profound effect in motivating reform. Some have had a lasting residue, if not resulting in immediate action, in the minds and emotions of the audience. Some appear to have entertained, but not informed or persuaded strongly enough to have had a discernible positive impact. Hollywood has at times demurred in addressing key controversial issues and has at other times declaimed strongly and courageously. Steven Spielberg said it this way: "We need to stop worrying only about making the Number 1 film for the July 4 weekend and realize we can all contribute something in terms of understanding the world and human rights issues."[29]

The important answer is that, given the power and influence of Hollywood feature entertainment films over the hearts and minds of people, moviedom's responsibility should be to help change beliefs and practices that are harmful to humankind by making pertinent and contemporary pictures of protest.

Notes

1 *"The Snake Pit,"* New York University Literature, Arts and Medicine Database. http://endeavor.med.nyu.edu/lit-med-db/webdocs/webfilms/snake.pit4–film-html.

2 *"The Snake Pit,"* IMBD User Comments. www.imbd.com/title/tt0040806/combined.

3 Semarne, Veda, *"The Snake Pit*: A Woman's Serpentine Journey Toward (W)Holeness,"* Literature Film Quarterly*, Vol. 22, No. 3, 1994. http://web19.epnet.com/citiation.asp?tb=1&ug=dbs+0+1n+en%2Dus+sid+78202.

4 *"The Snake Pit,"* IMBD User Comments.

5 *The Snake Pit.* www.reel.com.

6 Maltin, Leonard, *"One Flew Over the Cuckoo's Nest," Movie and Video Guide* (New York: Penguin, 2002), p. 1022.

7 Koller, Brian, *"One Flew Over the Cuckoo's Nest,"* October 10, 1999. www.epinions.com/mvie-review-5BC1-FB87094-3800E002-bd3.

8 Ebert, Roger, *"One Flew Over the Cuckoo's Nest," Chicago Sun-Times*, January 1, 1975. www.suntimes.com/apps/pbcs.dll/article?AID=/19750101/REVIEWS/501010348/1023.

9 *"One Flew Over the Cuckoo's Nest," Brain and Mind Electronic Magazine on Neuroscience.* www.cerebromente.org.br.

10 Kempley, Rita, *"Awakenings," Washington Post*, January 10, 1991. www.washingtonpost.com/wp-srv/style/longterm/movies/videos/awakeningspg13kempley_a0a0c9.htm.

11 Berardinelli, James, *Patch Adams.* http://movie-reviews.colossus.net/movies/p/patch.html.

12 *Ibid.*

13 Michell, Elvis, *"John Q," New York Times*, February 15, 2002. http://movies.nytimes.com/movie/review?res=9803EED.

14 Bordwell, David, *Film History: A Introduction* (New York: McGraw-Hill, 1994), pp. 76–7.

15 De Stefano, George, "Ungood Fellas," February 7, 2000, www.thenation. com/doc/20000207/destefano/2.

16 http://us.imdb.com/Quotes?0086250.

17 Ebert, Roger, "*The Insider*," *Chicago Sun-Times*, November 5, 1999. http://rogerebert.suntimes.com/apps/pbcs.dll/article?AID=/19991105/REVIEWS/9110503.

18 *Ibid.*

19 Dargis, Manohla, "*Thank You for Smoking*," *New York Times*, March 17, 2006. http://movies.nytimes.com/2006/03/17/movies/17smoke.html.

20 Maltin, Leonard, *A Civil Action*. *Movie and Video Guide* (New York: Penguin, 2002), p. 253.

21 Dargis, Manohla, *Michael Clayton*, *New York Times*, October 5, 2007. http://movies.nytimes.com/2007/10/05/movies/o5clay.html.

22 Ebert, Roger, "*Michael Clayton*," *Chicago Sun-Times*, October 4, 2007. http://rogerebert.suntimes.com/apps/pbcs.dll/article?AIUD=/20071004/REVIEW/710040302/1023.

23 Burr, Ty, "Out of This World" (Review of *WALL-E*). *Boston Globe*, June 27, 2008, p. D1, 14.

24 *Ibid.*

25 *Ibid.*

26 Schneider, Steven Jay, ed., *1001 Movies You Must See Before You Die* (New York: Quintet Publishing/Barron's), p. 618.

27 *Ibid.*, p. 608.

28 Davis, Paul, "Terrorism on Film." http://www.wickedness.net.

29 Thompson, Anne, "Plenty of Political Action at Oscars this Year," *Hollywood Reporter*, February 1, 2006. www.hollywoodreporter.com/thr/film/article_display.jsp?vnu_content_id=1001921711.

Selected Readings

Benshoff, Harry M. and Sean Griffin. *America on Film: Representing Race, Class, Gender, and Sexuality at the Movies.* Malden, MA: Blackwell, 2003.

Booker, M. Keith. *Film and the American Left.* (Summaries of films.) Westport, CT: Greenwood, 1999.

Buchheit, Paul. *American Wars: Illusions and Realities.* Atlanta: Clarity Press, 2008.

Buhle, Paul and Dave Wagner. *Radical Hollywood.* New York: The New Press, 2002.

Burgoyne, Robert. *Film Nation: Hollywood Looks at U.S. History.* Minneapolis: University of Minnesota Press, 1997.

Cameron, Kenneth M. *America on Film: Hollywood and American History.* New York: Continuum, 1997.

Carnes, Mark C., ed. *Past Imperfect: History According to the Movies.* New York: Holt, 1996.

Carrier, Jim. *A Travelers Guide to the Civil Rights Movement.* New York: Harcourt, 2004.

Christensen, Terry. *Reel Politics: American Political Movies from Birth of a Nation to Platoon.* New York: Basil Blackwell, 1987.

Cripps, Thomas. *Making Movies Black: Hollywood Message Movies from World War II to the Civil Rights Era.* New York: Oxford University Press, 1993.

Dickensen, Ben. *Hollywood's New Radicalism: War, globalization and the Movies from Reagan to George W. Bush.* New York: I. B. Taurus, 2006.

hooks, Bell. *Reel to Real: Race, Sex and Class at the Movies.* New York: Routledge, 1996.

Leone, Richard C. and Greg Anrig, Jr. *The War on Our Freedoms: Civil Liberties in an Age of Terrorism.* New York: Public Affairs Press, 2003.

Lowenstein, Frank, Sheryl Lechner, and Erik Bruun. *Voices of Protest: Documents of Courage and Dissent.* New York: Black Dog and Leventhal, 2007.

Mintz, Steven and Randy Roberts, eds. *Hollywood's America: United States History through its Films.* St. James: Brandywine Press, 1993.

Powers, Steven, David J. Rothman, and Stanley Rothman. *Hollywood's America: Social and Political Themes in Motion Pictures.* Boulder, CO: Westview Press, 1996.

Rampell, Ed. *Progressive Hollywood: A Peoples Film History of the United States.* New York: Disinformation, 2005.

Reed, T.V. *The Art of Political Protest: Culture and Activism from the Civil Rights Movement to the Streets of Seattle.* Minneapolis: University of Minnesota Press, 2005.

Rollins, Peter C., ed. *Hollywood as Historian: American Film in a Cultural Context.* Louisville: University Press of Kentucky, 1998.

Ross, Steven J. *Movies and American Society.* Malden, MA: Blackwell, 2002.

Schultz, David and John R. Vile, eds. *The Encyclopedia of Civil Liberties.* Armonk, NY: M. E. Sharpe, 2005.

Schneider, Steven Jay, ed. *1001 Movies You Must See Before You Die.* Happage, NY: Barron's Educational Series, 2003.

Wattenberg, Thomas E. *Unlikely Couples: Movie Romance as Social Criticism.* Orlando, FL: Waterview Press, 1999.

White, David Manning and Richard Averson. *The Celluloid Weapon.* Boston: Beacon Press, 1972.

Wood, Michael. *America in the Movies.* New York: Penguin Books, 1989.

Zaniello, Tom. *Working Stiffs, Union Maids, Reds & Riffraff.* Ithaca, NY: ILR Press-Cornell University, 2003.

Zinn, Howard. *A People's History of the United States: 1492-Present.* New York: Harper-Collins, 2003.

Index

Index 251

Index   257